PRAISE FOR VOLUME 3 OF DR. RAO'S COLLECTED WORKS

Pugnacious, entertaining, erudite, and insightful, John Rao never disappoints. This collection of writings takes you down memory lane in the company of one of the leading and most influential figures of American Catholic traditionalism—from the difficult years following Vatican II through the golden age of *Summorum* all the way to the present challenges, Rao has always been there, ready to speak up for all those who felt let down by the post-conciliar church, reminding us that even the present difficulties are just a blink in the two-thousand-years history of the Catholic Church. May many more letters scream out from Rocco's café!

—THOMAS CATTOI, William and Barbara Moran Chair of Early Christian theology and Interreligious Relations, Pontifical University of Saint Thomas, Rome

John Rao has played a key role in American Catholic traditionalism almost from its beginning: as a leader, scholar, organizer, publicist, and even liturgical acolyte! This volume, covering events from the 1970s to 2017, offers unique insights from a participant into not just the struggles and vicissitudes, but also the triumphs of Catholic traditionalism. To create his narrative, Professor Rao weaves together autobiography, travel reporting, secular and Church history, theology, liturgy and popular culture. And he vividly recalls for us dear departed figures who over the years have done and sacrificed so much for the traditionalist cause.

—STUART CHESSMAN, author of *Faith of Our Fathers: A Brief History of Catholic Traditionalism in the United States*

Having known Dr. Rao for 40 years, having read him and heard him lecture many times, I can assure everyone that his collected works represents a compendium of some of the best writing on, and analysis of, the Church in the Modern Age. As a leading figure in the traditional Catholic movement and as a scholar of Church history, Dr. Rao's works must be considered an indispensable part of any traditionalist's library. Dr. Rao knew personally and well many of the founders of the traditionalist movement such as Dietrich von Hildebrand, Bill Mara, and Michael Davies. Besides his many deep insights into the self-inflicted decline of the post-conciliar Church and the destruction of the Latin liturgy, Dr.

Rao demonstrates a wide civilizational perspective, especially in his trenchant critique of the so-called Age of Enlightenment and its cultural aftermath, making him a contemporary De Maistre. If you want true enlightenment, start reading Dr. Rao today!

—REV. RICHARD A. MUNKELT, Ph.D., Catholic priest, writer, and philosopher

YOUR STATUTES WERE MY SONG IN THE LAND OF EXILE: THE SORROWS AND THE JOYS OF THE BATTLE FOR A BIRTHRIGHT

For the Whole Christ

THE COLLECTED WORKS OF DR. JOHN RAO

VOLUME 3

Your Statutes Were My Song in the Land of Exile:

THE SORROWS AND THE JOYS OF THE BATTLE FOR A BIRTHRIGHT

ISBN: 978-1-998492-34-3 (pbk)
ISBN: 978-1-998492-35-0 (hc)

Arouca Press
PO Box 55003
Bridgeport PO
Waterloo, ON N2J 0A5
Canada
www.aroucapress.com
Send inquiries to info@aroucapress.com

CONTENTS

PREFACE

Your Statutes Were My Song in the Land of Exile

THE SORROWS AND THE JOYS OF THE BATTLE FOR A BIRTHRIGHT

IN HIS *COMMENTARY ON THE SONG OF SONGS* (1:1) St. Bernard of Clairvaux (1090–1153) exhorts us to praise God in all the gifts that he gives, since He is the source of our entire existence, making any ingratitude on our part worthy of severe punishment. Even when we are certain that we have been unjustly and unexpectedly deprived of our very birthright; driven from our homeland by those filled with nothing but contempt for our understandable shock and loss, it is to God and obedience to God's statutes that we must turn our eyes for the redress of our grievances and our return to our birthright. For Christian hope teaches us that in God's own time He will wipe away the tears of the victims of injustice, and that the joy that they will then experience will be immeasurably enhanced if they have recognized and corrected any of *their* failures to follow His precepts. For these may have sadly contributed to their robbery and their exile as well.

The articles in this third volume of the series "For the Whole Christ," extending over a period of eighteen years, are generally rather short pieces. Their focus is the horror of a variety of heroic men and organizations shocked by the unjust and unexpected theft of their birthright—in the form of the Traditional Roman Liturgy—and the contemptuous exile from the houses of worship constructed by their ancestors that was so long imposed upon them.

Sorrows, battles, and also some regrettable internal divisions are recounted herein. The reader can easily feel what can only be labeled the "outraged bewilderment" on the part of the militants of the movement: outraged, due to the realization of the extraordinary power suddenly exercised by a theological mafia seemingly determined to destroy the entire Catholic Tradition; bewildered, because of the sometimes frivolous and sometimes utterly pusillanimous submission to this arbitrary criminal will on the part of shepherds who ought to have known better.

Still, what predominates throughout the account of the struggle of this many-faceted *Exercitus Christi* for its doctrinal, liturgical, and devotional birthright is an abiding, zealous concern for the victory of the Statutes of the Lord—all of them, without exception. Thankfully, one finds here also an awareness that these statutes demand a spirit of reflection, meditation upon the teachings and examples given by holy men and women placed in similarly tragic situations in past eras, and an opening to self-correction, so as to make certain that the desire to defend the Faith not unwittingly put obstacles in the path of victory. And from this more conscious consultation of self-proclaimed traditionalists with the fullness of the Tradition the reader will perhaps discern that maturation in approach reflecting that coupling of outraged bewilderment with the humility and solid Christian hope and joy so essential to constructing a truly successful Catholic Action.

Clearly, my own personal experience with the Roman Forum lies behind what I have just discussed. This was founded by Professor Dietrich von Hildebrand in 1968 in order to support the Statutes of the Lord under serious attack in the form of the contestation by the ever more confident post-conciliar theological mafia of Pope Paul VI's encyclical, *Humanae Vitae*. Von Hildebrand understood that this was just the "tip of the iceberg," because connected with a progressive mentality threatening the dismantlement of all of the Church's dogmatic foundations, as indicated in his *Trojan Horse in the City of God*.

When I became a follower of the Roman Forum in 1970 the liturgical *Blitzkrieg* already launched during the Council and confirmed with the institution of the *Novus Ordo Missae* in 1969, was in full and seemingly irresistible advance. But von Hildebrand, already the author of a magnificent work entitled *Liturgy and Personality*, which identified most of the dangers connected with the promotion of a "personalist" and "pastoral centered" form of worship, realized that the love of the "Statutes of the Lord" demanded a full-fledged commitment to the protection and complete restoration of the Traditional Roman Rite. For it was primarily—in fact, almost exclusively—through the liturgy that the bulk of the faithful were presented with "the Truth that sets men free." Moreover, it was through the liturgy that *every* Catholic gained the grace coming from the Most Blessed Sacrament crucial for maintaining submission to that Truth. Hence, the perversion of the liturgy would inevitably have a disastrous impact even on those well-educated in the Faith who might delude themselves into thinking that their intellectual formation would alone protect them from succumbing to the *Blitzkrieg* in question.

All of the problems of defending the faith against external enemies and internal divisions of the *Exercitus Christi* became painfully clear to me in the course of the 1970s and 1980s. It was due to my conviction that the *sorrows* of the battle for our birthright—for the Traditional Liturgy and the Statutes of the Lord that this most effectively defended—required more of that reflection and meditation on the wisdom and actions uncovered by examination of the whole of the Catholic heritage that would enhance "outraged bewilderment" through "Christian hope and joy," immeasurably strengthening our fighting forces in the process. Hence, the systematic Church History and Catholic Cultural Seminars in New York City and in Italy that the Roman Forum instituted, with the full support of my irreplaceable predecessor, the tireless Professor William Marra, when I succeeded him as Director in 1991.

What I myself have rationally and culturally learned through these programs in the past thirty-one years, added and subordinated to the graces coming from the Traditional Liturgy and the confirmation of the Faith-in-Action that the ancient Roman Rite fuels and maintains, can be found in this volume. Whether we have lived up to what we have sought to do or not, it is my great hope that God's Statutes have been our movement's "Song in our Land of Exile," and that this volume will help make certain that my readers' real sorrows are drowned in Christian joy as we battle onward for the complete return of our birthright to the Universal Church as a whole.

I

From Hoboken to Eternity†

THE VALUE OF CATHOLIC TRADITIONALISM IN THE LIFE OF ONE TRADITIONALIST

1965–1969, THE YEARS I ATTENDED HIGH school, were among the most portentous in the entirety of Church History. Although born a Roman Catholic, and remaining a practicing one throughout that entire period, I have absolutely no recollection of my personal religious thoughts or inner life at the time. Oh, I do remember a few externals relating to those heady days of preparation for 1970s "renewal": sitting in a back pew with a friend, parodying one of the new, hideous hymns that we were expected to belt out with previously unimagined spiritual gusto; discovering that the class troublemakers were now considered heroes at the parish post-confirmation CCD classes; hearing clergy and laity say that this or that favorite sin was no longer an obstacle to going to communion. But try as I may, I cannot call up a single trace of any heart-felt reaction to the impending ecclesiastical disaster.

Nothing whatsoever seems to have interested me in those teenage years except for the fact that just at that moment modern American life was showering one after the other of its hitherto unknown, henceforth unmatchable, and rationally unquestionable gifts upon me. I was the recognized "star" at Indian Hills High School in Oakland, New Jersey—Class President for Life and, as my senior yearbook confidently told me, Most Likely to Succeed as well. My grades assured me entrance into top-notch universities, from which I saw myself one day emerging with an enviable law degree. This parchment, put both to energetic private use as well as public service would inevitably propel me into early riches, Congress (preferably the Senate) and eventually the White House.

† First published in *Love in the Ruins: Modern Catholics in Search of the Ancient Faith*, edited by Anne M. Larson (Kansas City, MO: Angelus Press, 2009)

The future was infallibly mine, with the only problem being the *embarras de choix* among the fruits that a free and happy society, the last and best hope of mankind, presented me.

But during my first semester at Georgetown University in Washington, D. C., this vision of the earthly paradise swiftly faded. An unexpected and thoroughgoing homesickness laid me low. To make matters worse, Georgetown's superb freshman academic program made it clear to me just how little I *really* knew in comparison to what I had been *told* that I knew, causing questions to pop into my head that had never troubled me before. Did I honestly want to be a lawyer? To what use would I put the riches that I presumed would flow like plunder from Persepolis into my pockets? What would I actually do on my first day as Head of State aside from wave to my admirers?

It did not take me long before I realized that I had no answer to any of these queries, and that, in fact, I had not the faintest idea whether I was preparing myself for heaven or for hell. The upshot was that by the end of the semester I had fifteen decent college credits under my belt and a one-way ticket on a Greyhound Bus back to the Port Authority Terminal. My stomach twisted into a million knots as the driver hit the Jersey Turnpike and I wondered what in the world would possibly come next.

Several months in the commercial world taught me that neither stomach knots would be loosened nor queries answered while working at my father's toy store. Hence, a decision to pick up the pieces of my aborted college education and carry them to Drew University in nearby Morris County. And it was through the experiences that some of the faculty of that secularized Methodist institution provided that the darkness began to dissipate. As it did, it threw a lot more light onto the back wall of the cave that I never imagined I was inhabiting . . . and would never have found a way to escape from on my own steam.

It was in the Hoboken Train Station, waiting to return to Drew after a day in Manhattan, that a powerful intellectual and spiritual freight engine bearing "every good and perfect gift" barreled directly into me. One of my professors, the late and sorely lamented James Lo Gerfo, had insisted upon a reading of St. Augustine's *Confessions* for his course on Early Medieval History. There I stood, under the departure announcement board, doing my routine academic duty, perfunctorily underlining some of Augustine's meditations, when a stray thought took possession of my mind, heart, and soul: what if these words were meant for my life instead of being meant just for my semester history grade?

That idea, quite frankly, made me sick to my stomach. Familiar Jersey Turnpike knots began to form again. Remembering their painfulness, but helpless to untie them and "return to normalcy," I took the first opportunity to run to the professor responsible for my condition and explain to him my discomfort. He then made certain that the journey that had begun in Hoboken did not end for me only at Drew.

Not that Drew itself was a bad place to pause for a while before changing from the local to the express. For it was here that I also gained the invaluable guidance of James Pain, a Methodist cleric and Chairman of the Religion Department. Dr. Pain had a profound interest in the search for God and a scholar's rigor in teaching the history of Christian belief and practice. Not only did he introduce me to a systematic study of Roman Catholic doctrine unmarred by dubious "signs of the time" and irrational swooning over the mysteries of the Omega Point. He also organized the semester abroad at Oxford in 1972 which led to my sojourn in that blessed environment for five further years of doctoral work. Even more importantly for this little essay, it was Dr. Pain who, during that first semester abroad, assigned me a paper on religious life in Britain. This brought me to a Tridentine Mass at Westminster Cathedral, an idle question to a member of the congregation regarding who could best inform me about current conditions of the Catholic Church in England, and the beginning of my thirty-two-year friendship with one of the greatest lay heroes of our time, the late Michael Davies.

But I am now getting far ahead of my story. So much more had already happened before that meeting with Michael in his suburban London house, all of which prepared me to appreciate what it was he had to say, about painful developments in the liturgy in particular. For in the months after my Hoboken experience, Professor Lo Gerfo had introduced me to two institutions which were to be central to my further spiritual and intellectual formation.

One of these was the two-year old Roman Forum, created in 1968 to defend Pope Paul VI's encyclical letter, *Humanae Vitae*.

and offering monthly lectures by Drs. Dietrich von Hildebrand and William Marra at a packed Keating Hall on Fordham University's Rose Hill Campus. The other was the Intercollegiate Studies Institute, whose summer schools provided access to the teaching of an extremely wide range of conservative academics, including those espousing the rich political and social thought of the European Catholic Right. Exposure to these organizations meant that I was present when von Hildebrand electrified the audience in the Bronx with his fervent call for a determined petitioning of Rome for the restoration of the "old Mass." It also meant that I heard Dr. Thomas Molnar, one of the most lucid and courageous of the ISI speakers, when he hammered at the dangers coming from the school of Leo Strauss and the first appearance in American rightist circles of what no one yet knew would someday dominate it under the name of "neo-conservatism."

Those years after 1970 were exciting ones indeed, and the reason for the excitement was the fact that I found myself in the middle of the budding Catholic Traditionalist Movement. Discovery and embrace of that Movement had come without my looking for it or expecting it, through personal confusion and happy accident alone. Nevertheless, it proved itself to be of central importance to the shaping of my life and the confirmation of my Faith—all of which indicates to me that I was led to Traditionalism through God's Providence.

Traditionalism proved its superabundant worth to me in four ways over the following decades, to begin with by teaching me the difference between a serious, open-minded, joyful intellectual endeavor on the one hand, and illogical, nostalgic, willful and closed-minded ventures on the other.

My introduction to the movement came through the influence of an eclectic mixture of Platonists and Thomists, with the Platonists, like Dietrich von Hildebrand and William Marra, in the dominant element. These men were not *Neo-Platonists* espousing some gnostic vision of contact with ever-greater corruption the further down on the Great Chain of Being from spiritual to material life one descended. Rather, they were Christian Platonists in love with God and man, emphasizing the goodness of Creation and the immense sorrow of the Fall. Most importantly, they were devout men who called attention to the supernatural light penetrating into every part of nature through the Incarnation, and the glorious role each of nature's elements, from the lowest to the highest, was called upon to play in the divine plan of "transformation of all things in Christ."

Such a teaching, fed in the years to come by a reading of works like Fr. Emile Mersch's *The Whole Christ*, and Werner Jaeger's study of *Greek Paideia*, introduced me to many truths: that nothing was superfluous to the task of raising the individual to God; that one needed solid theological, philosophical, political, economic, and aesthetic cooperation with supernatural grace, *all in the context of authoritative social life*, beginning with the family and moving upwards, if one were to succeed in this most exalted of enterprises; that men and women who *really* believed in the Incarnation and its consequences required a spirit of openness to sifting through all that nature had offered in the past—and might yet offer through unexpected future developments; and, finally, that all such labors demanded acceptance of one supreme condition: the necessity of keeping one's eyes focused firmly on the Christ responsible for God and nature's bounty; i.e., on the Christ who walked the earth and on that same Christ continued in His Mystical Body, the Church.

Hence the importance of the Traditional Mass, which von Hildebrand's books, such as *Liturgy and Personality*, made so wonderfully clear. Here one had the supreme "tool" for sanctification, with everything supernatural and natural ordered according to the proper hierarchy of values, beginning with the fact that it was aimed *primarily* at the worship of God, from which all things useful to mankind—all tools—only *secondarily* flow. All had its place in such worship—simplicity and grandeur, silence and public acclamation, humble recognition of unworthiness and rejoicing in superabundant love of the Almighty—in a dramatic and aesthetically brilliant presentation of man's relationship with his Creator, appealing simultaneously to eyes, ears, senses, mind, heart, and soul.

Tampering with such magnificence, under the guidance of a spirit that put the secondary teaching function of the Mass—and, hence, the service of man—above the truly overriding consideration of what most fittingly adores the Godhead, was thus the most certain means of failing to achieve *both* purposes: that of praising what is above and instructing what is below. The more

I understood this, the more the unfolding liturgical nightmare in the Roman Church became unbearable to me. My friend and I were instinctively right to laugh at those ridiculous hymns in our *Novus Ordo* training sessions after all!

Luckily, my courses with Dr. Pain back at Drew had drawn my attention to the many Eastern Catholic Churches of the New York metropolitan area and the possibility of living the solid, Incarnation-drunk liturgical life stolen from the Roman rite by a misguided "reform." Before I knew it, I was singing the Liturgy of St. John Chrysostom myself, and bringing my favorite Ruthenian priest to Drew to expose others to its beauty.

Still, as noted above, the years after 1970 acquainted me with two, contrasting, closed-minded approaches to wisdom as well—one that was primarily illogical and nostalgic, and the other determinedly willful in spirit. The first became ever more noticeable as Catholic Traditionalism and Conservatism parted their ways; the other, through wrenching daily contact with the "mainstream" Church and the development of its understanding of "renewal."

Dietrich von Hildebrand had begun the Roman Forum in union with the Catholic weekly newspaper, *The Wanderer,* and in conjunction with the creation of *Catholics United for the Faith.* This alliance was broken due to von Hildebrand's insistence on the need to criticize not the validity but the failings and inferiority of the *Novus Ordo* in relation to the Traditional Roman Rite of Mass. His former partners, conservatives as opposed to traditionalists, believed that loyal, orthodox Catholics were obliged to defend the reform of the liturgy, and did so, often enthusiastically. In the process, they accepted more and more changes that they themselves had bitterly fought when the revolution began.

It struck me that the conservatives' attitude concerning contemporary issues was in open and illogical battle with the historical traditions and saintly lives that they continued to praise . . . and which I honestly think, in their heart of hearts, they continued to prefer. Conservative grasping at bits and pieces of the ancient heritage—a *Kyrie* sung in Gregorian chant here, an old hymn there—in the midst of the general debacle seemed to me to "miss the point," and reflect precisely that "nostalgic" mentality that our common progressive enemies wrongly accused traditionalists of nurturing. Traditionalist concern was never for Latin or one specific gesture or another in the Offertory as such; it was a concern for *an organic liturgical whole aimed primarily at the adoration of God.*

Everything cherished outside of that whole was, at best, a pious nostalgia; something akin to a warm memory of a top hat, still worn with remembered pride, but now together with a new and absurd uniform of torn jeans and platform shoes. And this same illogical, nostalgic spirit seemed to reign everywhere that conservative Catholics of varied types congregated.

Willfulness was to be found in the "mainstream," expressed by the progressive ideologues choreographing the *danse macabre* that Catholic life in the 1970s had become. I simply found no means of engaging a discussion with whirling dervishes in the grip of renewal fever. All of their man-centered activities were defended by them with reference to the obvious guidance of a Holy Spirit whom I was said to despise; a Holy Spirit who had suddenly and inexplicably exchanged His friendship for Catholic Tradition for a Shiva-like passion for its annihilation. Mockery and distortion of Traditionalist arguments were the unchanging weapons in the progressive arsenal in those days, one favorite being the response to my justification for the old liturgy with the claim that I should then want my sermons to be delivered in Latin as well. It was clear to me that progressives did not seek assent to their positions through rational discourse; instead, they had passionately embraced the road to victory through the Triumph of the Will. "The Spirit and the *Zeitgeist* are One, and we are Its unquestionable Prophet!" was their war cry. And anyone doubtful regarding the validity of their *sutra* had to efface himself before its ineffable beauty and keep his bloody mouth shut.

As far as I was concerned, the only thing solidly intellectual and rationally useful that came out of my contact with the forces of renewal was the growth of my own library. For the Holy *Zeitgeist* had directed church after church, priest after priest, seminary after seminary, literally to toss into the rubbish bin beautiful altar missals, breviaries, copies of the Church Fathers, and major theological, philosophical, and historical treatises. They certainly were following a precedent started in the Age of Reason in doing this. After all, the eighteenth-century Enlightened Absolutist, Joseph II of Austria, had filled the foundations of state buildings in a similar spirit of spring cleaning, loading them up with the precious texts of suppressed Jesuit libraries. In any case, I scavenged the rubbish bins and swelled my shelves with all the discarded nonsense of nearly two millennia of Catholic thought.

Another thing that my Incarnation-drunk Platonist teachers had taught me was the crucial importance of examining the whole of the historical record, sacred and profane, in order to understand how Catholics had sifted the good from the bad in nature in past ages. This, they said, would help me to learn which paths to follow and which pitfalls to avoid in the future if I wished to live a Christian life in a Christian civilization. It was through his knowledge of the historical sources—in this case, Vatican One and its aftermath—that von Hildebrand was aware of the validity of his own nuanced position regarding Church law. Examination of the sources made it crystal clear that the Pope had the authority to impose the changed liturgy on the Church, and we Catholics had the duty to recognize its validity. On the other hand, it just as firmly showed that believers also had the right and the responsibility to criticize this action and beg that it be recognized as a mistake and overturned when convinced of its dangers.

By now, I was deeply interested in exactly how the Church had managed to get itself in the mess that I saw poisoning everything around me, and what it was that the faithful had done to emerge from similar crises in the past. Therefore, I set to work in Oxford on a doctoral dissertation that might satisfy my curiosity and enable me to contribute to the progress of the Traditionalist Movement in days to come. Step by step, this led me to a study of Catholic reactions to the Enlightenment, the problem of Naturalism, and the ravages of the French Revolution. It also brought me to investigate that deep fountain of lay and clerical interest in the Incarnation and its consequences that burst forth after 1848, feeding the *Syllabus of Errors* and Catholic Social Teaching, and providing the waters of Catholic speculation from which von Hildebrand himself had drunk. Step by step, this also pulled me towards my second, totally unexpected example of the importance of the message taught by the Catholic Traditionalist Movement: its effectiveness in showing how to deal with the reality of the devil.

When I finally found the theme for my doctoral dissertation, I was happily ensconced at St. Edmund Hall in Oxford. I lived in a room on Longwall Street overlooking Deer Park at Magdalen

College, and had worked out a routine that seemed destined to make me into the perfect Renaissance man. I labored each day at the Bodleian Library; took my exercise on Christ Church Meadow; enjoyed drinks and dinner with my friends in historic pubs; listened to the opera and committed the arias to memory before retiring for the night. Lent of 1975 was approaching, and I planned to cap my Florentine routine with a season of penitence that would enable me to enjoy the Easter Feast appropriately.

And then a crisis hit; an existential crisis of the sort that I had read about in Kierkegaard, but never prepared for facing myself. As with the experience in Hoboken, this crisis began with a sudden thought taking possession of me. The thought this time was of a saint who died and discovered . . . nothing. More specifically, it was the thought of a saint who could not even really discover nothing because of the total end of his consciousness that came along with his demise.

In short, I was seized with the fear that there was no God; that I had come from nowhere and was headed for nowhere. If this were true, if the Faith were vain, it was not just heaven that would be lost. There could be no enjoyment in even the simplest act of living here on earth. If eating, drinking, and being merry were not connected with a final supernatural purpose, none of them had the slightest significance for me whatsoever.

This was the most miserable experience that I have ever had to date. I was paralyzed, and the paralysis lasted quite some time, mitigated only by two lifelines. One was a mechanical commitment to continuing my doctoral work that allowed me to escape from confronting the vision of absolute nothingness for eight hours each day. The other was the inexplicable realization that every time I actually consulted my reason, this never failed to lead me to two conclusions: that there was indeed a God, and that if there were a God, that Catholicism in and of itself was worthy of the act of Faith I had once made in it. I could not escape the conclusion that my problem was that I could not bring myself to give credence to what my reason repeatedly told me to be true. I needed to find a way to *believe* what I *knew*, and then proceed from that *knowledge* back into my *faith*.

Three friends—Dietrich Warns, a fellow student from Germany, a good Franciscan priest whose name I never learned, and Dr.

William Marra's wife, Marcelle—finally showed me the way out of this abominable Black Hole. All of them insisted that I had come face to face with the reality of the devil, and the only thing that could effectively fight his call to *nothingness* was . . . *everything*. Everything around me, all of which was indeed real, was, they argued, continually speaking to me in varied ways of aspects of the message of Truth, Goodness, and Beauty that my re*ason* was willing to accept and pull upwards towards the thought of God. *Everything* around me was important to my spiritual cure, and *nothing* could be considered superfluous to it. I had now only to use this natural bounty on behalf of supernatural Faith.

After struggling with their advice for a while, I recognized that these friends were reinforcing exactly what I had learned in the Traditionalist Movement from the very outset: that Christ's Incarnation confirms the value of God's Creation; that all of nature is a powerful aid in the raising of the mind and soul to a desire for the supernatural; and that all of nature transformed in Christ was of an even greater—an infinitely greater—assistance.

So I dived back into the fullness of Christ, both through all that could in some manner be connected with Him naturally, as well as all that He was in and of Himself: the beauty of Oxford, Europe and Catholic culture as a whole; the wonders of the intellectual life; the warmth of friendship with others seeking the Truth; prayer; the life of an age-old liturgy which, through the Eastern Catholics and the English Indult, was mercifully available to me and provided me my daily spiritual food.

When I had regained my Faith, I regained the conviction of the value of my Reason. When I regained my Reason, I regained Reason's aid in confirming my Faith. And my Faith and Reason together warned me never again to abandon that message of the Incarnation and its consequences that Catholic Traditionalism *alone* had taught me to study and nurture; never again to abandon all the tools that had been shown historically to push men into the arms of Christ and keep them there.

By 1978, with my doctorate finished and my sense of how Catholics had fallen into their current predicament deepened, Oxford had become more dear to me than life itself. This alone would have made my departure for anywhere past the Ring Road quite difficult. Nevertheless, my return to the United States became particularly unpleasant when I began experiencing problems not only in explaining what I had learned along the Thames, but even in merely beginning a conversation about the life-and-death contrast of an Incarnation-minded Catholicism with a naturalist worldview.

Most painful of all was the fact that this difficulty was proving to be true with many traditionalists as well as conservatives and progressive ideologues, not to speak of colleagues, high school friends, and family members. Horrible to recount, I found that the same trouble was manifesting itself with each subsequent summer return to Europe and contact with Europeans outside my rather rarefied circle of former Oxford comrades. Chance (or Providence) guided me to an explanation for this phenomenon, and this explanation, which also came through the aid of Traditionalist thought, confirmed the value of Catholic Traditionalism for me yet a third time.

As soon as I returned from Oxford in 1978, Dr. Marra had begun to call upon my services as lecturer at the Roman Forum. One day, he commissioned a topic for a talk concerned with problems at Catholic University. As I developed this, it transmuted into a study of the Americanist crisis in the Church in the United States at the turn of the twentieth century. Confrontation of Americanism with the critique of its character that I found, once again, in the Incarnation-based thinkers to which the Traditionalist Movement had directed my attention, was startling. It unveiled the peculiar nature of the anti-intellectual, materialist, "pragmatic," but non-violent and seemingly "friendly" way in which the Enlightenment had made its progress in both Britain and the United States . . . to the most effective detriment of the Catholic cause known to history.

My study of Americanism helped to open my eyes to the explanation of many things: why my elementary and high school education had aimed me away from any serious investigation of the questions most important to life in general and towards narrow, mindless, materialist goals; why "pointless" intellectual discussions were generally avoided by American society; why both Faith and Reason failed to have a social impact; how a naturalist and revolutionary principle could find a way to masquerade as a solid bulwark of Tradition and the essence of patriotism; how "pragmatism" and the need to avoid "divisiveness" were used to prevent people from finding their way out of a spiritual dead end and back to Catholic sanity; how Europe, fearful that opposition to an American-inspired Pluralism would be construed as sympathy for Nazism and Communism or simply outright insanity, was also won for the cause of mindlessness.

Walter Matt, the founding editor of *The Remnant*, was so eager that I continue with the critique of Americanism that this lecture had begun that he insisted I publish a brochure on the subject; hence the start of what is now a regular collaboration with that journal. "Everybody in the world is infected with this Americanist virus," Dr. Marra told me. "Your life's work has been laid out. I don't envy you."

Such foreboding predictions proved to be miserably accurate, especially with respect to the strong hint of possible frustrations in my work. Filled with missionary zeal, I initially managed to intrigue a rather wide range of people and organizations regarding my labors, thus obtaining invitations to speak almost everywhere . . . once. After that, oversized *persona non grata* mats were laid at many a formerly friendly door. Bit by bit, the invitations degenerated from microphones at elegant Opus Dei parlors with wine and cheese receptions to those at suburban firehouses and out of the way catering halls with snacks of stale donuts and bad coffee.

Perhaps the most depressing aspect of this drudgery was the fact that Catholic traditionalists themselves were often among the least responsive to my arguments. Rather than being willing to listen to proofs that Americanism and Pluralism were the most effective tools for leading them into acceptance of the Enlightenment naturalism that lay behind our contemporary crisis, liturgical as well as theological, they often waved me away as a dangerously treasonous kook. Instead, they took refuge in explanations of the ecclesiastical cancer, accurately identifying one or the other head of the revolutionary hydra that had affected them personally, while neglecting and even cooperating with other manifestations of that very same beast in different realms.

Moreover, separation from the mainstream of life, while totally understandable, seemed to me to be making traditionalists stranger and sadder rather than wiser; hence the expansion of the influence of those who thought that they could deal with the disaster by acting like Protestant atomists in little houses on the prairie; of others, Rousseau-like anarchists committed to "unschooling" their children; of pseudo-fascists speaking of the *Triumph of the Will* and blaring out hard rock on car radios while claiming to be militants determined to crush the menace of liberal theology. Meanwhile, despite what one can now in retrospect perceive, hopes for official Church support for the revival of the Traditional Mass appeared to be ever more groundless as the '70s turned to the '80s. "The movement," as one of my friends quietly sobbed, "is stationary."

By the mid-1980s, I began to wake up each morning thinking I was dead and in hell. People my age in New York City were starting to make Big Time Bucks, buy luscious apartments, and get full view boxes at the Opera. They would shout hello to me from their limousines on their way to Lincoln Center while I sat on my tenement stoop drinking jug wine and listening to fading, crackling, spliced tapes of Don Giovanni. Most Likely to Succeed indeed! Traditionalists were losers and I was one of them. Tradition, above all else, was supposed to be tied in with a normal human life. What was normal about the way that I was living? Surely, it was time for a return to real normalcy! "Back to mainstream living!" became my motto.

And so I took a vacation from the stationary Movement and its seemingly hellish frustrations. Articles for *The Remnant* lapsed into silence. My trips back to Europe turned away from contacts with exotic traditionalist cells and towards the Riviera, for basic, healthy, physical exercise. I took to jitterbugging rather than lecturing, preparing gourmet meals from scratch with fresh ingredients rather than polishing notes lambasting Cardinal Gibbons and Bishop Ireland. In my hunger for normalcy and longing for a return to the mainstream of life, I even did something I never would have dreamed possible just a short time before—I abandoned my Eastern Catholic churches and became a lector for the *Novus Ordo* at my local Greenwich Village parish, Our Lady of Pompeii.

Not that I cut off all my ties with the Movement in those years of backsliding. My companions were still almost exclusively traditionalists, thus giving my escapade the telltale tinge of a day of hooky from a school which would inevitably call me back to its classrooms. Moreover, aside from Dr. Marra, whose summons to lecture for the Roman Forum I could never turn down, another force entered onto the scene to help to keep me honest during this winter of my discontent. This was the SSPX, in the person of the then Fr. Richard Williamson at the Society's seminary in Ridgefield, Connecticut.

Now although I had always been a deep admirer of Archbishop Lefebvre, I had never been a parishioner at a Society Chapel. Nor have I ever become one since, although I attend Mass at St. Nicholas when in Paris and at other SSPX churches as need arises. I never attacked the Society's path to dealing with the nightmare of the late twentieth century Church. I just had a different path myself. It always seemed probable to me that there could be more than one return path to ecclesiastical sanity. Moreover, I was and remain one of those people who has often been quite stunned by some of the things that the now Bishop Williamson has said regarding the Church and the world situation.

Nevertheless, his intellectual curiosity, his pastoral solicitude for my soul, and his personal friendship pulled me back from playing with a pointless existence that could easily have slid into the despair that once wore me down so miserably in Oxford. He actually did want to hear what I said about Americanism and Pluralism, and invited me to talk to his seminarians about their dangers. More than once, and in pleasant settings to boot! Further still, he wanted me to lecture not only on contemporary evils, but on my own field of expertise, on Church History in general, as well. This forced me back to the sources of the Tradition for another and still more comprehensive "refresher course."

Once this refresher course began, I quickly had to admit that even if the Movement were all too stationary, the mainstream was hurtling yet farther into Outer Space on its journey to nowhere. Really, no matter how much I had wanted to be "part of something," and recognized that traditionalists were suffering due to their isolation, I never could flee from the fact that the world at large was nothing other than acceptable society's Twilight Zone. Grateful as I was to the fine pastor of my parish church, which was infinitely saner than most around me, it just could not become my permanent spiritual home. Attendance at family funerals in that ecclesiastical wilderness west of the Hudson, outside relatively conservative New York, showed that liturgies were degenerating at an ever-greater pace. The presence of pianos in the sanctuary had begun to give what ought to have been a somber setting the flavor of a tacky cocktail lounge. Each time I spoke with rarely seen relatives and old acquaintances at these events, whole new chunks of doctrine, morality, and history seemed to have disappeared entirely from their collective memories.

All this meant that when *Ecclesia Dei Adflicta* was finally published, and St. Agnes Church in New York City decided to take advantage of it to restore the Traditional Mass to its Sunday liturgy, I needed only one week to "jump ship" and exchange my lectern for a St. Andrew's Daily Missal. Within a fortnight I had donned an acolyte's cassock. A short time after that, I was writing for *The Remnant* again, renewing my contacts with Michael Davies, accepting lecture invitations, and, eventually, working—till they, alas, tired of me—with *Una Voce America*.

This does not mean that the situation in the Traditionalist world had perceptibly improved in the years of my vacation, from 1985–1988. In some respects, the same partial explanations for the collapse of Christendom were being proclaimed, rehashed, and commented upon even more loudly, insistently, and pedantically than ever before. And the exacerbation of these evils that would come from uncontrolled blogging were as yet still lurking, unimagined, in the technological underbrush.

But it was now that Catholic Traditionalism made its fourth self-validating appearance in my life. This time it appeared to give me advice regarding how to deal with the problems of Catholic Traditionalism itself! My recent "refresher course" in the fullness of the Tradition, urged upon me by Bishop Williamson, had given me the final push to listen once more to what it was that that Tradition had to teach. Traditionalism again reminded me that one had to "dive in" and use all the natural and supernatural tools available to a man if he were to defeat dangerous influences of each and every sort. This meant that dealing with the continuing "problem" of traditionalists was, in fact, nothing other than a variant of dealing with the existential crisis troubling me at Oxford. My fellow traditionalists had to be exposed to more than a lecture, more than an intellectual argument, in order to be won over to an understanding of the evils of an Americanist and Pluralist world. They needed to have the totality of Catholic Faith, history, and culture placed before their minds, souls, and body to make the point that my mere words could not describe. My duty was to find a way to create a holistic environment in which they could live, for a time, in a microcosm of a truly Catholic order. Then, by confronting what they experienced and learned with their ordinary daily reality and its erroneous teaching, they might come to make the same kinds of judgments respecting the deleterious effects on Christendom of Americanism, Pluralism, and the non-violent, "friendly," Anglo-Saxon path to Enlightenment that I had made.

Dr. Marra gave me the means to move forward with this project when he decided, in 1991, to put me in charge of the Roman Forum. This allowed me to gather the funds to create an annual "Catholic Commune" which, like the Chartres Pilgrimage, whose treasures I discovered about the same moment, could shape a "time out of time" leaving an indelible imprint on those who participated in it. I had tried something similar, on a much smaller scale, in Venice, in 1985, just before I threw my hands up and went on vacation from the Movement, leaving the project stillborn. This time, the concept was to come together in a more lasting and fruitful form.

Once again, a chance (or providential) visit to the Institute of Christ the King at Gricigliano in Tuscany, introduced me to Cardinal Alfons Stickler, and the beauty of the Solemn Pontifical Mass of the Traditional Rite. Cardinal Stickler, with the encouragement and aid of the Institute's superior, Mgr. Gilles Wach, accepted the Roman Forum's invitation to come to St. Agnes in February of 1992 to inaugurate the work of our "Catholic Commune"—a seminar inspired by Dietrich von Hildebrand's "Incarnation-drunk" vision. This seminar, meeting annually at Gardone Riviera, on Lake Garda in northern Italy, would allow traditionalists a chance to live a "time out of time" where Catholic principles reigned supreme; where they could eat, drink, sing, play, study, and worship, as Traditional Catholics, with all that their heritage had to offer them, placed at the center of their existence. In New York, I had only myself to count on to lecture and appeal to the intellect; in Gardone, I had all of nature and supernature as my senior partners. If nothing else would break through a parochial spirit limiting Traditionalist understanding of contemporary reality, I was certain that this could do so. If exposure to the light could have an impact on a spirit as weak and wobbly as mine, surely it could make the same impression more speedily and firmly on others made of stronger stuff.

In the summer of 1982, I found myself in Paris with an

unexpected sum of money at my disposal. I decided I wanted to live a week enjoying everything that the *ville lumiere* could legitimately offer me. Up to that point, I had been traveling on the cheap and was in a desperate state of personal disrepair. Once I bought a pair of shoes without holes in them, I realized how ridiculous my worn-out trousers appeared. When this problem was remedied, my wretched shirt clearly stood out in all its misery and had to be replaced. That done, I quickly perceived how badly I needed a decent haircut. Everything bodily in order, I marched off to my first museum and immediately recognized that I was terribly, terribly lonely. In short, my decision to enjoy Paris properly caused me to see that much more work was required of me than I at first had bargained for.

When I hopped on the train from Hoboken in 1970 I first got off at the stop marked Catholic Traditionalism. Here I met serious men of joyful spirit; men who understood that all of us make mistakes and backslide in our efforts to do the Good and take possession of the Beautiful; men who emanated a truly noble sense of humor about their own limitations as they played their part in the Drama of Truth.

What my Incarnation-drunk Catholic traditionalists taught me when I arrived at their destination was that Tradition and Traditionalism were not an end in themselves. They were valuable precisely because they were always a way station; a way station to Christ, to Christ's Mystical Body, and to an understanding of just how much every aspect of grace and nature must be nurtured and loved as a means of leading us to the light of the Beatific Vision.

In other words, embracing Tradition was like embracing Paris, and coming swiftly to the realization that one's work had just begun when the initial decision to open his arms was taken. The trip begun in Hoboken had to continue ever onward and ever upward. To turn my back on this lengthier journey would be to abandon life with the Father of Lights and eternal joy. To turn my back on the Traditionalism that inspired it would end with life in an arrogant, unenlightened, and ultimately *unnatural* nature left to its own self-limiting devices; to eternity in a self-created hell.

2

Dr. William A. Marra[†]

TRAVELER ON A CATHOLIC ROMAN ROAD

MANY UVA MEMBERS KNEW BILL PERSONally. Many of those who did not are nevertheless aware of his work as a philosopher at Fordham University in the Augustinian-phenomenological-von Hildebrandian tradition, as one of the founders of the Roman Forum, as a broadcaster for Drama of Truth, and, of course, as an international lecturer strongly defending innumerable beleaguered Catholic causes. What I should like to do for the benefit of those few for whom he may be merely a name, and also for the sake of rendering justice to a man who cared nothing for recognition and honors, is to describe what I believe the message of his life was, and what it has taught his friends who now feel so lonely without him.

Bill Marra's life reminds one of a journey on a Roman road. Like a traveler along an ancient republican or imperial highway, he went from his starting point to the conclusion of his earthly pilgrimage directly, single-heartedly, and with no doubt as to his destination. Anyone who listened to what he had to say and followed where he went understood that there was a journey calling to be made, that it actually did go somewhere definite, and that one could be confident that the particular route offered was secure and expeditious. He followed a *Via Appia* in a twisted, macabre modern landscape.

But Bill Marra's Roman road was constructed out of Catholic rock. This meant that it was not a human one, certainly not his own. It was that of Christ and Christ alone. As all who knew him will, I am sure, attest, he had to be among the most unselfconscious and personally disinterested men. Friends will remember that he often engaged humorously in an hyperbolic boasting (he would attribute traffic jams in New York City to press leaks of his presence therein) that was funny precisely because he was in

† Slightly altered name of a eulogy in *Una Voce Newsletter*, Spring 1999.

truth so genuinely humble. The successes he achieved were for Christ, not for himself. And it was to Christ that he constantly turned for maintenance.

Spared the effort of observing himself constantly, this traveler on a Catholic Roman road spent his time examining the sights along the path of his journey. Viewing things in Christ, he then saw what the self-conscious neglect: a world populated by lovers or potential lovers of God, presented with an endless variety of God-given means by which to nourish and enrich this startling romance. Because everything along the journey was precious to the greatest Lover of all, Bill believed it should be precious to him. He had to open his eyes to its particular message. This lay at the base of his phenomenology, and, again, as I am certain all can testify, this made him the easiest man to approach and to engage in discussion. One always was aware that Bill was not trying to score points in an argument, but to get at the truth. He had an amazing, unflagging enthusiasm for teaching the truth, so that it was in character that he should have died driving home from a stint of lecturing in Alabama. No matter how many lectures he gave in his incredibly busy career, he never seemed to tire of answering the same questions by a constant stream of people newly converted or newly awakened to the Faith, the intellectual life, or the urgencies of a given battle. In all the work he did for various Catholic organizations and causes, he never lost sight of the fact that the goal of the work, the point of the "cause," was to instruct, convert, give comfort to and save individuals and promote the kingship of Christ.

This sometimes made him a bad businessman. He gave away stacks of books and tapes; he would fundraise for one organization at an event sponsored by another. The organizations or events were never his main interest: they were the platforms from which he preached to individuals. His motto was a Catholic variant of "no enemies on the Right," and he worked anywhere he saw an opportunity to teach the Faith.

The message of the Marra road was therefore anything but monotonous. Though the journey was long, the highway was open—he was always looking for new companions, always ready to encourage love, always joyous, always expecting the unexpected experience, and yet always sorrowful for those who opted for the somber anti-Catholic track to nowhere. For this tragic perception also came through travel along Bill's pathway: an awareness, as the name of his radio and television shows underlined, that the romance of individuals and God in a world filled with aids to love was a Drama of Truth that had to be confronted moment by ever distinct unrepeatable moment in time, and that, dramatically, the kiss of Faith could be spurned. Bill's message, while joyous, was one that warned of and lamented unrequited love.

How many souls were, are, and will be borne down that straight, unselfconscious, disinterested, loving, joyful, dramatic Catholic Roman road that Bill Marra taught us to follow? How many people's awakening to God is owed to him? How much faith was sustained by him through his tireless trudging through this and other continents? How often have those who have despaired felt ashamed at their lack of hope and regained confidence in conversation with him? I know a few of them, myself included. But all of them? That is a secret locked in Christ. Suffice it to say that anyone reading this brief eulogy who himself has been borne down that road is not lacking for company.

Bill Marra felt a link with a more vibrant Catholic past to have been broken when his mentor, Dietrich von Hildebrand, died. All of us with Una Voce now feel that same sense of loss of moorings now, with Bill Marra's departure. In praying for the repose of Bill's soul, let us also pray that we can continue his arrow-like, confident, unselfconscious, and truly open-minded work. To his widow, Marie, to his family, to all his friends and admirers, let us promise that we will at least try to do so, and hope, in return, that we will one day see again a man whose personality stood out so strongly because he hid himself in Christ.

3
Charting a Course for Una Voce America†

I MUST BEGIN BY APOLOGIZING FOR MY rather lengthy delay in responding to all of your very kind words of welcome to the Presidency of Una Voce America. The delay had its reasons, including work involved in preparing for the 1999 Dietrich von Hildebrand Institute in Gardone, the publication of my book, *Removing the Blindfold*, and the conclusion of the academic year. Now that I have a little more time at my disposal, a somewhat more "catholic" introduction of myself than a basic biographical sketch can give seems in order. Through this, I hope to leave you with a broad sense of my personal understanding of the nature of the mission of which Una Voce is a notable part and where I think we ought to be headed in the coming years.

Although I am a cradle Catholic, my real awakening to the Faith dates to the years between 1970 and 1973. It was at that time that I met Dr. Dietrich von Hildebrand, Dr. William Marra, and Mr. Michael Davies. Toward the end of that period, I started my doctoral studies at Oxford. And it was at Oxford that I encountered the books of Fr. Emile Mersch on the doctrine of the Mystical Body of Christ which helped me to put the contemporary problems of the Church in historical perspective, get a glimpse of their full significance, and begin to see the kind of work that I myself ought to do in the future.

Mersch's writings, which my own book will explain in much greater detail, opened my eyes to the awesome mystery of the Church and the consequences for all of nature of acceptance or rejection of participation in her life. This was due to the fact that they underlined the essential character of the Church as something much more than a purely legal structure focused on saving men from an unfavorable juridical decision, important though this structure might be. Mersch emphasized the Church's

† First published in the *Una Voce America Newsletter*, Summer 1999.

existence as Christ-continued-in-time (the "whole Christ," to use St. Augustine's terminology), acting to perfect the universe that He Himself created. Insistence upon the central character of the Church as Christ-continued, as His living Mystical Body, clarifies the exalted dignity of the Christian mission, demonstrates the cooperative labor of supernatural grace and the natural world, shows the need for the individual to work within an authoritative community for his own benefit, and also opens one to the endless diversity of ways in which different persons, different periods of time, and different initiatives can be utilized to glorify the Trinity if only they are incorporated into the life of the God-Man. Finally, an understanding of the Mystical Body lays bare the error of modern, secularized, libertarian society, since it teaches that any attempt to leave nature and the individual to their own devices is bound to lead to a failure to understand their true destiny and talents, and end in self-defeat.

On a historical level, Mersch's writings were important to me in revealing the full glory of the Greek and Latin Fathers, to whom this role of the Church as Christ-continued was primary. They illustrated the significance of the revivification of the study of the Fathers in the course of the past five hundred years, the period which historians generally speak of as the modern era. This revivification is not the only blessing that the Church has received in modern times. It is linked with and has helped cause other valuable developments in modern Catholicism, not least of which is a greater appreciation for and reception of the Eucharist. When we are tempted to fall into despair, and compare our world unfavorably with the Middle Ages, it is necessary to remember that much of what stirs us to commitment to lay action today is a desire to restore all things in Christ which is actually a product of a more conscious modern Catholic militancy reflecting a deepened understanding of the nature of the Mystical Body. This is what electrified St. Ignatius Loyola and the Jesuits; this is what lay behind the doctrine of the Sacred Heart, and made propagation of that devotion so popular from the 1600s onwards. This is what one finds working through Pius IX's *Syllabus of Errors*, Leo XIII's social teachings, Pius X's program for the defense of the Church, and Pius XII's encyclical on the subject of the Mystical Body itself. This is what also inspired the liturgical movement of the nineteenth and part of the twentieth century as well—the need for everyone to understand and to tap into the riches of Christ in His Church through the liturgy, for the sake of the sanctification of the individual and the lifting up of the whole world to the greater glory of God.

Having noted this background for my own awakening to the Faith, allow me to make the following five points with respect to my understanding of what it means for our own labors now:

1. I am certain that no one in our organization presents our work as some rearguard nostalgic activity. Still, it is necessary energetically to note that Una Voce is the healthy heir of a vibrant Christ/Church-centered Catholic liturgical revival and movement of lay action developing out of the nineteenth century; a liturgical revival and movement of lay action, part of which has unfortunately lost its moorings and contributed to the chaos we see around us today;
2. Despite very strong appearances to the contrary, time is on the side of our cause. The more that the forces we oppose break with the Church and adopt modern secularist libertarian ideas, the more they fall into an irrational self-destructiveness that distances them from anything which is true and beautiful even on a natural level alone. This means that any young mind and spirit earnestly seeking guidance will more and more see that there is nothing to be gained from listening to them, and everything, in contrast, to be won by opening the heart to the school of thought we represent;
3. The advantage of time can only be of use to us if we make certain that we turn every moment that we are not engaged in opening up dioceses to the Traditional Mass into an opportunity to learn more about the liturgy, Christian spirituality, and the history of the Church in general. This will enable us effectively to guide the remnants of a collapsing official Catholic population and potential converts down the proper pathway;
4. Charity, patience, and openness to the surprises of time and nature as a whole ought to make us ready to adopt a wide variety of strategies and be prepared to deal with an unexpected diversity of personalities to spread acceptance of the Traditional Mass. In other words, no one and nothing moral ought to be excluded from our calculations in moving forward. The whole ecclesiastical framework is in such a state of flux

that one cannot be sure any longer what someone who seems like he should be our opponent thinks, whether he thinks at all, or what his reaction would be to specific kinds of arguments or pressure. Therefore, let a thousand initiatives bloom, or, to quote Napoleon, "plunge in, and see if any specific strategy works." Our need to be firm on principle must be matched by an equal flexibility on practical approach;

5. While excommunicating no one who does not excommunicate us, it has been and must always continue to be the policy of Una Voce to work patiently and lovingly, with all its infinite frustrations, within the structure of the Church.

These are, of course, very broad statements of policy: the need to see ourselves as part of a historical development, to recognize the bankruptcy of the forces we are opposing, to dedicate a great deal of time to education, and, in effect, to be ready for anything. It is difficult for me to be more specific than this at the moment. My own work as president will have to evolve in character as I gain a greater understanding of the shape of all your activities through time. It seems to me, right now, that one general Una Voce America conference a year dealing with the character and history of the liturgy would be a good means of giving us a sense of being a unified group. This could be organized in conjunction with CIEL and my own Dietrich von Hildebrand Institute, and be both a high quality scholarly event and a backdrop for an annual Board of Directors meeting. Such a conference requires time to think through, but there is no reason why one could not be organized within the next year.

4
Letter from Dr John C. Rao

SEPT. 23, 1999

His Eminence Jorge Cardinal Medina Estevez
Congregazione Per il Culto Divino Palazzo
delle Congregazioni Piazza
Pio XII 10
Vatican City, 00193

YOUR EMINENCE:

I am writing this letter in my capacity as President of Una Voce America. In doing so, I know that I am representing both the deep respect that our organization feels for the Congregation that you head, as well as the very serious concerns that it has regarding Protocol 1411.

By this time, I am certain that you have received many letters expressing anxiety with respect to the effects that Protocol might have on the particular mission and future of the Priestly Fraternity of St. Peter. Fears will undoubtedly also have been indicated about the impact that the Protocol could have on people who have always been critical of the 1988 Indult and its reliability. These anxieties and fears are common to Una Voce America as well, and are therefore the main reason for my writing.

Allow me, however, the opportunity to strike another note, one that is of vast consequence to me as a professor of history at a Catholic university and as a father of a very young family. Although it may not involve a matter that can be weighed by canonical norms, it does, at the very least, represent a major lay concern in a Church recently rededicated to the overriding importance of pastoral considerations in her everyday life.

It is a sad fact, confirmed by large numbers of my colleagues in both confessional and secular education in the United States, that the overwhelming majority of young people in this country are receiving woefully inadequate instruction of all kinds. This failed education has left them not only indifferent to theological, philosophical, moral, historical and aesthetic questions, but often ignorant even of basic reading and writing skills. In many respects, a truly "dark age" is forming around us, and one that is made all the more frightening in that it is nevertheless accompanied by a considerable mechanical knowledge bereft of higher guidance.

Hence, it is a special joy to see the awakening of any questioning mind and spirit to the realm of truth, goodness and beauty when one does encounter it. And my experience has shown me that such minds and spirits have, without exception, found that attendance at Masses said by priests like those of the Fraternity of St. Peter, as permitted under the 1988 Indult, provides them with an opening into the broader world that their ordinary education and the surrounding culture has unfortunately denied them.

Students whom I have brought to the celebration of Holy Mass according to the 1962 Missal, at churches approved by the local Ordinary, have here encountered everything that is, ironically, almost impossible to find in the average American environment, academic or otherwise. They have been exposed to people familiar with Hebrew, Aramaic, Greek, Latin and Arabic languages. They have met scholars in patrology. Through lecture series and personal conversations they have become aware of and interested in Church History, the oriental liturgies, mystical theology, music and art. Attendance at this Mass has given them knowledge of the tremendous problem of abortion and euthanasia, since churches where Fraternity priests (and others like them) are active are invariably strongholds of the pro-life movement. For some, attendance here has been the first experience that they have had of real participation in a multi-racial community as well. In short, I have become dependent upon the atmosphere of churches where the Mass permitted by the Indult is offered for the opportunity it has demonstrably provided for introducing the young to civilized life in general. Here, they have found real love for the mind and spirit, respect for the past, recognition of the realities of modern life, and true diversity—all, I should like to add, in the context of an atmosphere of lay-clerical friendship and obedience to the Holy See. Everything that the Second Vatican Council could have hoped for regarding the creation of an educated, active laity, participating in the liturgy, is flourishing under these conditions. I should hope to see this atmosphere continue and grow stronger still, for my students' sake, and, in the long run, for the education of my own children also.

As a historian and as a father, therefore, I feel justified in adding to the most obvious concerns of Una Voce America with respect to the future of the Fraternity of St. Peter and the credibility of the Indult as a whole, a deep fear regarding the impact the Protocol might have on serious education. I should very much regret tampering with something that works so well to awaken people from intellectual and spiritual slumber; something that introduces them to the whole civilized heritage of the hunt for Truth, Goodness and Beauty. I should very much dislike leaving them with one less defense against a hopelessly inadequate educational system and the ever more barbaric environment around them. It is my firm conviction that anything disturbing the life of communities working under the Indult of 1988 would have precisely that effect.

My prayer as President of Una Voce America is that priests such as those of the Fraternity of St. Peter may continue to prosper within the framework in which they have labored so successfully up to this date, and that nothing will be done that could hinder their effective functioning under authoritative leadership. I know that they, like all of us, accept the difficulties that they are facing as part of the mystery of God's Providence, and that they will grow through them as has everyone who has worked sincerely for the renewal of Christ's Church. In the hope that my prayer will be answered, I remain

Yours truly,

John C. Rao
(D.Phil., Oxford) Assoc. Prof.,
St. John's University, NYC
President, Una Voce America

5
Curial Commission or Soviet-Style Bureau?†

As most of you are probably aware, Fred Haehnel and I were the American representatives at the International Una Voce Federation meeting at the Domus Pacis in Rome on November 13–14, 1999. Over twenty-five nations are now members of the Federation, new delegations from Argentina and Singapore being present for the first time at this year's gathering. Most of the participants, Fred and I included, arrived earlier and stayed longer than the official two day conference, partly to be able to get a better feel for the overall situation by further consultations with our fellow delegates and with others outside Una Voce in Rome.

Saturday the 13th was taken up with the presentation of official reports, both written and oral, Fr. Joseph Bisig's account of the current state of affairs in the Fraternity of St. Peter and a presentation by Mr. William Hudson on the life of the Institute of Christ the King.

As usual, the American scene compared rather favorably with that of most other countries. Delegation reports emphasized a range of problems. Some lamented the general growing indifference encountered by traditionalists as well as everyone else in the ever more devastated vineyard of the western Catholic world. Others complained of open hostility on the part of many bishops, some of whom are even willing to call upon state assistance to hamper the Traditionalist Movement. The Czech delegation recounted one incident particularly annoying to me in my capacity as Director of the Dietrich von Hildebrand Institute. Cardinal Vlk, Archbishop of Prague, postponed permission for use of the 1962 missal because of reading Dietrich von Hildebrand's The Case for the Latin Mass, claiming that "the author publicly advances the opinions of the schismatic archbishop Marcel Lefebvre," and that it was thus his

† Altered name of a report on the FIUV Conference in the *Una Voce Newsletter*, Spring 2000.

duty to prevent the faithful from being "confused" by such "non-authentic interpreters of doctrine."

Fr. Bisig's comments were realistic in their awareness of the gravity of the problems facing the Fraternity and traditionalists in general. Nevertheless, they underlined the overwhelming sense of all the conference participants that, hard as the immediate future may be, we will be able to see things through, so long as we stay united. The theme of unity should, I think, be taken very seriously by traditionalists as grounds for meditation in this upcoming Lenten season. It would be very wise indeed for each of us to resolve not to criticize one another at this juncture lest we end up harming our own cause by internal dissension without our opponents having to lift a finger. Self-destruction is always a real possibility in our current situation. Restraint in open debate within the traditionalist camp may take some effort, but it would be a useful spiritual exercise and might perhaps contribute more to final victory than anything else. I am not urging such a moratorium in perpetuity and in private, but only for the time and in the public arena.

A certain progress was reported by some participating Una Voce national chapters in comparison with the 19th meeting. Australia led the list, announcing the happy arrival of the Fraternity in the Diocese of Melbourne. The situation in the Netherlands and in Italy also seemed to be somewhat improved. Poland presented a most impressive report, including a video cassette and elegant book on the Mass celebrated in Poznan in July of this year to commemorate the 900th anniversary of the liberation of the Holy Sepulchre from Muslim control in the First Crusade. A counter-cultural event if there was one!

Sunday, November 14th, began with a Missa Cantata sung by Fr. Bisig. The day's session saw an address by His Eminence Alfons Cardinal Stickler on the dichotomy between the desires of the Council Fathers with respect to the liturgical reform—desires which he, as a peritus, was well placed to gauge—and the reality of the deformation which actually took place. It was following upon this talk that the Ecclesia Dei Commission's clarification of matters concerning Protocol 1411 and fallout from it was read. A general discussion of plans for the future closed the International Una Voce Federation meeting after dinner that same evening.

I would like to make a number of comments about the Ecclesia Dei Commission's clarification, the complete text of which can be consulted on the Una Voce website. My comments will not be those of a canonist competent to dissect legal documents and arguments. Thankfully, we do have people within the Federation who can make such observations, and make them well. Rather, my remarks will be those of a historian concerned to place events in historical context.

It is impossible to discuss this document without noting in its words and manner of presentation one basic fact: it is contrary to the expressed purpose of the Second Vatican Council. Laymen would be hard pressed to find in its content and approach the spirit of openness and pastoral awareness which one would presume to be more of a sign of acceptance of the Council than the ritual formalism of concelebration. Moreover, one could readily conclude from it that the iron curtain of clergy and laity so lamented by critics of pre-conciliar days had not been opened a fraction of an inch in the past thirty five years. "You" (the laity) and "us" (the clergy) came through with absolute clarity. Obviously, we would all agree that such a basic distinction is true with regard to state of life and function within the Church, but not with respect to our common concern for the Church's survival and our common commitment to spiritual growth. At best, the approach can be labeled impolitic. It reminded me of complaints about the British government's first propaganda efforts during the Second World War, when posters exhorted the population: "Do your duty so that we (and who are we?) can win."

Unfortunately, the Ecclesia Dei clarification is all too obviously a reflection of one of the most basic problems not only of recent Church History but of the past two centuries and more of revolutionary change: namely, the simultaneous reference to contradictory themes as a basis for authoritative action. This works, effectively, to allow a revolutionary authority to act arbitrarily, and to sow such confusion in the minds of those trying to defend order and tradition that it can even paralyze their opposition entirely.

In this particular case, "signs" and "law" are set against one another in order to permit arbitrary action. Hence, signs of the times, such as concelebration with a local Ordinary, are elevated to tests of loyalty freeing one from the suspicion of schismatic tendencies, despite the fact that legally no one is supposed to be forced to concelebrate. One wonders what other future signs may eventually be evoked to indicate true union of traditionalist priests with fellow clergy in a given diocese. On the other hand, law is also emphasized, but law which could be placed in a proper perspective by a reading of the Church's history and consideration of her pastoral sense alone. Among the legal matters mentioned are, first of all, the supposed inadmissibility of any lay concern for the internal affairs of a religious community, and, secondly, the unacceptability of referring to negotiations with Mgr. Lefebvre as a means of understanding the final agreements of 1988 establishing the Ecclesia Dei Commission and the erection of the Fraternity of St. Peter.

That the laity certainly can be involved in the internal affairs of a religious community in an inadmissible way is no doubt clear. Lay pressure led to the destruction of the Society of Jesus in the eighteenth century. Unfortunately, the Church succumbed to this pressure, praised it, and thwarted efforts to prevent it. Luckily, however, other lay involvement, even on the part of non-Catholic laity, helped to maintain the Society in its time of troubles until the day that Rome officially restored it in the early 1800s. Indeed, the whole first half of the nineteenth century (regarding which the Catholic world suffers, as one writer has noted, a "collective amnesia"), is replete with lay involvement in the work of reviving religious communities and shaping their character, whether the laity concerned were princes, journalists, or simply members of various lay-clerical circles in Germany, France, and Italy. Praise of the laity's role in this regard is a matter of public record. Does such praise always have to come after the fact? Does it have to pass through some Hegelian flip-flop in which lay activity is first identified as having been illegal, only afterwards being honored as a work of the Spirit?

The Commission's clarification makes reference to the right of every faithful Catholic to appeal to the Holy See, though it does so only in speaking of the actions of the sixteen disgruntled priests of the Fraternity. One wonders what kind of matter the laity could bring, in appeal, before the eyes of the Holy See other than what traditionalists have done concerning 1411. If the laity cannot approach the appropriate commissions and congregations of the Holy See with reference to the affairs of a religious community that baptizes it, gives it the sacraments of Penance and the Eucharist, marries it, educates its children, buries it, and is mentioned in its wills, what else could it ever legitimately bring up? All other issues pale in significance compared to these.

Moreover, treating the negotiations of the Holy See with Mgr. Lefebvre as though they have no bearing on the character of the Fraternity seems to me to be historically absurd. Indeed, when certain traditionalists criticized the 1988 agreements, claiming that they would lead to some different end than that sought after by Mgr. Lefebvre, they were, at that moment, thought of as revealing a suspicious anti-Roman spirit which probably masqueraded schismatic tendencies. It is precisely to such background negotiations that the Holy See has appealed in the past when complaining of the violation of Concordats by given nations looking for loopholes in the letter of the law. Hence, to take but one example, it always understood that Napoleon's "Organic Articles" did not flow from the Church's agreement under the French Concordat to allow police measures to protect public order, because the discussions leading to that document's acceptance did not envisage the deductions contained therein.

The effect of this simultaneous appeal to signs and law, common to much modern revolutionary discourse, is to create grave confusion in people's minds. This is especially true with regard to traditionally-minded individuals who do accept the validity of both the letter of the law and the movement of the Spirit in history. One is never sure what ground he stands on in petitioning for redress of grievance. When a stand is taken on the ground of clear legal evidence, pastoral signs are evinced as being superior to such pettifoggery and hairsplitting. When pastoral needs are called forth, they are swept away with reference to the LAW in capital letters. In the final analysis, it then seems to be the case that the authorities can do whatever they wish to do under whatever rubric they choose to operate. Those that complain can then always be accused of some form of disobedient, schismatic behavior, as, indeed, traditionalists of the most loyal stamp often are. In this context, Cardinal Bilio's critique of exaggerated Ultramontanist activity at Vatican One might justly be recalled: "this is not the way to handle the affairs of Holy Church." It is reminiscent more of the attitude of Soviet officialdom, which treated Russians who sought protection for their rights as stated in the Soviet Constitution as traitors to that Constitution—for having the temerity to request that its precepts be honored.

The Ecclesia Dei Commission is upset about tendentious use of material on the internet. That there is such tendentious use of material in this medium is, I think, indisputable. It is for such reasons that traditionalists have always warned against a too facile embrace of the wonders of the modern world, internet among them. Still, one powerful means of rendering incorrect reports harmless is to treat loyal Catholics with respect, not immediately to label them as schismatic in tendency, to answer their requests for information and help, and to listen to both sides of any given story. The Commission's record in this regard is not sterling, to say the least.

After due reflection on these questions, it strikes me that Una Voce America—and Una Voce International as a whole—should utilize the right of every faithful Catholic to appeal to the Holy See—a right noted in the clarification itself—respectfully to request a change in spirit, and, if necessary, personnel in the Ecclesia Dei Commission. Since a "pastoral sense" is now a recognized sign of unity with the Second Vatican Council, such a sense would seem to be the minimum requirement for any papal commission: especially one dealing with people who have made a special point of defending the divine authority of the See of Peter. Long live Christ the King!

6

The Good War and the Rite War[†]

A LARGE ARMY OF HISTORIANS, POLITICAL scientists, sociologists and psychologists repeatedly informs those who take theological and philosophical issues seriously that they must judge the true character and validity of their cherished principles "in context," with reference to the environment in which these were born, grew and thrived. As a historian myself, I cannot help but agree. Indeed, I would underscore the need to apply the same criterion to the investigation and judgment of every matter of significant concern to anyone. As a result, it seems to me that much more attention ought to be paid to the broad context in which the attack on the Traditional Mass—the Rite War—came to life and prospered than traditionalists in general are wont to devote to it.

Tackling this context is a complex task, as this essay will indicate. Part of its complexity is due to the fact that its context is steeped in blood. For behind all of the scholarly, spiritual and pastoral factors playing their admitted roles in the destruction of the Roman Rite lies also the tremendous influence exercised by the dramatic events and consequences of the Second World War.

Actually, the drama of the Second World War stands behind and influences every aspect of life in contemporary western society even more than do most current events. Our world feels permanently threatened by Blitzkrieg. One need only pick up a copy of a major daily newspaper or, better still, its Sunday book review section, in order to test this truth. The specifics of the war years and the struggles leading up to them are the stuff of regular reminders and admonitions used perhaps more than any other tool to explain and shape the flow of present-day political and social life.

Obviously, part of the power of the Second World War in this regard is due to its intrinsic importance, its injustices and its brutally inhuman crimes. Many nineteenth and twentieth century Catholics had predicted that precisely such a conflict would emerge in a world that sought to banish religion from the public forum

† First published in the *Latin Mass Magazine*, Spring 2001, 34–38.

and that reduced the problem of morality to individual choices and social contracts subject to the most grotesque desires and the strongest wills.

Still, the Second World War gains its force from another source as well, from its usefulness to Marxism-Leninism and Pluralism, the two ideologies emerging victorious out of the conflict, as a propaganda tool demonizing all of their opponents, whoever they might be, and thereby shoring up their already dominant position still further. They had fought the Good War versus the forces of evil. By repeatedly evoking the struggle and horror of that conflict and their central role in bringing it to a conclusion, the victorious ideologies were able to drive home the argument that everything non-Marxist and non-Pluralist was *ipso facto*, National Socialist; that anyone who opposed bloodshed, genocide and Hitlerian politics in general had better fall in behind their banners and shudder at the thought of breaking rank. Awe before the power of the forces that had fought the Good War destroying Nazism, and terror at the prospect of being identified as a Fascist, then silenced several generations of anti-Marxists and anti-Pluralists into acquiescence in the policies sanctioned by them.

Catholics were among the most seriously affected by this awe and acquiescence, and for at least five different reasons. First of all, many Catholics followed Marxist or Pluralist guidance out of the same psychological drive that leads most people to accept the validity of whatever force dominates their environment at a given moment. The difficulties of explaining a Christian position built upon theological, philosophical and cultural arguments rejected by the victors from the outset either as pure products of class consciousness or as being dangerously divisive frustrated a second group of Catholics into silence. A third Catholic element, related to the previous group, did speak out against whichever of the two victorious ideologies it deemed more dangerous, while keeping quiet about, forgetting, and eventually even praising the errors of the other. Yet a fourth segment of the Catholic population, ashamed by the fact that some fellow believers had indeed been attracted by Fascism, or had seen in it a useful tool against a more fearful Marxism, enthusiastically embraced the message of the victors to compensate for sins which, uncontested, might be used as a pretext for casting aspersions upon the whole Church's honor.

And, finally, the atmosphere created by the Good War allowed Catholics actively committed to Marxism or Pluralism an audience and impact that they otherwise might never have had, especially if these activists had done something courageous during the great conflict that gave them enormous prestige in the postwar world. It is with this last group that this essay must concern itself.

Who were these Catholics who actively aided the ideologies emerging victorious from the Second World War? They were people influenced by certain twentieth-century efforts to improve evangelization and Catholic Action who began to explain their desires in conjunction with the philosophical-political-social theory called Personalism, tapped into the heritage of the Abbé Félicité de Lamennais (1782–1854) while doing so, and found encouragement in the speculations of the Jesuit, Pierre Teilhard de Chardin (1881–1955). Let us look at the history of this activism, since it throws a good deal of light upon the battles and outcome of the Rite War.

Interest in the improvement of evangelization and Catholic Action can be examined together under the heading of zeal for the Missions. Nineteenth and early twentieth century Catholics began to speak of the existence of the Outer Missions (those focused on bringing the Faith to non-Christian peoples) and the Inner Missions (those aimed at the secularized populations of what were thought of generally as already Christianized lands) as two parts of an overall enterprise of evangelization. Some of those engaged in such labors, building upon the experience of generations of missionaries in the tradition of Matteo Ricci, became more and more convinced of the need for a deeper effort to "get under the skins" of those whom they were trying to evangelize—to "inculturate" the Faith, as one would say in our own day, so that Christianity did not appear to them to be an alien force, but something best suited to their own development and perfection. The names Charles de Foucauld (1858–1916) and Vincent Lebbe (1877–1940) are very important in this regard with respect to the Outer Missions, while the Inner Missions took a great deal of inspiration from men like Joseph Cardijn (1886–1967) and his conception of a Catholic Action specialized according to the nature of the groups it targeted.

Personalism, as it developed in the 1920s and 1930s, perhaps ought to be referred to as a movement rather than a specific idea. Many circles of thinkers used the term and some of the themes associated with it, and it is in this sense that Jacques Maritain (1882–1973), principally thought of in conjunction with the related but more structured vision of Integral Humanism, may be cited as a Personalist. Still more tied to the specific term Personalism is the figure of Emmanuel Mounier (1905–1950), editor of the journal, *l'Esprit*, and destined, like Maritain, to have a wide influence beyond Europe in radicalizing the Catholic camp after the Second World War.

Personalism has its roots in much nineteenth and early twentieth century thought concerning the importance of "vitality" and "action" as guides to truth, Lamennais' heritage playing a major role in transmitting such interest among Catholics. The interest in vitality and action was enlivened still further by meditation upon the experience of front-line soldiers during the First World War, who heroically sacrificed themselves together in a common cause despite their divisions into so many different religious, political and social factions at home. Insofar as one can synthesize a complex and often very confusing vision, Personalism argued something like the following: The individual, trapped inside himself, is a dead man. To develop into a true "person," capable of fulfilling all his potential and destiny, he must dive into a deeper life beyond himself, into the life of the group, the life of the community. Which group? Which community? Precisely a group or community which, by its vitality and effective, cohesive action, shows itself worthy and capable of drawing the individual outside himself.

A Christian Personalist would consider even an individual believer who submitted to the teachings and rituals of a Church outside of himself to be a crippled personality if his spiritual and secular life continued to be lived basically on his own. "Tridentine" Catholicism, with its emphasis on private devotions and concern for individual sanctification, was accused of encouraging just this sort of crippled behavior. A full grip on the Christian message and a full perfection of personhood required self-loss and a complete donation to Christ as revealed in the vital, active community or communities around him. Tie Personalism and the twofold movement of evangelization together and the missionary's program then becomes clear. He must "get out" of himself and his narrow presuppositions about Christianity, and give himself over to the vital, effective, cohesive, active group or culture to which he is sent. The spirit of Christ that is revealed by each of them is to be nurtured by him and brought to its innate perfection. In helping it along, he is "witnessing" to his presumably still more complete Christian Faith in a quiet, humble, and ultimately more successful way, and yet actually learning things about Christ that he could never otherwise have known outside the group.

The Second World War sparked a deeper and more radicalized alliance of the Outer and Inner Missions with Personalism. It demonstrated to Catholic activists how little they had really achieved in the way of influencing the many specialized groups with which the war now forced them into even closer contact and under much more difficult conditions, whether in the army or in forced labor camps in their home countries and in Germany. Many of those experiencing the hostility or indifference to Catholicism on the part of soldiers and laborers from a myriad of social and ethnic backgrounds began to argue for a total immersion in the milieu to which the activist was sent. This immersion demanded a root and branch obliteration of all previous education and practice that gave the militant missionary a different character from someone from the milieu in which he was to operate; it was to be a total immersion perhaps necessitating a greater or even complete reliance upon that specialized milieu for teaching the message of Christ. The awesome drama of the new kind of evangelization this would entail began to be linked with a faith in an evolution towards a greater universal knowledge and manifestation of the love of Christ as argued by Teilhard de Chardin. Studies on the worker-priest movement, especially that of Emile Poulat (*Les prêtres-ouvriers: Naissance et fin*, 1999), are particularly helpful in tracing such developments.

World War Two also served as a vehicle for spreading the message of this more radicalized alliance. It did so partly because a number of its advocates eventually became active on anti-Nazi journals or in partisan, anti-deportation and anti-forced labor movements, thereby gaining prestige as heroic exemplars for future generations. It did so also because it brought to power Marxists whose vitally and cohesive action was seen by many Personalists to be a clear sign of the presence of that spirit of Christ to which militants had to witness and help perfect for the sake of the Faith. Moreover, the Good War promoted Pluralists, who justified and praised the existence of a variety of different milieus and the validity of the messages that they all proclaimed, and Christian Democratic movements which always carried at least a germ of Lamennais' influence in their train. Hence, both Marxism and Pluralism helped the radicalized cause. Moreover, the War and its use as a symbol by the victors gave to this cause a wonderful propaganda tool: the ability, if other arguments failed, to demonize Catholics opposing it as Fascist brutes.

Whatever the true merits of inculturation may be—and I think that there are many—its historical alliance with Personalism and radicalization in the context of the experiences and aftermath of the war have been a disaster. A Pandora's Box of problems has been opened in consequence. By insisting upon an unprejudiced dive into the vital, active milieu in which the spirit of Christ is taught, no contact with a vital, active historical Christ outside of and above these milieus is really permitted. The objective reality of the Incarnate God-Man is thus ultimately called into question, the very concept actually being identified as merely a "western" understanding of the work of the spirit in human life. No culture is allowed the possibility of making an objective contribution to human life capable of influencing another one, Greco-Roman civilization undergoing the supreme punishment of being stripped of all right to speak any message whatsoever, given its use for precisely this supra-cultural mission in the past. All cultures become like ships passing one another in the night, with no philosophy, no theology and no Christ as polar star above them by means of which they might navigate with precious cargo safely from port to port.

Finally, the call for unquestioning faith in the spirit of Christ operating in the vital active communities one encounters, unguided by a historical Christ and the objective achievements of any historical cultures, is a recipe for self-lobotomy. It denies all merit to reason and logical judgment, which many Personalists sarcastically denounced as just another piece of the useless baggage of the crippled individual who needs to be dragged into the supra-rational vitality of community-minded personhood for his own benefit. And it is no wonder that they do so! For the more one encourages abandonment to a spirit that neither dogmatic Christian Faith nor objective norms of reason and science are allowed to judge, the less one will see what that "spirit of Christ" really is to which one is obliged to "witness." Indeed, it can at times be something good and blessed by the hands of God. But practically speaking, under such influences, and in our day, it is most often a "spirit" inspired by a libido for the base and the ugly that is rejected as sinful or blasphemous by the Christian Tradition, a force manipulated by strong individuals and groups who themselves arbitrarily define the specifics of that providential spirit to which they demand all others bend.

Here, as far as I am concerned, is the essence of the horror unleashed by opening up the Pandora's Box of this radicalized alliance. All calls for submission to vital, active, effective community guidance from the time of Lamennais to that of Mounier have entailed, first, the destruction of any means of distinguishing between a good and bad manifestation of communal energy, and, next, the determination, in practice, of what is or is not acceptable on the basis of the imposition of the will of charismatic interpreters of the "right kind of vitality." "Getting outside of oneself" ends in immersion in the interior life of "vanguards of the people" who insist upon faith in their judgments as though they were not really their own dicta but those of the community, itself pressed forward by the mysterious designs of Providence.

But turning inward, away from the focus on the truly other, involves, as Dietrich von Hildebrand so well described in Transformation in Christ, a deeper and deeper plunge into the untutored self and its temptation to view what is cheapest, most immediately impressionable to the senses and most parochial as somehow more "real," more rewarding and more expressive of the will of God. This, Professor David White notes, helps to explain why Dante's Inferno is more appealing to our contemporaries than the Paradiso.

And this is why certain priests in German labor camps treated the hell that they endured therein as providing a more clear teaching about the reality of life than the refined peacetime world from which they had come. Christian order had to be built upon the vivid context of experienced hell; the man who wished to found that order upon reflection aiming upwards was merely a slave of the crippled past. I do not in any way deny the significance of the experience in focusing someone on existential questions; the crux of the matter is whether that overpowering hellishness should become the supreme and sole guide to the construction of Christendom.

It is crucial to recall that all of this emphasis upon vitality, charismatic leadership and effective action was of central concern to twentieth-century Fascism. And, therefore, it ought not to come as a surprise that many of those involved in the developments discussed above had a great interest and sympathy for fascist movements of all kinds, tempered only by a dislike of Nazi racism, and, of course, an ultimate rejection of a force that proved itself to be insufficiently vital to dominate the world. What is perhaps more startling is the ability displayed by those expressing such sympathy to ride the wave of vitality into either the Marxist or the Pluralist camp after the War, to disassociate themselves in the mind of the public from a philo-Fascist spirit, and even to use the accusation of Fascism against others as an effective club to brutalize and silence their enemies. That cudgel has been used to great advantage, in the Americas as much as in Europe. Pity the poor opponent who wanders into the realm of the radicalized Personalist evangelist interpreting the desires of his community! He is like someone going to a dinner party given by a man who has declared cannibalism to be the expression of his and all his other guests' deepest spiritual longings. Terrified at the thought of criticizing his host's proclivity lest he be identified as an unrealistic, shriveled-up individualist lacking faith in the action of the Spirit, and a Fascist to boot, the poor soul is eaten alive at the command of the only real representative of the Triumph of the Will who is present. At least the victim can console himself with the thought that he is not alone in his misery. The same fate befalls practically every enemy of the dominant forces of contemporary western society, characterized by people gleefully making willful "choices" destroying the lives of others.

But how has the Good War, in sparking and serving as a vehicle for the radicalized alliance of evangelization and Personalism, affected the Rite War? How could it not? Everything, from dogmatic theology to catechetics to popular devotion has been affected by it, and the liturgical movement, a number of whose advocates interacted with missionary and personalist circles, more than most. A Catholicism that is obliged not merely to take into account but to bend to what is defined as the "spirit of Christ" waiting to come to perfection in each and every vital, active group and culture that it encounters, is bound radically to alter its liturgical practices as well. It is bound to continue to do so each time a vital, active interpreter of spirits identifies yet another energetic community with a message to which the missionary must witness. A Catholicism that is told that in order to confront and develop Christ fully within these milieus it must abandon, as insensitive prejudice, all education and tradition standing in the way of a wholehearted acceptance of their messages, is stripped of any means of judging whether it really ought to be open to each and every aspect of liturgical inculturation. Indeed, it is deprived, in the long run, of any means of nurturing a memory of its past teachings, and any connection between the *lex orandi* and the *lex credendi* whatsoever. The liturgical movement merges with all other movements in Church life into one, uniform, Self-Lobotomization Movement. Leave Faith, Reason and History behind, ye who enter it!

Everything I have noted as a consequence of the radicalized alliance of evangelization and Personalism has manifested itself clearly in the Rite War. Individual devotion has not been helped, but drowned in communal rites. These are diversified *ad infinitum*, as each parish and each proclivity discovers its own startling new spirit, needs and message to teach—the more Spartan, the more drab, and, in fact, in many cases, the more grossly sensual, the more identified with what is truly "real." This began by tapping into many soldiers' memories of hearing Mass on the back of a jeep, amidst their comrades, with the sounds of artillery around them (and probably praying more devoutly than ever before), contrasting the "truth" of that experience with the "artificiality" of the liturgy and parish life under normal peacetime circumstances, and calling for reform to recapture the lost ties with a more serious "reality." It has translated in the United States (and elsewhere) into endless liturgical revolutions "listening" to every "need" from the homosexual to the capitalist (with the latter making good money off of each change in calendar and ritual practice). Everywhere these new rites are invented not spontaneously out of communal desire, but in typical revolutionary fashion by vital teachers of the will of the community, as illustrated by the silencing I once witnessed of a Hispanic group singing traditional hymns to the Madonna so that it could be forced to stutter other hymns unknown, yet declared to be more consonant with its true spirit by the liturgical experts who had created them out of the blue. Everywhere, the starting principle of the more serious liturgical movement—the need to go back to the ancient sources—has given way to a reliance on no sources except those of the interpreters of the community, and a demand for "faith" in the manipulated spirit and signs of the times that these reveal. And luring behind it all lies the threat of chastising whoever would criticize such changes not on the basis of what such criticisms really are—a call to true faith, to objective use of reason, and to a respect for tradition that any real culture (like the Chinese) always takes seriously—but as something racist, elitist, restrictive, anti-pluralist, or, in a word, Fascist.

A study of the broad context in which the Rite War has been fought thus reveals a great deal about the nature of the victory that has temporarily been won by the innovators. It is a victory that, despite the contribution of scholars and pious men aware of the reality and value of liturgical developments, has been shaped, in practice, much more by events and a mentality connected with the Good War. It is a victory that has placed the wrong spirit in charge of the most sensitive aspects of Christian life, one that allows for an irrational, cheap and willful program to be promoted in the name of fulfilling all that is best in human nature and dearest to God's heart. It is a victory that inverts reality and answers rational criticism with propaganda slogans and a Nietzschean disdain disguised as enlightenment, strong with the confidence of the victor who knows that he defines the meaning of words for the mass of frightened mankind. Let us hope that awareness of this context may help to free men from fear, and that the Rite War will end in a victory of Tradition calling attention to the failed promise of the Good War, so that the Truth may really overcome the Triumph of the Will.

7
Change and Changers†

TO SAY THAT WE ARE LIVING IN CONFUSing and rapidly changing times is to state the obvious. To determine an appropriate response to this overwhelming sense of often incomprehensible flux is another story entirely. Unfortunately, the success rate in the Response to Change Game is not a particularly impressive one.

Some people, disturbed by the uncertainties and nightmares of unbridled change, are convinced that they are living in the end times. After condemning the disastrous flux around them, they predict imminent Divine Judgment of one sort or another upon it and then avoid petty battles with the admittedly distasteful foe. While understandable, this is not an appropriate practical response to our dilemma. For, although the end times will certainly one day be a reality, a focus upon their approach does not help us to deal with the question of where to attend Sunday Mass until the axe falls. Much less does it enable us to confront the truth that our own individual date with eternity may be just seconds away, reducing the grander picture to a matter of considerably secondary personal importance.

Most of our contemporaries, however, do not respond to rapidly changing times in the same dramatic and apocalyptic manner. Instead, they draw the rather banal conclusion that everything and everyone must, of necessity, change along with observable changes in society, whether they approve of these or not. Hence, the presumption by many Catholics that a world which is continuously evolving along materialistic, hedonistic, anti-intellectual, pluralist lines requires a liturgy (or liturgies) marching happily, unquestioningly, or grudgingly in step with it. This is not a rational position, but, rather, one reflecting a disturbed psychological state inviting medical intervention. Nevertheless, it is a viewpoint that has been ably exploited for over two hundred years by men for whom change has become a religion, and often a personally profitable one as

† First published in the *Una Voce Newsletter*, Spring 2001.

well. There is, however, another approach towards dealing with a rapidly changing world different from one of abandonment of all human hope or unquestioning acceptance. It is that of thoughtful examination of the transformations around us, on the basis of our faith, our reason and our knowledge of history. Such examination, now as ever, puts the horrors of the present into a calmer perspective, relativizes specific changes and recognizes that many of these are misplaced and wicked, calling for stubborn opposition with every ounce of energy we can muster.

Una Voce represents this third approach towards facing change in the liturgy. While admitting the nightmarish character of the liturgical chaos into which we have been swept, it is not prepared to close up shop and run for the hills. While agreeing that we, as mortal, historical beings, do indeed live in a world of change, it is not ready to make that change into an idol before which everything substantive and beautiful must scrape and bow. And seeing, as it does, hideous deformities in liturgical changes which must be reproved by anyone who understands how a destruction of what is most rooted in a given people's beliefs and culture amounts to annihilation of that people as a whole, it is and always will be committed to the fight for the Traditional Mass.

We cannot claim to imagine the precise way in which our struggle will end. That outcome is in the hands of God. The restoration of the Traditional Liturgy—which we believe to be essential to our survival as a distinctly Roman Catholic community—will take place in a Church and in a world which will inevitably be different from that of 1969 or 1963 or 1958. But one thing is certain amidst that uncertainty. Our labors will not have been in vain. We will not have fought illicit change to no effect. For history is not somehow made purely by people who foment change; it is made by those who oppose it as well. Western civilization would be a quite unrecognizable force today if the medieval world had been shaped only by the irresistible changes caused by German barbarian invasion and not also by the superior spirits and intellects battling vigorously to Romanize and Christianize them, and to restore the Empire while doing so. It would be unrecognizable had there been only supine acceptance of the winds of Protestant change, and no Jesuits or Council of Trent to stand in their way armed with weapons built from the Catholic Tradition. It has been one of the most useful tricks of the high priests of the religion of Change to claim that they are the sole real makers of history, and that the rest of us are mere obstructers of the inevitable. This is indeed one of the "big lies" with an unfortunately long record of success behind it.

So fight on, Una Voce chapters—the battle for the future of the Church and the world continues. We are defending a liturgy with a tested ability to teach and to unite us with the dead and those yet unborn in a glorious hymn of praise to God; a liturgy which only evolves organically, in order better and more beautifully to express unchanging Truth, out of solid roots untouched by the picks and shovels of irrational idolaters of change; a liturgy exercising an incalculable impact on all of civilization. The history which is made by men and women dedicated to its survival and victory is history with a long life ahead of it. The history made by professional Changers is the really valueless product. To paraphrase the Italian poet of despair, Leopardi, it comes from nowhere, is going nowhere, and has nothing to hope for either now or in some nonexistent future.

8
Nowhere to Run†

ST. JOHN CHRYSOSTOM HAS A WONDERFUL passage in his conclusion to the Homilies on Romans (32), in which he describes the astonishment and delight with which friends and fellow believers will greet one another in Rome on the day of the Resurrection. This meditation of the Patriarch of Constantinople came to my mind as I began to prepare a brief description of the meeting of the International Federation of Una Voce on October 13th and 14th, 2001 at the Domus Pacis in Rome, since something of the same spirit of wonder in the face of renewed life seemed to me to characterize that gathering. Why should this have been so? Because of the contrast of atmosphere between this year's session and the one that preceded it. Quite frankly, the cloud of Protocol 14:1 hung heavily over the 1999 meeting, bringing with it the fear of death for the fraternities and institutes preparing priests to say the Traditional Mass. And yet, two years later, Una Voce delegates found themselves back together again in the Eternal City, far from dead and even entertaining guarded hopes for the future.

Four factors, aside from the normal joy accompanying reunion with people of like mind, worked in tandem to give substance to this feeling of resurrection. The first was the sense of continuity and growth instilled in the delegates by the presence of our President Emeritus, Dr. Eric de Saventhem (a man who never abandoned the struggle for the 1962 missal, even in its moments of greatest vulnerability), alongside representatives from new national Una Voce chapters, such as that of Finland. Very encouraging reports on the progress of the Fraternity of St. Peter and the Institute of Christ the King provided a second encouragement to a federation which believes that it is defending not only a living, perennial tradition, but also precisely the liveliest elements in the contemporary Church. A third aid to a vision of revival was the splendid Sunday Solemn High Mass celebrated by a priest from

† First published in the *Una Voce Newsletter*, Winter 2001.

Gricigliano at the Church of Gesù e Maria on the Via del Corso, and accompanied by the music of the Una Voce Rome choir and organist. Finally, a feeling of renewed calling to an ever more necessary mission in the midst of a continuing ecclesiastical crisis was stirred by Alfons Maria Cardinal Stickler's address at the Open Forum at the Domus Pacis on Sunday afternoon. Conscious of the justice of our cause and the solidity of Christ's promise to uphold his Church, he emphasized his personal conviction that the Third Millennium would indeed see the definitive victory of the Catholic message.

Nevertheless, my resurrection analogy can only be taken so far. St. John Chrysostom was speaking of the real thing; I am merely evoking a feeling at a conference of a federation that is forced to confront daily and generally highly unpleasant earthly realities. And the reality, for Una Voce, is clearly still one involving patient, persistent, and often thankless battle. A sense of realism, consonant with a Christian hope that refuses to be cheapened by the banal "optimism" of the modern spirit, was also, therefore, omnipresent in Cardinal Stickler's words. He insisted upon unflinching recognition of the depth of the current ecclesiastical disaster, not simply in the realm of the liturgy, but in other spheres as well. His Eminence lamented the tragic dechristianization of that very Europe which had brought the Faith to the rest of the globe, but which was itself now in need of evangelization.

This realism was matched, both in public and private statements, by the concerns of the delegates regarding the possible continued effects of Protocol 1411, the problematic character of the Ecclesia Dei Commission, and the fallout from the so-called "Reform of the Reform" upon our efforts to maintain the 1962 missal. The more subdued tone with which discussion proceeded, in comparison to the 1999 conference, seemed to underline a realization, as the Una Voce America report states, that we are frozen in a situation requiring some dramatic authoritative action to thaw. Unfortunately, such measures do not appear to be imminent, especially given the failure of negotiations aimed at reconciling the Society of St. Pius X.

In other words, to summarize my central point, the Roman meeting reflected our happiness to be alive, but, barring unexpected events, our recognition that we have a long road yet to haul. At the risk of belaboring and exaggerating the argument, I might add the darkly humorous comments of an elderly Italian friend with whom I dined one day. "I was born in one world conflict," he said, "lived through another, experienced the evils of both the Communists and the Nazis, and suffered through the Second Vatican Council. All that was missing was a Muslim Holy War, and now I'm facing that. You are only fifty years old. Good luck!" Hangman's humor, indeed.

But grim reality in no way kills Christian hope, which knows that God can accomplish what is beyond human ability alone to achieve. And, in fact, Cardinal Stickler's hope-filled address had the ultimate aim of urging all of us on to faith-filled action. He stressed that we must do everything in our power to make clear to people the nature and extent of the devastation that the Church is experiencing, and avoid anxiety over the question of personal success or failure in this common enterprise. The new *Latin Mass Magazine*, he explained, was an excellent example of how this work could be done justly, respectfully, and effectively. Enumerating the articles in the last issue one by one, he had especially kind words for the homeschooling movement as a force for keeping the Faith alive under difficult circumstances.

Mention of the *Latin Mass Magazine* and the homeschooling movement brings us back to the American front of the international traditionalist battle. I should like to conclude this article by noting that our own national struggles appear to be designed to respond to the call for renewed action while also insisting upon the maximum development of a virtue which I, personally, do not possess to any memorable degree: the virtue of patience. Not that traditionalists the world over do not find their practice of this virtue tested. We, as Catholics, are members of a Church in which authority lies unquestionably with the hierarchy. Nothing permanent and good in the Roman Catholic Church can ever be accomplished without the support of the bishops and the pope, and obtaining this, as innumerable historical examples indicate, can often take a great deal of time, during which an impressive number of ulcers can develop. Most countries have suffered more in this regard than we in the United States have done. Rather, American traditionalist patience is particularly tested due to the perplexing and wearisome attacks that we have to endure from the conservative and neo-conservative Catholic camp.

I must confess that I have been sheltered from such outbursts for a long time, because I have been somewhat buried in my own historical studies. Nevertheless, while in Rome, I finally read a compilation of some of these attacks, completing this with an examination of certain conservative websites upon my return to New York. Annoyed incredulity are the only words I can summon to describe my reaction to the vast bulk of the complaints against us that I found therein. Our sin against the Holy Ghost seems to be our failure, enthusiastically, to accept as a given the superiority of absolutely everything emerging from Rome. The numerous historical struggles of both laity and clergy to move Roman authorities to correct horrendous mistakes for which the latter themselves have often been responsible apparently offer no model for their loyal Catholic descendants to follow. Presumably, the conservatives would permit us to join the Church in praising the efforts of dead heroes, but to do nothing, while alive, other than to glorify as the height of human and divine wisdom what these very saints found horrifying when confronted with similar problems in the past. What makes this particularly offensive is the fact that "loyalty through acquiescence to abuse" is promoted at a time when the Church is priding herself on a new openness to reason, history, and lay action—and demonstrating it by condemning much of her own tradition.

One wonders when the statute of limitations on criticism runs out. Will the conservatives allow us to fight against the current disaster ten, twenty, fifty, or one hundred years from now, when the ecclesiastical climate alters? Will we then be able to view the decisions of Vatican II and their practical implementation with the theological and historical rigor which everyone allows a scholar like Hubert Jedin to have done with the much more openly dogmatic Council of Trent? Or is this the one era in two thousand years over which historians of the papacy such as Ludwig von Pastor could have shed no tears whatsoever? Frankly, despite my own annoyed incredulity, I think that patient silence is the proper response to most of these attacks. It does not seem to me that any reasoned argument would dent the armor that withstands the testimony of endless pages of Church History. Nor do I think that the cause of the 1962 missal is helped by the wasting of effort to demonstrate that we are the "good traditionalists," different from those others with whom we do, indeed, very often disagree.

We will always be considered beyond the pale for failing to treat our own flawed age as uniquely irreproachable, while every other period is run through the mill. Una Voce's renewed life since 1999 ought best to be used by following Cardinal Stickler's advice: to continue, unceasingly, to present the evidence of a disaster which no false optimism can profitably hide; to beg our ecclesiastical authorities to do something about it, especially in light of our special mission, by seeking permission for the Traditional Mass; and to exercise true Christian charity in all our undertakings, while declining invitations to illustrate this charity by abandoning entirely our plea to the hierarchy to protect the flock it was sent to guide. The disaster affecting the Church is not the product of a traditionalist imagination gone mad. It is real. We have no other choice than that of patient persistence in bringing this reality before unwilling eyes. And in a dechristianized world, we have nowhere to run if we refuse to do so and continue to wish to live.

9
Drinking the Dregs†

"IF CONTEMPORARY SOCIETY DOES NOT DISintegrate," an old departed friend of mine argued twenty four years ago, at the time of Paul VI's death, "it will be an insult to my Reason as well as to my Faith." He said this not as though he were filled with joy at the thought of the problems that would inevitably flow from social collapse, and for innocent and guilty alike, but out of a growing exasperation at the fact that anything so badly flawed and corrupting as modern civilization could continue to survive much longer. I recall his words frequently these days, and should like to make some comments upon them which I believe to be pertinent to the life of Una Voce America and International. I do this with some trepidation, however, since I feel as though I am either repeating what I have already said before, or, perhaps, simply belaboring the obvious.

First of all, it seems to me that my friend, were he still alive, would now feel that his natural and supernatural faculties had finally been given their due respect. Anyone with eyes to see what is happening in the globe at large today must realize that Faith and Reason have not accepted being mocked. A world that has indeed disdained them is disintegrating around us at an almost incredible pace. Church, state, and economy are in such wobbly and fluid conditions as to make the mortally-ill civilization of 1978 appear positively vigorous, coherent and full of promise in comparison. Institutions and individuals wander from disaster to disaster like madmen, punished, on the one hand, by their failure to heed the laws of God, and on the other by their indifference to the wisdom and warnings of Socrates, Plato, and Aristotle. Surely, one would be tempted to think, anything as religiously confused as the modern progressive clerical establishment lies exposed to an imminent *coup de grace*. Inventing novelties at will, mired in sexual and financial scandals, losing the allegiance of layer after layer of the faithful, including the enormous number of Hispanics

---

† First published in the *Una Voce Newsletter*, Winter 2002.

who have defected to evangelical Protestantism and Pentecostalism, burying the name of Christ Himself in ecumenical abandonment to a pluralism that cannot get enough of Catholic self-humiliation, it has forgotten the nature of the Church's most basic work and why she alone can accomplish it. There is nothing but an embarrassment of choice regarding which of the other equally disturbed forces of our disintegrating culture might administer the final blow to this decrepit and inept band before succumbing to its own justified demise in turn.

On second thought, however, one needs to recognize that the final agony of modern anti-Catholic, anti-rational society, and the progressive clerical establishment that has become its ally, may last longer and involve still worse consequences than any of us would particularly like to contemplate. Yes, the chief principle on which modernity has been founded—the idea of the self-sufficiency of a natural world which is depicted sometimes as a predictable machine and sometimes as a fountain of innumerable, unpredictable, but justifiable passions—is erroneous and contradictory; it was bound, from the outset, to miserable failure. Nevertheless, it has been promoted openly for some two hundred fifty years by now (and in intellectual circles before that for much longer), with each generation of its opponents—our spiritual ancestors—incorrectly predicting its immediate collapse.

That this fate has not yet befallen it is, I think, due to many reasons, only two of which I will note here. One of them is the simple fact that it is human beings who are the agents of ideas, and many of these flawed and irrational creatures have often worked in practice against the development of the logic of the principles that they espouse, generally as a result of the continuing strong effects of traditional values upon them. They have delayed the harm of modern poison by a frequently unconscious recourse to its traditionalist antidote.

A second factor involves a failure of imagination on the part of the opponents of modernity; an inability to see just how elevated the civilization that they loved really was, and just how far they could descend before the chasm labeled total chaos opened up underneath them. I know this lack of imagination very well, since I suffer from it myself. It explains to me my surprise, every four years or so, by a qualitative decline in an educational system which

I already thought had hit rock bottom. Apparently, "the powers that be" are able to mine, with every generation of new high school students, the lodes of the logic of decay in areas where digging had not yet begun. With the realization of the potential for a still deeper descent into darkness comes the feeling, perhaps most effectively expressed by Saint Catherine of Siena when trying to woo the Papacy from Avignon back to Rome in the 1370s, that the worst of one's contemporary ecclesiastical scandal has not yet unfolded. She had the Great Western Schism lying in the wings. What rough beast slouches towards the front pages of our major dailies and prime time television screens to frighten still more blood from our already overly pale cheeks?

One thing that rarely, if ever, seems to change through all the evidence of decay and disintegration is the confidence of our opponents in their own erroneous views, even when these lead to the destruction of what they themselves claim to desire. Their tenacity is not surprising; it forms part of the very essence of modern ideology, whose peculiarity was vividly captured by an anecdote cherished by one of my undergraduate professors. He repeatedly told us the tale of a man who wakes up and informs his wife that she is dead. She ignores him at first, but, given his insistence on this absurd theme throughout the day, grows alarmed and invites a physician friend to dinner to help her convince him of his madness. Over coffee, the physician asks his friend whether or not dead men bleed. "Of course not!," he responds in annoyance. The physician then takes his finger, pricks it with a pin, and squeezes out a few drops. "What do you think now?," he triumphantly inquires. "Look at that!," his friend exclaims. "Dead men do bleed!" No evidence to the contrary can convince the ideologue that he is wrong. "So much the worse for the facts!," Hegel is apocryphally said to have snarled to a critical student seeking to refute the philosopher's theories with reference to mere truth.

Unfortunately, the most painful examples of this ideological behavior in face of the evidence come, once again, from the ranks of those who call themselves conservatives; those who, as Louis Veuillot complained in the nineteenth century, are so good at conservation that they conserve, indiscriminately, good and bad alike. Una Voce members know exactly what I mean in this regard. Having started with an exaggerated understanding of the infallibility of the Church at large and the Papacy in particular—a position precisely rejected while defining the dogma of Papal Infallibility at Vatican One—they have deemed themselves obliged to accept the revolutionary principles of the progressive establishment, follow these wherever they lead, and praise the consequences that have been drawn from them as an integral and holy part of Sacred Tradition. Hence, the Catholic Stalinism that has become the distinguishing mark of some of their more virulent spokesmen; a Stalinism that purges the Old Guard, invents explanations for bizarre policies on all levels of Church activity that bear no relation to their actual genesis and blames abuses on traitors, wreckers, and Catholic Trotskyites. This Stalinism has succumbed to a cult of personality so completely that it could already commission a hagiographic biography of the next Pontiff, all of whose actions can be attributed to genius and the Holy Spirit, leaving a blank space for the name to be inserted upon his election.

The one element that adds a curious contradictory touch to this approach, indicating that the real heart of the conservatives is still with true Tradition, is the continued appearance of articles and advertisements in their publications dealing with the life and heroes of the Church before the Second Vatican Council, as though these have not, in practice, been "whited out," like doctored photographs from the Soviet era, by anyone who really grasps the current party line. Admittedly, even those of us—like Una Voce members—who do take all the evidence seriously, might be tempted by the sheer quantity of bad news into adopting false conservative positions as well. We might want the relief that comes from giving exaggerated significance to a hopeful sign here and attributing abuses merely to the fluke of a bad bishop or an undetected conspiracy there. Then we, too, might be able to enjoy seeing the best of times in what are actually the worst of times. Even more horribly, the inundation of bad news might attract us to the flip side of the conservative attitude, the one which presumes the Pope to be above all criticism, sees that such criticism is nevertheless due, and concludes that the See of Peter must be vacant.

Such temptations have to be fought, and, once again, in the name of all the evidence. The evidence of Sacred Tradition shows us that the Church is still the Church, and her authorities still her authorities. It reveals to us where her indefectibility lies and what its boundaries are. It teaches us that her fallible, human character has been badly vitiated by alliance with the revolutionary principles that have plagued the other institutions of the western world for so very long now, bringing the string of consequences which have recently plunged us further into chaos, and which could propel us still deeper into the pit. It leaves us with our Faith unscathed because it demonstrates that nothing has happened that could bring our Faith into question. Neither our Faith nor our Reason has been mocked. "Thank heavens I believe in God," my deceased friend also once said. "It has saved me from the foolishness of believing in men." The evidence has illustrated to us that it is foolish mankind and not divine institutions which is to blame for our troubles.

One thing, therefore, that Una Voce members need not stir up is any existential angst in the midst of disintegration. All that we see happening around us was bound to happen. Our task, as ever, is that of collecting the evidence, presenting it before the proper authorities with a constant demand for redress of grievances, avoiding false explanations and false hopes regarding who is or is not on our side, drawing profit from whatever crumbs of cooperation come our way, and doing the organizational work to keep together the broken shards of Catholic structure and culture that we encounter and can reshape. I know that all of you are doing this already, as the excellent national conference in California has recently so well demonstrated. The seeds laid down in seemingly infertile soil today will blossom beautifully when rained upon properly in the future. Dry spells may still lie ahead, but they only presage the inevitable day when the Church turns right side up again.

10

Roma e Mia Homa

(An Esoteric and Carefully Deconstructed Allegory in One Act)

PREMIERE AND FINAL PERFORMANCE

Tenth Anniversary of the Summer Symposium, April, 2002

FORLORN CATHOLIC GIRL: Another skull-cracking migraine. Perpetual dyspepsia. An ever-augmented sense of loss, abiding ennui and loathing. The cause? Would you like to hear? No? Perhaps I'll tell you anyway. Why shouldn't you be as miserable as I am?

"THE MODERN CATHOLIC"
(To the Tune of "Somewhere Over the Rainbow")

I'm a modernized Catholic, up to date;
All my chains have been shattered, no Pope controls my fate.
I've abandoned my Latin and my Greek;
No Augustine or Thomas, I'm no doctrinal geek.

I'm now ruled by the People, votes pour in;
Liberals count all the ballots, somehow they always win.
Far away from the Papists, free I breathe;
That's at least what they've told me, pers'nally I'd rather leave.

For being psychoanalyzed, professionally stripped of my Tradition;
I gradually have surmised my Liberators planned for my complete submission.

Somewhere, back in the ghetto, Catholics play;
There's Indulgence for sinners—yearly, by month, by day.
Somewhere, things have a meaning, Truth is found;
When nuns preach at the pulpit, eggs teach them to sit down.

Oh Catholics must still congregate and logic'lly debate around the bottle;
While some they excommunicate, and most they urge to procreate, like Aristotle.

Somewhere, handshakes are shaken outside church;
And confessional schedules need no computer search.
Somewhere, laymen keep quiet, bishops bish;
Is there no way to realize my deep Platonic wish?

GUIDE: Young lady, why are you crying? Your essential wish can be turned into a substantive reality. Look at this letter I have received. (*The guide shows her a* very wide letter *with the word* "Generous" *written boldly on it*). A Commission has been established which can give wide and generous permission to all Catholics who wish to return to the ghetto to do so forthwith. Permission is being granted every day. Imagine! No more Liberators! You can go back to a place where you can say whatever you think! You don't have to smile all day long! Or tell everyone to have a nice day! You don't have to use code words like "pepperoni" when you talk about burning heretics!

FORLORN GIRL: Can this really be true? And, if so, how do we get to the Commission?

GUIDE: It's easy! You just follow Anathema Road!

FORLORN GIRL: Follow Anathema Road?

WE'RE OFF TO THE COMMISSION
(*To the Tune of "We're Off to See the Wizard"*)

Follow Anathema Road.
Follow Anathema Road.
Follow, follow, follow, follow, follow Anathema Road.

We're off to the Commission that gives a Permission a Day;
We're sure to gain a place to say whatever we wish we may!
Whatever, whatever we wish we may, the Commission that
gives a Permission a Day;
Will find a spot where we can pray and play—
And pontificate in a Catholic way!

We're off to the Commission that gives a Permission a Day!!

THE FORLORN LADY AND THE GUIDE MEET THE APOLOGIST

THE APOLOGIST: I'm so sorry that the Third Macedonian War lasted as long as it did. And I apologize still more vigorously for the War of the Spanish Succession. And I am deeply, deeply ashamed of the fact that Barcelona lies in northeastern rather than southwestern Spain, and that shallots go well together with peppers and onions.

FORLORN GIRL: This is clearly another modern psychologically rehabilitated Catholic. The Liberators have done a fine job with him!

GUIDE: But let us tell him the wonderful news! Oh, good sir!

THE APOLOGIST: I am a "sir," and I am so deeply sorry for it. In fact, I am ashamed to have a body forced to take either male or female shape. And I neglected to mention that I shudder in horror over the interruption of the Han Dynasty by a mercifully short-lived usurpation which I must have in some way prepared.

FORLORN GIRL: But you do not have to be sorry anymore. The Commission that gives a Permission a Day is allowing all of us who want to go back to the ghetto to do so, merely by asking. It's all so easy. There, back in the ghetto, you only have to apologize for the things you do wrong! Would you like to come with us to get Permission?

THE APOLOGIST: I'm sorry to say that I would!

THE CONSERVATIVE CATHOLIC: Just wait right there! What makes you think that you have the right to ask for Permission? I mean, wouldn't the Liberators have given it to us already if it were permissible to have it? Let's give them the benefit of the doubt, please! Just because something was good for us for 1900 years doesn't mean that the Liberators were hasty in taking it away! Come, come! A little patience in adversity!

GUIDE: *Showing him the wide and generous letter.* But look at this! Isn't that official enough?

THE CONSERVATIVE CATHOLIC: *Becoming hopeful.* I must say, it seems so. I'm feeling the slightest *frisson* of hope!

FORLORN GIRL, GUIDE, AND THE APOLOGIST: Then come with us!!

"WE'RE OFF TO THE COMMISSION" (ANEW)

ARRIVAL AT THE COMMISSION

FORLORN GIRL: This must be the Commission. *She knocks on the door and speaks to the secretary, who wears a big button saying 'Helper.'* Excuse me, magnanimous and pastoral gentleman, is this the Commission?

THE HELPER: Yes.

GUIDE: Are you the Secretary?

THE HELPER: Yes. My name is Secretary Sqwakins. But I prefer to be known as 'The Helper.' I help Catholics to become truly, truly free.

FORLORN GIRL: And will you help us?

THE HELPER: Oh most certainly. What else am I here for? What do you seek?

ALL: Permission!!

THE HELPER: No! Beat it, losers! Go trim your fingernails!

FORLORN GIRL: But the wide and generous letter says that you give a Permission a Day!

THE HELPER: Oh? Have you tried reading it backwards? Tell me what it says then.

GUIDE: It says: "Yad a Noissimrep a sevig taht Noissimmoc eht."

THE HELPER: You see? What could be clearer? It says "don't bother us. Fit in. Keep your mouth shut. Beat it. Take a pill or two. Go to the Mall. Shop. Take the Global High Road to the Omega Point."

THE APOLOGIST: I am so sorry that I unnecessarily took up your time and, by not shopping, have contributed to a current economic downturn useful only to terrorists.

THE CONSERVATIVE CATHOLIC: And I would like to say that your words are golden and harmonize neatly with everything that has ever been taught since the time of the Council of Nicaea. Now could you please beat me with a studded stick?

FORLORN GIRL: Wait a minute! I've dealt with your type before. You're not really a "Helper"! You're one of the Liberators!

THE HELPER: Nonsense! Look at my button! Does it not say "Helper"?

FORLORN GIRL: *Grabbing hold of the identification button, turning it over, and revealing the word "Liberator" on the other side.* Look!!!

THE HELPER: A slight semantic problem. It deconstructs to 'helper' in my idiom.

GUIDE: *Pushing everyone away from The Helper.* There is only one way to deal with this type!! *He pulls out a portrait of Pope Pius IX.* Look directly at this image of Blessed Pio Nono!!

THE HELPER: *Shielding his eyes.* No, not that! Anything but the Grand Mufti of Obscurantism! The most triumphalist Pontiff in history! Aaaargh! I must flee!! *He runs away.*

"BRAVO, PIO NONO!"
(*Sung to the Tune of "Ding, Dong, the Witch is Dead"*)

Bravo, Pio Nono, he made the phony Helper go;
Bravo, we'll deal with him no mo'!
We knew he was our foe, when he said no, we had to toe,
Toe, toe the line that's caused our woe!

He's gone where the Liberals go—below, below, below;
And so, we sing, of Blessed Pius, Pio. . .

Pio, Pio Nono, the Pope who always said—NO, NO!!
He tossed the Liberals out the door.
Way back in days of yore, in eighteen hundred sixty-four;
When they would spout errors galore!!

He sent them where Liberals go—below, below, below;
And sealed their fate, with eighty condemnations.

(*while waving their handkerchiefs*)

Bravo, Pio Nono! Progress gets the old heave-ho;
And modern civ'lization takes a blow!

FORLORN GIRL: Stop the music! We've come all this way for nothing. We still can't get back to the ghetto. We'll never return to the place where we can say what we wish to say and be what we want to be once again. Not to speak of one where we can smoke in a restaurant!

THE CATHOLIC FAIRY: (*as the good witch, carrying a basket*). Fear not! You saw how The Helper fled before the portrait of Pius IX. Look in this basket. It is filled with items dear to Blessed Pio Nono's heart. A Catechism of the Council of Trent. Devotional cards. Scores of polyphonic Masses. Several comprehensive syllabi of errors. This is all you need to get back to the ghetto. You never needed Permission from the Commission in the first place. Just hold this basket in your hand and repeat after me: "There is no place like Rome; there is no place like Rome."

ALL: There is no place like Rome; there is no place like Rome; there is no place like Rome.

FINALE: "Oh There's No Place Like Rome"

(*To the Tune of "Oh, There's No Place Like Home"*)

Oh, there's no place like Rome when it goes Baroque;
For a fresh start, or when the last bell's rung.
For an auto-da-fe or Goetterdaemmerung;
Give me Rome, Mia Homa, Rome sweet home!

THE END:
DEO GRATIAS

II

Una Voce and the Habit of Error†

"ADDING INSULT TO INJURY" IS A SAYING whose significance and pain all believing Catholics have to confront whenever any issue of intellectual, political or social importance is discussed. In fact, this phrase needs to be altered where Catholics are concerned to indicate the triple insult regularly tossed at them by opponents intent upon doing them injury. To begin with, they find themselves denied credit for noble developments in western civilization for which their religion bears a great and even overwhelming responsibility. Secondly, they face the accusation of having engendered most western evils, and often precisely those which, in truth, Catholicism has actively opposed from the outset. And, finally, Catholics are insulted by being expected to accept as proof of their omissions and commissions arguments which are lacking both in seriousness and logic, usually presented by critics who are living off of past Christian glories and lamenting horrors which they themselves have caused. Unfortunately, many—probably the vast majority of Catholics—find confrontation with both their injury and three-fold insult something easy to take in stride.

Listing one's personal experiences of this phenomenon can be an illuminating, though ultimately lugubrious undertaking. I myself have heard academics laugh incredulously over the mere suggestion of a Christian association with learning, thereby betraying an abysmal ignorance of the Church's central role in the birth and nurturing of the university in the Middle Ages. The same sort of uninformed critics have expressed to me their revulsion over a Catholicism which they claim to be a fellow-traveler of environmentally-destructive technology, even though our religion has been on record, since the seventeenth century, as a prophetic voice against science and materialism run amok. And behind such erroneous charges, I generally have found a tissue of mere assertions which often amount to a variant of the old "it could

† First published in the *Una Voce Newsletter*, Spring 2002.

have happened, it should have happened, it really did happen" argument. Each man feels these injustices most keenly in his own particular field of activity; the idea that the very educators whose distorted world view is the catalyst behind the destruction of learning dare to sit in judgment over Christian contributions in this realm feeds my special rancor as a teacher.

Two fresh wounds involving the turning of reality topsy-turvy were opened for me recently in my own living room. One was inflicted by an episode of the television series, Law and Order, concerning a pro-life activist who kills an abortion doctor and is brought to justice by a team of police investigators. We are introduced here to Christians whose actions, while perhaps debatable, seem perfectly logical—the central figure, for example, becoming violent due to his anguish over the abortion, against his will, of his own child. The police investigators, in contrast, come across as being cold, cynical and deceptive men who believe that anyone connecting ideas with consequences, and allowing something so petty as his own child's murder to influence his future attitude towards abortion suffers from psychological disturbance. Bursting in upon a homeschooling, pro-life family during lessons, these Stalinist apparatchiks interrogate the mother regarding the perilous lack of rock star posters in her daughter's room, obviously equating freedom from the Zeitgeist, the spirit of the times, as synonymous with madness. Guess which group represents reason and openness to the complexities of life in contemporary society? No contest! The logical Christians, struggling to protect their liberty, are uncomprehending neanderthals; the storm troopers of mindless conformity are the ones who stand guard over free thought, diversity and the good life in general.

The culprit behind the second wound was a disturbing satire, The Truman Show, dealing with a man whose entire life has been orchestrated by a super-producer who places endless obstacles in the path of the hero's efforts to escape from his environment. This environment is a deadeningly one-dimensional, secularized, materialist, vulgar but "peaceful" middle class world, dominated by its overbearing but loving Führer-director, for the delectation of consumers of media bilge. Christianity is not directly mentioned in the film. Still, the miserable society which is satirized seems to be an allegory for the ordered universe protected by the loving

Creator God and providential Lord of the Scriptures, which is now shown for what it really is. And yet, orthodox Christianity never inspired or could give birth to the hideous culture laid out, brilliantly, in all its horror before us. Ironically, the hero, who decides to "become his own man" and flee the "Old World" of the director-God on a boat called the "Santa Maria," is headed for precisely what he wishes to escape. For, whatever The Truman Show had in mind, it is the society that abandoned the old Catholic world for puritanism, secularization and the victory of media over message that creates the monstrous conditions that the film rightly deplores.

Perhaps, by this point, I am nitpicking. There is no wonder that everything is depicted in topsy-turvy fashion in our brave, and by the twenty-first century, not so new world. Already, in 1848, Catholic writers were noting contemporary society's marriage with the illogical; its inability to pronounce a single intellectual statement that was not in contradiction to itself. How could it have been otherwise? For modern civilization, while inheriting from its Christian and Greco-Roman past a respect for reason, freedom and even progress, has, by rejecting God and the natural laws of the world created by Him, left itself with nothing to protect these goods than irrational wills irrationally at war with one another. Insane contradictory principles can only produce mad arguments and art works to underline them.

Moral theologians and experienced confessors have long noted the distinction between a sin in and of itself and one that has evolved into an habitual flaw. Although the habit is more dangerous, given that it indicates a deeper penetration into the heart of the soul, it nevertheless makes repetition of the specific corrupting action less free, more mechanical, and even unconscious. This is still more true if the habit is ingrained in an entire society, and taught to all its subjects in manifold ways from earliest youth, as Plato indicates in The Republic.

Here, I would contend, lies the gist of the problem. Modern man has now lived for some centuries with all of the contradictions of a basically irrational, willful world view that nevertheless still wants to see itself as the protector of reason and freedom. He has become familiar with the defenses thrown up by his civilization to prevent the unmasking of absurdities for what they are. In other words, he is used to existing in a society that has contracted the habit of error. This habit is incorporated into all the basic rhythms of life, is taught to children as a given and a good, and is taken for granted by many of the Catholics whom we at Una Voce are trying to address as much as it is accepted by everyone else.

An essential part of this habit of error is the teaching that Traditional Catholicism is an enemy of all that is decent. Every argument or historical event, even those that actually confirm the opposite conclusion, is made to prove this "truth." Evidence, often of the most circumstantial variety, can be pulled from out of nowhere at any time to demonstrate Catholicism's evil in one manner today, and in an absolutely contrary way tomorrow. Unfounded ridicule is accepted and used as though it were scientific methodology, statements of blind faith in anti-Catholic dicta as if they were rigorous judgments following investigation of first principles. If the Catholic responds ably in his religion's defense, a society and souls gripped by the habit of error will shut out his words or hear in them only what is required to maintain their addiction. Any dent made by an apologist in the armor of error on Friday will be forgotten by a diet of habit-reinforcing television viewing and a few painkillers on the side during the weekend. By Monday morning, it would be as though the work of battling the habit of error had never been undertaken before.

Two conclusions that can be drawn from the existence of this "habit of error" have been useful to me in maintaining my own equilibrium in what I consider to be an era more intellectually and spiritually troubled than any other in human history. I draw attention to them now in the hope that Una Voce members engaged in the nuts and bolts struggle for the progress of the Traditional Liturgy may also find therein some help for the shoring up of their commitment and sanity in times of trial.

The first is the recognition that it is highly unlikely that many people caught up in the net of confusion constituting what passes for wisdom in the last few centuries are ever going to grasp the full nature and extent of the absurd life that a habitually erroneous society teaches them to live. Even with the best of intentions, the grind of daily activity can prevent drawing the requisite judgments about the world around us on the grand scale that is needed. I remember, in this regard, the bewilderment of a very fine priest from lower Manhattan who had been awakened to the nightmare of his particular parish's religious decline. His response to the late Dr. William Marra's cataloguing of the identical problems at his own university in another part of the same city was an astonished "all the way uptown as well?" Dots on the horizon may be noticed by those with eyes to see, but it is perhaps too much to hope that they will generally be connected to reveal the complete character and dominion of the rot whose rhythms have been imprinted in our souls for all too long.

What this means is that we are engaged in a struggle of little steps, akin to that fought by soldiers in the trenches during the First World War. We must be ready to work with whatever tiny signs of understanding and cooperation come our way, and give heartfelt thanks to God for them when they arise. The fact that a given bishop or priest might come to see even a partial value to our arguments concerning the importance of the Traditional Liturgy is, given what one faces in a world engulfing us in the habit of error, a marvelous achievement; their failure to understand how concern for the Traditional Liturgy implies commitment to a proper catechetics, sound theology, a correct idea of Church-State relations and an accurate estimation of the causes of the rise and fall of Christendom as a whole is indeed upsetting, but, alas, a "high class" problem. Let us indeed pray earnestly for a general enlightenment tomorrow, but bless any patron contributing in but a microscopic way to giving us access to the Traditional Liturgy today. One step forward alone, in the civilization of habitual error, is a mammoth victory, justifying a lifetime of praise for the authority responsible for it.

My second conclusion, tied intimately to the first, is probably best introduced with reference to the parable of the Prodigal Son. For years, this parable left me as troubled as it did the loyal son who wondered why the fatted calf had never been slaughtered for him and his friends. Eventually, a good comrade pointed out a second possible meaning to it. My problem, she said, was that, although I was justifiably frustrated over the successes of those who really indeed were squandering the Catholic inheritance, I took for granted, as a given, that I was its sound defender. Was I really as solid as I seemed to think that I was? For one thing, my bitterness, my despair and my desire for vengeance were not fruits of the Holy Spirit, and were weakening my own right to function in the apostolate that I had chosen. And how could my own imperfect soul stand up against the other temptations of the age? Maybe both the loyal son and I were ourselves actually more prodigal than we realized, and a plate of fatted calf would be on the table for us once we came to our senses and shaped up.

Building upon that line of thought, what I really mean to say is this: just as we are all "ordinary" sinners, even in the best of civilizations, we all, in addition, are rattled by living in a society wedded to a habit of error. This is why anyone who consciously wants to be a good Catholic, must make a still greater effort, both spiritually and intellectually, to enrich his soul with the life and wisdom coming from our Faith. It is our special duty, as people seeking consciously to fight for orthodoxy in a troubled age, to learn ever more clearly what that orthodoxy is really all about, and not simply assume that we are committed to Christ because we say that we are. "If you cannot make progress in a substantive way," a priest tired of hearing my repetitive confessions once told me; "make progress in humility." If we cannot make even miniscule progress, at the moment, in a given effort to gain permission somewhere for the Traditional Mass, well, then, let us try to make progress in breaking any ties that we may still nurture, not only with "ordinary" sin, but with the habit of error. God may want us to work on ourselves first before allowing us an objectively deserved victory. It is to a world afloat in a sea of errors that Una Voce sailors set sail to do battle. Once we make certain that we are not ourselves serving in the navy of the enemy, and that we are ready to welcome with open arms whoever courageously takes but a single step in the direction of the traditional boat, then maybe, Lent behind us, we can sit down at the table of the fatted calf together and hone down the final points.

12

Una Voce and the Interregnum[†]

AN INTERREGNUM, WHICH I WOULD DEFINE very broadly as the time between two periods of effective rule, is a horrible thing. The reason for this is quite simple. Interregna, historically, have all too frequently been moments of terrible doubt regarding the true possessor of real authority in a given country, causing its inhabitants to trudge along a political, social, and moral path which seems dreadfully uncertain. Place an intelligent individual in the midst of an interregnum and he will sooner or later realize that events around him are not necessarily being shaped by the officially recognized regent or ineffective ruler. Rather, he will see that, more often than not, policies are being dictated by the clash of self-serving, politically shrewd, and often hidden cabals, feeding on that widespread confusion which generally paralyzes the good as well as the weak. A well-intentioned person, demoralized by his helplessness under such conditions, is bound to understand what others in analogous situations before him have grasped: that only the accession of a firm, clear authority will put the dangerous manipulators who thrive in an interregnum back in their appropriate place.

We faithful of the international monarchy of the Roman Catholic Church are, unfortunately, living in an interregnum of a sort that we could not charitably wish upon the worst of our enemies. This interregnum, like all others, has created a playground for the manipulative to enjoy their destructive games. Unlike the average interregnum, however, the one affecting Catholic Christendom is much more complex in nature, involving three layers of confusion of authority. All of these have cooperated in opening the door to a twisting of the Christian message by parochial interest groups of heretical or morally dubious intent in a way that is unparalleled in Church History.

One cause of the Catholic Interregnum directly concerns John Paul II. Although the Pope's immediate, poignant medical condition

† First published in the Una Voce America, Winter 2003.

certainly has contributed to the problem of anarchy within the Church, I would nevertheless argue that the entirety of the present pontificate has, in many respects, been one long, extremely perilous interregnum. For, despite media and liberal Catholic insistence upon a supposedly oppressive centralization of power encouraged by John Paul II, the past quarter of a century has actually seen the progressive slippage of effective authority from the hands of the legitimate Pope, and that both in Rome as well as away from the Eternal City.

Not the least of the factors responsible for this abandonment of control has been what Michael Davies has labeled the "Opiate of the Popes"; that endless physical movement that has made of the household of the Papacy an enormous and continuously active Travel Agency, always preparing, entering upon, or assessing the results of a voyage. Constant excitement over the tour business has had the unfortunate side effect of blinding the highest authorities to the manifold set of more humdrum, down to earth disasters caused by Church Renewal. It has also led to the serious neglect of the day-to-day administration of the Church, a fact recognized by the scholarly world as well as by those of us who might seem to have a special axe to grind. And failure to administer firmly has meant that all of the specific subordinate organs of Church authority, from Roman dicasteries to local bishoprics and parishes, have had the opportunity to become little makeshift "papacies in their own countries." The pope who has been seen the most in Church History has actually reigned considerably less than most of his predecessors over the course of the last century.

This practical incentive to the creation of an interregnum has been exacerbated by a forty-year theoretical stimulus stemming from the call for collegiality emerging out of the decrees and "spirit" of the Second Vatican Council. I must confess that the idea of collegiality, in and of itself, does seem to me to have a certain merit to it. The exaggerated Ultramontanism of the nineteenth and twentieth centuries may indeed have worked to create in many places an episcopacy that was often incapable of acting with an energy suitable to confronting new or peculiar local situations and temptations. Nevertheless, collegiality, as a working principle, has not generally yielded positive results. Far from engendering a cooperative hierarchy harmoniously laboring together for the common good, it has presented to the world the spectacle of a Church apparatus whose various parts interpret, and then follow or thwart, both the central authority and one another at whim. Moreover, collegiality has fatally weakened all local defense against the third and most important force responsible for fomenting an interregnum in Catholic Christendom: those Enlightenment-inspired conceptions of freedom and democracy which now thoroughly dominate all western rhetoric and public life.

Generations of Catholic thinkers before the Second Vatican Council, from the eighteenth century down to the 1950s, had cogently argued that such conceptions were self-destructive as well as wrong; that they led precisely to the opposite of what they claimed that they provided. The fathers of Catholic Social Doctrine repeatedly warned that Christian acceptance of a definition of freedom and democracy which denied man's limitations, his dependence upon God, and the reality of human sinfulness, would quickly cause the Church herself to be twisted to the purposes of individuals and self-interest groups motivated by the strongest and most insane ideas and passions. This is exactly what has happened in our Catholic Age of Aquarius, and especially to bishops. "Liberated" from the discipline of a centrally-unified and anti-revolutionary phalanx, subjected to the same daily dosage of "enlightened" propaganda on the local level as the flocks that they were supposed to lead, and regularly flattered for their courageous kowtowing before the spirit of the age, bishops have allowed their own power and dignity to crumble along with that of their papal "taskmaster." As predicted and feared by many anti-revolutionary writers, the statements and policies of local prelates have thus become, in practice, whatever those most passionately breathing down their necks and claiming to represent the vanguard of freedom and democracy in their dioceses wish to make of them. Such figures include Church bureaucrats, journalists, politicians, investment and advertising consultants, and purveyors of all types of vicious utopias and utopian vices.

Any intelligent man or woman coming to grips with these three layers of interregnum-producing obfuscation, must, therefore, continuously ask himself the question "who" and "what" he is really obeying when he follows the endless contradictory commands of a crippled Church at cross purposes with herself. Is he truly submitting to pope and bishop, and legitimate ecclesiastical decree? Or is he, ultimately, cringing before the whims of some general secretary or master propagandist, Stalin or Trotsky-like in his hunt for power, whom the weakness of the official authorities has permitted to rule and pontificate erroneously in their name?

One does not make a pope or a bishop an effective power by repeating and intensifying the number of panegyrics sung in his name. If this were the case, the Emperor Valentinian III, increasingly incensed as he more and more lost control of the Empire in the West in the fifth century, A. D., would have been an infinitely more successful ruler than an Augustus or a Trajan. It is usually the case historically that a greater frequency of praise and exultation indicates a closer approach to an abyss. And this is why the unending chorus of hosannas to Church Renewal, maturation, freedom, and democracy which has provided the background music for our troubled era actually points to the death, on a human level, of Catholic Christendom.

The next Pope, were he to be a truly reigning pontiff, would have to direct his attention to one major task: the end of this three-fold cause of interregnum. To do so, he would have to commit himself to a more permanent stay in Rome, working diligently to clean up the administrative Stalinism and rhetorical Trotskyism that have devastated the Church; to a cultivation of an honestly cooperative spirit of collegiality, one which allows for local initiative while not permitting defiant insubordination; and to a concerted effort to critique the reign of Enlightenment ideals which have turned the Church Militant into a discotheque filled with shrieking, willful adolescents, with villains at the sound controls, madly cranking up the decibel level.

Will he do so? Could he be successful even if he did? On the rational, natural level, it seems that one should doubt it. All of the illicit secular groups that have benefited from the interregnum—and, again, they are the dominant forces in contemporary Western Civilization—are united in standing guard against the election of a man who would finally see the modern world of freedom and democracy for what it actually is: an enormous fraud. Frightened or opportunist prelates have grown too used to the "powers" that have enabled them to serve whatever their secular masters demand of them to remember what real Catholic dignity and courage are.

Well-intentioned members of the hierarchy, backed by conservative lay Catholics who are convinced that they must see genius in every action of the hierarchy, are still themselves too steeped in a routine round of praise for the current leadership to be expected to abandon, consistently, the forward march to the destruction of all remnants of Church authority.

But what, exactly, should Una Voce's role be in this terrible period of interregnum? Is there anything positive that we can do in the midst of a recognition of our basic weakness? Allow me to reiterate a policy composed of three parts, all of which I think that I have called attention to in earlier articles; all of which, as recent discussions on the internet have indicated, many chapters have already thought through and adopted on their own.

To begin with, Una Voce must always keep in mind that our ultimate goal in an interregnum is the restoration of the effective authority of the pope and the bishops over Christ's Church, so that that Church can once again become the light of the world. Therefore, let us constantly praise and encourage whatever hopeful words and deeds emerge from official sources that work towards that end. There have been a great number of these recently, as all of you well know. I say this because the history of so many Catholic movements which began with a concern for a reestablishment of rigor and discipline in the Church—that of Jansenism and the Ultramontanism of the Abbé de Lamennais being primary among them—ended with the promotion of a theology of the superior prerogatives of the outraged laity destructive to the true structure of the Mystical Body of Christ. Good news tending towards the rebuilding of solid authority should get from us the positive press that it deserves.

Secondly, however, Una Voce must never lose sight of the sad fact that the forces promoting the Catholic Interregnum are enormously strong. Our outright opponents have regularly shown themselves capable of circumventing the most favorable initiatives coming from above, even to the point of audaciously and illogically using them against us. Many of those prelates kindly disposed to the Traditional Liturgy do not themselves generally understand the full nature of the modern fraud underlying Church Renewal, and can easily become confused in following up their more constructive actions, quickly backtrack and become lost in contradictions. What we would really like is for King Richard to come, exile Prince John from the realm, and tell Errol Flynn that he can go, marry Maid Marion, and live happily ever after, all in one fell swoop. But our Prince Johns, Guys of Guisbourne, and Sheriffs of Nottingham are still too vigorous for the film in which we unhappily star to finish all that neatly.

Under these circumstances, Una Voce chapters must become even wiser than serpents. What this means, in practice, is a much more conscious policy of trying to ignore or circumvent the interregnum manipulators in prelates' clothing; perhaps a doing of what Rome has indicated we have a right to do, and a reacting to what happens only afterwards. Efforts to ask the assent of the legitimate local authority when that authority actually is exercised by illegitimate spokesmen of the Age of Aquarius is generally an enormous waste of time. When the late Dr. William Marra wanted a traditional Requiem Mass for the funeral of Fr. Vincent Micelli, S. J., he let the hostile chancery popelets know that he was aware that they were making decisions on their own steam, and gave them to understand that he was going to have the service he was insisting upon barring direct, authoritative intervention from the Ordinary. He had his Mass. Like minded traditionalists with clerical fellow-travelers working in parish churches ceased worrying about asking permission to bury their dead decently thereafter. When Cardinal O'Connor gave his personal approval for a Traditional Mass for my wedding, countermanding the initial negative dictate of his own bureaucracy, a number of priests of my acquaintance stopped asking approval for a similar privilege for other couples. After all, the chancery "authorities" would have definitely refused them, and they might not have had the opportunity that I had had to reach the archbishop who would undoubtedly welcome their request.

I do not mean to be flippant about this, since I am fully aware that the situation in New York is much, much better than the torturous circumstances faced by many chapters elsewhere on a day- to-day basis. Our opponents do indeed have fangs that they like to keep in shape by using regularly, and problems will arise from a policy of leaping first and looking second. Nevertheless, it is important to bear in mind that the opposition expects a certain type of reaction from us which we have to ascertain and then avoid, turning to new and inventive ones instead. Adopting unique strategies, attacking on different fronts, seeking help from unexpected sources, appealing to be placed under more favorable jurisdictions, all can throw the Aquarians off balance, and even provide a little humor in our basically humorless task. It would be difficult to specify exactly what might work under each peculiar circumstance, especially because of the varied personalities involved, diocese to diocese, and parish to parish. The main point is simply this: our enemies, while strong, are not as wise as they think they are, and the conscientious options open to us are frequently greater than we are wont to contemplate. We cannot afford to indulge in scrupulosity. I would myself be happy to offer specific groups suggestions on how to develop a looser conscience in this regard.

A policy both of thankful encouragement of hopeful signs from above, as well as thoughtful risk-taking from below is, I think, one that is in line with the spirit of the XVI International Una Voce General Assembly which took place at the Domus Pacis in Rome on October 11th and 12th. This meeting, attendance at which was wider than usual, saw the entrance into the Federation of three groups: Una Voce Nigeria, Pro Missa Tridentina, a German association which has been a long-term friend and fellow-traveler of our international organization, and Inter Multiplices Una Vox, the Italian group responsible for the Solemn Mass at Santa Maria Maggiore on May 24th. It also led to the election of our new Federation president, Ralf Siebenbürger, the head of Una Voce Austria. After formal business was completed on Saturday, and Sunday Mass was sung to a packed congregation at the Church of Gesù and Maria, accompanied by the magnificent Una Voce choir of Rome, an Open Forum informed the membership of the activities of a variety of specific societies and individuals during the last two years.

For me, what stood out most clearly was the positive contrast of this meeting with our last, much more gloomy gathering. Two years ago, we were, in effect, lectured regarding limitations on the traditional movement by the representatives of a Commission that was supposed to be assisting us, but was itself hoping that we would stop being unpleasant and go away quietly. This October, the serious limitations that we feared might cripple us two years ago, were seen to have been to a large degree illusory. Proof after proof of a changed and much more enlightened attitude of Rome on our behalf was adduced or even visibly apparent to our own eyes. That evidence included numerous public statements of Cardinals and Roman Congregations, the recounting of all the events leading up to and accompanying the liturgy at Santa Maria Maggiore, our own Mass at the Hungarian Chapel in St. Peter's, and the very presence of Fr. Josef Bisig as its celebrant as well. Dr. Eric de Saventhem summarized the new situation perfectly in noting that Rome has given us a golden opportunity for proselytizing our cause anew. In fact, one could perhaps say that Rome has admitted practically all of our theoretical arguments in defense of the Traditional Liturgy, even to the point of arguing that the statements of Vatican Council guaranteeing "citizenship" to the "other rites" in the Church could be used not simply by Eastern Catholics, but by the defenders of the ancient Roman Rite itself. There are many new tunes on the old piano that are worth learning and blasting to the skies so that everyone can join in and sing them.

On the other hand, the continued existence of the kind of interregnal obstructionism that I addressed above, was obvious in the tales told by some of the representatives of various countries and groups at the Open Forum on Sunday. It was even clear at the Mass in St. Peter's itself, whose time and duration were the object of the kinds of petty persecution one might hope to encounter not from fellow Catholics, but in a satirical novel about the foibles of a civil service gone bonkers. Inventive strategies and positive interventions from unexpected sources also were recounted at the Open Forum, including one involving a Russian Orthodox appeal on behalf of "real Catholics" that traditionalists would find helpful.

But I mentioned three components of the Una Voce role in this dreadful period of interregnum. What is the third? Forgive me for beating what might seem to be a dead horse of mine, but it remains, now as always, that of a good-humored patience. Malcolm Muggeridge said that humor lies in recognizing the difference between aspiration on the one side and performance on the other. Certainly few groups could have higher aspirations than we do—nothing less than the restoration of Christendom. Fewer still could be going about their activity with smaller numbers and means at their disposal. Perhaps God has recognized that we need this drilled into our self-willed heads just a tiny bit longer, so that we can emerge, like Gideon, as victors against impossibly greater odds; victors with a good-humored awareness of their own flaws and dependency upon higher authority.

Numbers, for one thing, do not count for overly much in a revolutionary environment. Revolutions are made with limited adherents and they are undone with limited adherents. Our international treasurer, Fred Haehnel, and our secretary, Leo Darroch, have alone done the work of battalions. So has our first President d'Honneur, Dr. Eric de Saventhem, whose faith-filled patience carried us through many years in a wilderness of seemingly endless horizons. And so has Michael Davies, our second President d'Honneur, named as such at Dr. de Saventhem's initiative at the October Assembly, at the end of his seven years of remarkable service as leader of our Federation.

I do not think that there is a man or woman among us—and small in number as we are, we still represent a sizable crew—whose life has not been shaped, and his vocation as a lay activist awakened and clarified, through Michael's work. His influence on me began thirty-one years ago, in London, at a meeting to discuss the situation of the Church in England for the purposes of a paper that I was writing. That influence has not yet ended today, whether it be through his books and articles, his advice regarding ways to make my writing style more readable, or his stimulation of my eight-year-old son's appreciation of whisky, which has, thankfully, been kept as of now to the intellectual level alone. All of us have been shown the incredibly positive snowball effect that one eccentric Welshman can have. As we salute him for his years bearing the yoke of the International Federation's presidency, let us assure him that we won't grumble too much about being so alone in our own activities; that we will move forward as a merrier and more patient little band, even as we engage in a bit of honest and productive mischief. Besides, maybe King Richard will come along and end our miseries swiftly after all.

13

Saved by Sophism, Doomed by the Familiar†

IN 1991, I FINISHED A SATIRICAL NOVEL attacking everything that I thought to be corrupted by modern civilization, starting from my own profession and concluding with the absurdities perpetrated by contemporary Church and State. My interest lagged after its completion, at least until last month, when I finally encountered an agent who offered to try to locate a publisher for it. Since I did not have a computer over a decade ago, I sat down to the task of pumping the rather lengthy text into my laptop. My one great fear was of the root and branch editing that might be required in order to update the characters and the context of what I presumed would appear to be a story all too bound to an already vanishing era.

But editing has proven to be far from the existential difficulty that I at first had contemplated. The substance of what I said twelve years ago demanded almost no alteration. The tainted meat of the modern world was exactly the same. And tainted meat is just as vile, whatever the name it goes by, on whatever table it is served, and whatever the time set for dinner. My fears of extensive labor on the guts of the book had been put to rest. I realized, as I typed along, that I, ironically, had been "saved by sophism."

What is sophism? The word itself means "wisdom," but its use and abuse in classical Greece gave it a more negative connotation. To make a long story short, sophism is the substitution of an obsession with what the world calls "success" for a dedication to the discovery of substantive eternal Truth. This obsession with success is then itself defined by the sophist as the only wisdom worth having, any other knowledge involving a painful waste of time and a futile journey to cloud cuckoo land. And here, indeed, lies the great psychological advantage possessed by the sophist in his battle with the lover of real truth; his appeal to the individual's dislike of

---

† First published in the *Una Voce Newsletter*, Spring 2003.

the delays that the study, meditation and self-questioning towards which the honest theologian, philosopher and preacher directing him may entail, along with his terror of missing the opportunities for power and wealth that immediate, unconsidered action offer.

We traditionalist Catholics have, to a large degree, been fighting against sophism for the last forty years. The "pastoral" considerations that were said to have guided the Council were, while theoretically valid ones, very much dictated, in practice, by a sophist mentality; by a concern for success in a contemporary pluralist society which first disdained all dogmatic questions, and then declared its "pragmatism" to be the only unquestionable truth worth taking seriously. The result has been the corruption that is the constant accompaniment of a purely sophistic approach to truth: a short-sighted selling out of all that is meaningful and makes life worth living for immediate, superficial and all too perishable glitter; the abandonment of our Catholic birthright for a biblical mess of pottage, and not even a tasty one at that. I have tried to describe the influences lying behind these developments, and the reason for their strength, both in my pamphlet on Americanism and in articles in the *Latin Mass Magazine* on the theological-philosophical minefield labeled Personalism.

Depressing as the situation may be, it at least means that we at Una Voce who are fighting against contemporary corruption have had our intellectual burden lightened. Like me, with my task of editing, we have all been "saved by sophism" from a great deal of painful labor. Practically everything that has been offered us, in the name of the spirit of the Second Vatican Council, indicates enslavement to the sophistic dogma of pragmatism, and reveals itself to be a superficial blip on a consistently unchanging phenomenon; yet another marketing ploy for a civilization in love with tinsel. While we are bombarded with what, on the surface, may seem to be endless new ideas and programs, each of which has to be studied and critiqued on its own merits, these, in reality, reduce to nothing more than boring, repetitive appeals to a worship of the god of immediate impact and worldly success, whose character never changes, and whose prizes are actually nothing but perishable carnival trinkets. It is as though we were expected to be unceasingly overawed by access to an infinite number of channels on a television which we already had learned, by experience, would forever transmit the same pointless schlock.

Whatever intellectual labor might be required in this thankless battle generally lies in recognizing sophism for what it is, and not taking its call to time consuming investigation of its never changing novelties at face value; after that, the rest is easy. The guts of our task never change. Anyone who is nervous about being able to judge whether the latest supposedly earth-shattering change is worth considering or not should read Plato's dialogues dealing directly or indirectly with sophism; especially the Protagoras, the Gorgias, and the Republic. There is no need to be afraid to do so. This is not modern philosophy. It actually can be understood! In fact, the characters and events described therein will make you think, while you are studying it, that you are reading a copy of today's newspaper. And what you will take away from it is a deeper understanding of how a right reasoning man can know whether he is or is not dealing with someone or something valuable, even without being an expert on the specific subject in question; whether, for example, he is confronting a true physician or a quack doctor, despite the fact that he has not got the faintest idea what a tumor is, or how to remove it.

Resistance to the dominance and temptations of the sophistic environment in which we wage our difficult war will also make the real problems and substantive novel situations which face the Church stand out with all the greater clarity. For such dilemmas do, indeed, exist, just as they did in the less than perfect days before the Council as well. It is precisely because Una Voce has always understood this truth that it has never suffered from tunnel vision, or the condition of nostalgia which is falsely attributed by our opponents to all traditionalists indiscriminately. We know that we have never been working in a perfect ecclesiastical climate, and that we never will be. Difficulties with new names in new places do indeed emerge at every turn of the corner.

Given this fact, we are all then obliged to do the kind of editing that I did find myself obliged to work at in completing the novel: namely, abandoning specific names and surrounding events which were no longer of significance, and, most importantly, not resting content with familiar passages which further examination revealed to be mediocre, contradictory, and harmful to the basic argument. We, also, have to make certain that we are never lulled by familiar names, slogans and positions into contentment with a bad strategy for defending what we love; that we are careful that no such satisfaction ever leads us to contradict the task that we have set ourselves, causing us actually to destroy the principles that we wish to protect. All of us, like novelists correcting their work, must be constantly aware that that which we are used to is not necessarily the same thing as that which is correct and efficacious; that the customary, as Pope St. Gregory VII noted in his battle with the Holy Roman Empire in the 1000s, is not always synonymous with Catholic Truth. It would be tragic to be saved by sophism, only to be doomed by the familiar.

I say this, as I believe that I have reiterated a number of times before, because, psychologically, it is all too common a phenomenon to equate the familiar with the true. There are many things that can seem to be part of Sacred Tradition because people are used to them for a relatively long period of time, or due to the fact that they are commonplaces which are imbibed along with the air we breathe and the food we eat. If we stubbornly refuse to test these apparent "givens" against the standard of Catholic truth, because to do so would be tantamount to questioning our immediate "tradition," then we have ventured into an ideological acceptance of what is familiar as the grounds for determining the norm. Before we would know it, we would find that the real Truth and true Tradition, which could be known, but were being avoided, were step by step being replaced by an uncritical acceptance of all that which was merely familiar and customary around us. The effects for the essence of the Catholic Faith would, in consequence, be devastating.

Contentment with the merely familiar can cripple us in all aspects of our lives as Catholics, but what we are concerned about at Una Voce is the specific problem of a familiar environment hindering our work for the restoration of the liturgical tradition of the Western Church. Here, the danger lies in the sacralization of two things which appeal to us either because of the particular historical circumstances of our battle, or simply because of the fact that we are fallen, willful, human beings: the pre-conciliar world, and our own individual preferences. Even if we are fully aware of the difficulties this divinization may present on a theoretical plane (and, as I indicated above, I think that we are conscious of its dangers), on the practical, pastoral level we must nevertheless always remind ourselves to stand on guard against it as a subtle, all too familiar siren song.

American Catholicism in the 1950s and early 1960s was not a model for the world, whether on theological and pastoral grounds or, generally even more, on liturgical ones. In this regard, I remember both the late Dr. William Marra telling me that he had heard every error popularized at the Vatican Council taught openly by teachers and colleagues of his in the 1940s and 1950s, while Dr. Dietrich von Hildebrand lamented the painful banality of what he frequently heard from the pulpits. Sloppiness at Low Masses and inattention to ceremonies and proper music at High Masses was very common. It was a shock to me, born in 1951 and a regular attendee at my parish church, when I learned, in the late 1960s, that it was not only Protestants who had a musical tradition. I had not even been informed of the existence of Gregorian Chant, much less that of polyphonic music. In fact, I don't believe that I ever heard the name of St. Thomas Aquinas mentioned. St. Augustine I knew of from my public school history classes. As one Una Voce leader summarized his experience to me, the 1950s, in many respects, was actually a period of decline, covered over by a great deal of success on the statistical level. Still, there remains a temptation to look upon this period as a norm for restoration purposes. One can see this readily in a number of Catholic circles, where everything, from clothing to the look of the photographs printed in bulletins, seems as though it emerged straight from 1958.

This leads us directly into the question of individual preferences. Just as one passing moment in time can be divinized—in this regard, chiefly because it is associated with the era before the official assault on the Traditional Mass—familiar, but narrow, personal likes and dislikes can dominate our vision of how the liturgy and its supporting pillars must be restored. And yet no particular hymn, devotion, responsorial approach, scriptural/catechetical/historical text, political position, article of clothing, choice of home or attitude towards alcohol, smoking, or child rearing practice, however familiar and dear to the heart of an individual who may very well be sincerely devoted to the Traditional Mass, can be praised and used as normative for restoration purposes if further examination reveals it to be sloppy, inadequate, intrusive, or downright sectarian and abusive. To do so would be to sacrifice the Truth for the mere semblance of a "tradition"; to miss certain developments in contemporary research which are solid and good; to avoid battle strategies which might actually succeed in winning over our fellow Catholics. It could even lead to a stubbornness of the sort that caused old British Catholics to disdain the efforts of St. Augustine of Canterbury and the Irish monks to convert the Anglo-Saxons. They were too familiar with them as "the Enemy" ever to wish to see them transformed into friendly, fellow believers.

The Catholic Church, the Mass, and Una Voce are bigger than the 1950s, the United States, and the personal preferences of people who prefer to live in the country or the city. They require no one to dress as an Amish or a gentleman from the Eisenhower era or in a tasteful style from 2003. In all things that we do, we must have only one, infallible guide: Catholic Tradition in all of its fullness. Let us pray that we will always be able to edit our thoughts and our behavior along with its dictates, both as individuals and as a nation. It cannot fail us, either in our path towards liturgical sanity or in our attempt to live a broadly human life, free from enslavement to a loathsome civilization based on sophism.

14
On the Rocks[†]

SINCE 1979, THE YEAR I BEGAN WORKING at my university, my summer months have regularly been spent in Europe. They have involved stays of at least several weeks each in France, Germany, and Britain, after rather lengthier periods in Italy with the Dietrich von Hildebrand Institute. This routine has proven to be a valuable experience for any number of reasons. One of them has been the repeated opportunity it has given me to get a sense of new developments in a variety of sister western nations. Another has been the chance to retain the impressions thus gained by departing before a too great familiarity with local conditions begins to dull appreciation of any novelties, and judgment of their long-term significance. Two such judgments concerning matters of central importance to the mission of Una Voce have impressed themselves firmly on my mind after mulling over the sense of what I have seen during this summer's wanderings.

The first of these is the ever more inescapable realization that we are living through a change of epoch perhaps as great as that from Antiquity to the Middle Ages, one which is bringing to an end the world formed by the Reformation and the Enlightenment, and dragging down the remnants of Catholic civilization with it. Such a change has, of course, been in preparation for some centuries already. Still, its approach has accelerated considerably over the course of the years since 1914, and that acceleration was stimulated still further by the collapse of the Soviet Bloc from the 1980s onwards. Today, literally everything in Europe, from the composition of given nations' populations to their most basic everyday habits and assumptions is in total question. This startling reality causes even what seem at first glance to be the most newsworthy decisions of leading men of our day to diminish in importance. Many of them, upon further consideration, can be seen to reflect the preoccupations of an already lifeless and disappearing culture. Rather than truly shaping history, they remind one of the

† First published in the *Una Voce Newsletter*, Summer 2003.

petty intrigues engaged in by irrelevant courtiers at the palace of a Roman Emperor whose realm has already passed into the hands of the barbarians. Change sits confidently at the steering wheel of the Old Continent. Both a superhuman foresight would be required to predict the final direction that it will take, as well as the faith of St. Augustine's City of God to believe that it will all work out in the end according to the designs of Divine Providence.

The Roman Catholic Church was instrumental in bridging the enormous gap separating the ancients from the medievals, and thus saved what was best in the Greco-Roman past to be merged together with the hidden benefits that would one day be discovered in barbaric German culture. That same Church, in Europe as in the United States, is, in contrast, a cipher in our own age of epoch change. Everywhere that I have been, the "official" Church shows herself to be spiritually, intellectually, aesthetically, politically, and even economically carried away by events rather than mastering them. And yet, everywhere I have traveled, the panegyrics proclaiming the immense success of Church reform would appear to indicate her unparalleled efficacy. Here, too, images from collapsing Antiquity come to mind, in particular the propaganda pouring forth from fifth century Ravenna, adulating the glories of the holders of the imperial title at the exact moment when the antics of the Roman authorities had come to mean about as much as the pronouncements of the hosts of television talk shows.

But that brings me to my second point. In an age of epoch change, that which is truly essential and seriously capable of carrying the greatness of the pasts into an uncertain future stands out with greater clarity to all those with honestly open hearts and eyes. To paraphrase a comment of Dr. Alice von Hildebrand, substantive things repeatedly reveal their contempt for servile adulation of the "signs of the times," and questions regarding whether they are ahead of their times or behind them. Meaningfulness regularly proves itself to be an attribute of whatever sublimely transcends that which is merely "timely."

None of the hymns, prayer services, liturgies, and socio-political programs of the modern Church possess any formative significance and staying power, precisely because they are purposely designed to do nothing other than follow the example of what seems to be most "active" and "energetic" in our culture at any given moment.

Determined to do nothing but learn from the environment rather than in any way to teach it, they are swallowed up by the various "mystiques" that they try to imitate. Odd contradictions thereby emerge, my personal favorite being the iron-clad union of Church and State which has developed through progressive Catholic commitment to the seemingly opposite secularist principle of their absolute separation. All too swiftly, Catholic initiatives "fall behind" the erratic alterations of the willful and flighty unreligious society that the supporters of timeliness worship. They then become yet another batch of sore thumbs used to illustrate the Church's intrinsic inability to keep pace with change. This engenders a new and frantic round of timely reforms to a western world which is, as noted above, itself already irrelevant and dying. If the fifth century Church had taken the modern Catholic path, Pope St. Leo would have sallied forth from the gates of Rome to give the keys of the city to an "energetic" Attila the Hun rather than to try to convince him to go away as quickly as possible. And that seemingly invincible conqueror, welcomed into the Eternal City, would have himself soon been swept away by some other momentarily powerful barbarian, proving that the opening of the windows to the "fresh winds of Hunnish change" would have been an enormous and pathetic waste of time. Meanwhile, those pointing out the failure of the policy of servile accommodation with the powers that be would have been chastised as being "deaf to the promptings of the Holy Spirit" and "disrespectful of the wisdom of a holy pope."

Impotence amidst epoch change shouted out from every corner of the lands that I regularly visit this summer. Passing through villages where I was unable to buy a bottle of wine because the food shops were all in the hands of Muslims, visiting couples who would never dream of marrying or baptizing their one and only child, hearing the criticisms of people incapable of understanding how my wife and I could tolerate the prospect of the imminent arrival of a third infant, and threading my path into houses of worship through groups of threatening and abusive native youths controlling the steps and portals, I found confronting such change the ever saccharine, ever smiling, ever optimistic Church of No Hassles. And it was this toothless wreck that tried to respond to the draft of a European Constitution which left out any reference to the Christian heritage in its statement of the formative influences on our civilization, by begging, pitifully, for at least a shred of historical honesty, and often with the hideous argument that honor should be given to religion for the hand that it had had in creating the very Enlightenment that has systematically sought to crush it. Where, in such uncontrolled flux, was the transcendence that stands calmly above one's times, offering something meaningful to guide them and confidence to judge them?

There was, of course, one representative of such transcendence available, and, luckily, there were many places in Europe where it might be located. In a world of epoch change, abandoned by a Church which feels obliged to offer herself to be drawn and quartered by whatever force seems to be powerful enough to require accommodation, the Traditional Mass of the Roman Rite stands out as a solid, meaningful, eternal rock around which to throw one's flailing arms and flagging spirits. Happily and confidently above its times, it escapes that superficial spirituality of the passing, cheap sensation that sends honestly hungry hearts on a desperate hunt for anything whatsoever which smacks even slightly of substance—as is happening en masse in prisons around the globe, where inmates find that Muslim preachers give the guidance and the answers denied them by ecumenical chaplains and liturgies from Outer Space. Classical, discrete, and coherent, it escapes entirely the truly reactionary trap fallen into by those who would slap a few Latin words here and there onto the carcass of a liturgy condemned to a rap dance which alters with every slightest breeze. The Traditional Mass was there, even if the labor of finding it sometimes took an entire day of investigation and travel. And the message that it sent out was that of the Permanent Things. Everywhere, it breathed the spirit of the Church of Pope St. Gregory the Great, who sponsored spiritual programs that aimed to conquer a frightening new world in the making rather than simply "listening" to it and following its violent and pagan teachings. That spirit made it overwhelmingly clear, once again, that here, amidst its prayers and ceremonies and the Christian vision that gave them birth were the answers and the promise of hope in a time of cultural collapse that the Church of No Hassles could never give.

This is why I think that the Mass celebrated at Santa Maria Maggiore on Mary 24th was so valuable. Many motives may have entered into the permission and stature given by Rome to that ceremony. It in no way indicated the end of our troubles. Opposition to the Traditional Mass is strong enough to guarantee us a longer period of wandering in the wilderness than we might wish to contemplate. Nevertheless, it encouraged our colleagues in Europe enormously, illustrated just how much ground we have gained since 1988, when such a ceremony would have seemed to be nothing other than the dream of the most clueless utopian, and revealed a perhaps unconscious realization on the part of a number of ecclesiastical authorities that without the spiritual depth that it possesses, the Roman Catholic Church is doomed to be swept away by the same floodwaters of epochal change that she herself has helped to unleash. Merely by taking place, the Mass at Santa Maria Maggiore has entered into our dossier proving the legality of the ancient Roman Rite. And, most importantly, the flag of transcendence, substantive meaning, and permanence which it flew had to have stirred the hearts of an unknown number of clerics and lay people who were hunting desperately for spiritual guidance, were shocked by the contrast between the Traditional Liturgy and a modern counterpart which is anchored to nothing, and are now destined to become our future friends and allies.

Some time ago, in a previous article, I noted that we, in our frustrating and often unrewarded battle for Tradition, are building the future every bit as much as those who constantly claim that they are "forward looking" in their approach. In fact, we are constructing that future even more securely than any self-proclaimed futurists, both because we are more consciously aware of the fact that modern western culture is in free fall, and because we know what we want and where we ought to be headed.

Our familiar world may be shipwrecked and lie in pieces on the rocks, but those rocks can still include the solid granite of the Roman Rite and the teaching it enshrines. And on those rocks we can revive Catholic civilization, ever ancient, ever new. Where else could we turn to do so?

15
Forty Acres and an Indult?†

WHEN I FINALLY REACHED THE POINT OF expecting absolutely nothing from contemporary life, I began to believe that I had at last made substantial progress towards becoming a mature, contented, modern man. There are, of course, certain peculiar benefits that accompany such a state of zen hopelessness. One of them is the strangely comforting sense of stability that emerges from the feeling of knowing "what's what" about the world, dismal though that knowledge might be. Another, quite different by-product of the embrace of existential numbness is giddy propulsion to seventh heaven on those completely unforeseen occasions when any grounds whatsoever for rejoicing seem to be given. Sorting out whether or not to succumb to the temptation to abandon the comfortably foreseeable lessons of a bleak environment for happy indulgence in an unanticipated but potentially flawed joy is not, however, a simple task. And this is doubly true when it involves the question of taking flight from the predictable gloom of a flat and dreary ecclesiastical landscape for a long-term fling in an unexpected liturgical paradise.

Many of us actually live in such Edens, given the regular opportunity that we have to attend Mass in the Traditional Roman Rite. I myself am among those so blessed. The vision of my oasis surprised me when it first emerged on the arid Church horizon of 1989, and its failure to dry up continues to astonish me today. My gratification is all the greater since the Traditional Mass became available without my having had to exile myself from my home in Manhattan, or even to leave it at the crack of dawn every Sunday morning for some Homeric commute to a chapel in the wildwood. In short, in matters liturgical I have been enjoying not only a rare seventh heaven experience, but one that has lasted for fifteen years. To stretch an analogy from the 1860s Reconstruction Era, I at times feel like a traditionalist Catholic equivalent of a man freed from decades of slavery and guaranteed his forty acres and

† First published in the *Una Voce America*, Spring 2004.

a mule. My forty acres is New York City; my mule is the Indult that has enabled me to make my homestead productive spiritually. Should the producer of a documentary called "Gone with the Church" wander my way, I could recount to him the gripping tale of the miraculous intervention of the Roman carpetbaggers who liberated me from slavery to the local meanies with the clauses of Ecclesia Dei, thus holding out the hope for a secure possession of everything that I could possibly desire.

Nevertheless, seated cheerfully in my apartment and on my church pew, I began to wonder this past year if my giddiness had not been hoisted on its own petard. Maybe I was being a bit too harsh with myself, but I seemed to have learned to combine naïve enjoyment of my oasis with a cynical acceptance of the continued suffering of my brethren still wandering in that big, bad, outside liturgical desert, about which I knew "what's what." My calls for prudence, I thought, while perhaps sensible, must have rung hollow in the ears of believers who realized that they came from a contented man who did not have to pay any price for them. Besides, I thought, those who lived "on the outside looking in" could easily have burst my exuberant bubble merely by pointing out the weaknesses of the "carpetbagging" responsible for the creation and maintenance of my own oasis, and the continuing threat of deadly raids organized by my neighborhood Ku Klux Klan to punish uppity Tridentine collaborators like myself.

And then again, I had to admit, I really didn't even know "what was what" out there any longer anyway. Precisely because of my academic historical work and the availability of the traditionalist niche that I happily inhabited, I had become generally oblivious to the specifics of the deteriorating existence of "the others" in that mysterious black hole called Ex-Christendom. Just as my contact with contemporary television was limited to those moments on annual flights to Europe when boredom reduced me to watching any drivel to while away the time, my association with the outside, contemporary ecclesiastical universe was restricted to occasional observations of the Church situation on the Old Continent, and the marriages and deaths of relatives in the New World.

Although during the last few years, no relations have married, in the last several months very many of them have been dying. Attending their funerals has been, dare I say, a mortifying experience, but one that at least enlightened me about the reality of the situation in our spiritually and sociologically meaningless "normal" parishes. I am sure that everyone reading these pages knows what I mean, liturgically, so I will not dwell on it, but I cannot resist a few comments regarding the banality of it all. Who could possibly want to live at all if one's final fanfare were so miserably atonal? Schmaltzy cocktail piano music played from the sanctuaries evoked memories of a visit to a third-class bar around my corner the night the main pianist took sick and people in the audience began singing theme songs from situation comedies of the '50s and '60s to fill the gap. Clearly, the contrived whisper used by the priest at one travesty was somehow "in," though reminiscent not of the celebrant reciting the Old Canon, but of the ghoulish taunting utterances of the devil in The Passion. An elderly couple, the extraordinary ministers on the same occasion, swung their arms this way and that in what was supposed to be an approved liturgical fashion, though it recalled to me a geriatric gymnastic display, perhaps a preparation for the parachute jumping and mountain climbing that insurance companies tell all of us we will be enjoying in our peppy 'nineties.

Still, what really made an impression upon me on these excursions into the dying or already dead outside world was the progress of the mentality dominating the second stage of our four-decade ecclesiastical revolution. The first act of that nightmare was a Reign of Terror, under which believers were outrightly persecuted by the proponents and manipulators of change. With time and greater understanding of pluralist methodology, came wisdom in revolutionary oppression. Hence, the expansion of the concept of the "Catholic Salad Bar," religious pluralism's pathetic answer to the spiritual appetite of the age, to include some traditionalist offerings in aisles stocked with truncated dogmas, ambiguous moral choices, and outright heresies. Space was thus allowed, as the late Dr. Marra said, "for everything, even the Truth."

Investors in the Liturgical Corner of the Salad Bar accepted the need for room for the Traditional Mass, though not generally because of any conviction regarding its innate, substantive value. Some were disturbed by a liturgy that had spun totally out of hierarchical control, and convinced that encouragement of a more historical form of worship would be valuable in reestablishing internal authority and equilibrium. A number of others were eager to assure access "to everything liturgical, even that which is traditional," in order to demonstrate that our Millennial Paradise had the ability to choreograph all beliefs and practices in one harmonious dance.

People whom I met on my voyage to Ex-Christendom had perfectly adjusted to the demands of the expanded cafeteria in a way that I found startling. In the first stage of the ecclesiastical revolution, the reaction of my relatives to my efforts to escape from modernity was akin to that of normal men and women when faced with the ranting of a dangerous lunatic. Now, in contrast, all was sweetness and light. Yes, most of them had no idea what the Traditional Roman Rite or the *Novus Ordo* signified. But, after all, so what if I attended the former? Did I not have a right to do so? And think the Catholic thoughts that corresponded with it? Could I not dress my salad with solid oil and vinegar if both were offered on the condiment line? So long, that is to say, as I left them the opportunity to choose Paul Newman's Own? And the different faith that had accommodated it? It was with this choice echoing in my ears that I ran back, panting, to my once carefree niche, a sadder but wiser man, certain that my earlier worries were indeed justified, and with eyes sharpened for signs of any fragility that could bring my paradise crumbling down.

Now all of us are aware that the most obvious of the limitations of Roman "carpetbagging," one that parallels the experience of its nineteenth century predecessor, has been its woeful incompleteness. Despite a decade and a half of legal grounds for change, many dioceses just refuse to be reconstructed, and outside intervention has never been strong and thorough enough to overcome their ingrained hostility to Ecclesia Dei. Roused hopes of the traditionalist downtrodden have regularly been crushed, and often arrogantly so. Humble petitions continue to be met with stepmotherly disdain and blatantly lame and lying excuses. All too many Una Voce members personally bear the wounds of this reality, and frequently relate to me the course of their fruitless confrontations with the appropriate authorities in painfully vivid e-mails.

Moreover, it is not as though the proponents of the Reign of Terror which has persecuted Roman Catholics in the name of the Goddess of Change since the 1960s have completely lost their hold even in those dioceses where the Traditional Mass is permitted.

Their continued antagonism has made certain that our lives remain difficult. Those of us who have weekly Masses find it next to impossible to obtain daily ones. Holy Week services, marriages, funerals, and especially Confirmations, are, in most places, hopeless dreams. Repercussions threaten cranky traditionalists. Parishes so malcontent and potentially schismatic as actually to request what Ecclesia Dei offers can find obstacles placed in the path of the smooth functioning of ordinary pastoral activities, with offending clerics cast out from polite society to deal with the noonday devils on their own. A laity already exhausted from the tortures of their daily business labors can be reduced to absolute prostration by the evening hours required for petitioning and letter writing Ku Klux Chanceries.

But to top it all, *pour comble de malheur*, peril threatens now through seduction by the false promise of the augmented Salad Bar. Accommodation to its spirit would disfigure us beyond repair, convincing us, as it desperately wants to do, that our freedom to enjoy the Traditional Rite must be accompanied by a violation of the whole concept of the Church as a historical community with a common message and a common understanding of the theology underlying justifiable ceremonial differences. It would put us in the same boat as Viennese aristocrats in white tails and top hats who are permitted to organize an Opera Ball, merely to be driven mad by the realization that its Hapsburg glories could be recaptured only at the price of permitting ambiguous clowns and tramps and revelers dressed in drag to enter and whirl about alongside them.

In fact, a number of stockholders in the Liturgical Corner were willing to invest in a space for the splendors of the past only under the presumption that this would prove to be their ultimate undoing; in the hope that toleration of traditionalists' whimsy would isolate them in tightly-knit conventicles where they could be watched more closely, and multiply endlessly in peculiar sectarian factionalism. Liturgical Traditionalism might thereby be exposed as a particularly quirky position in an Alice and Wonderland of thousands of varied lifestyles and value options, a dynamite-looking dud easy to implode and bring down damage on its own combustible hideaway alone. The less of a threat to the establishment that it was treated, the more certainly that it, too, would swiftly be *Gone with the Church*.

The seductive character of the siren song of the Salad Bar is more than understandable. Customers have been lured to dine on the deadly banquettes of the Liturgical Corner with great success ever since Opening Day. These have included honest, conservative-minded people unaware of just how much their health is impaired by breathing its polluted atmosphere. All of us who have endured decades of Ecclesiastical World Wars might be more than ready to succumb to its charms in exchange for even a limited taste of the old, lost tradition, and a maintenance of just a trace of unjustifiable Zen giddiness. We ought to tie ourselves down and stuff up our ears so that we do not leap to embrace the Salad Bar's wares.

But what does all this mean for my Forty Acres and an Indult? With the ever-present dangers threatening from the outside world more clearly in my mind, am I not to allow myself a moment's peace to enjoy something in which I actually do have an opportunity to take delight? Many of the opponents of the Indult Mass have suggested as much, but I personally do not share their view. Indulgence in some liturgical happiness in our admittedly flawed oases continues to be more than justifiable. Nothing whatsoever could ever make me regret the interference in my life of the Roman "carpetbaggers" and the blessing that was and is Ecclesia Dei. Limited though they were, they have made my life richer. Much more importantly, however, they have given me the chance to offer a few people who are not capable of worrying about the rest of mankind—namely, my own children—something of a normal Catholic childhood and catechesis. They have provided necessary standard operating procedures and proving grounds for the training of the confessors of the future. Therefore, in exchange for my cooperation and interview, I would insist that *Gone with the Church* not portray my benefactors badly. I would demand that its producers avoid caricaturing those of us who have gained something from Ecclesia Dei either as an ignorant, inferior, obscurantist breed, useful on screen only for the post-conciliar version of a racist belly laugh, or as wretched crumb-gatherers, indulging slavishly in a trifling concession. Even crumbs have a certain value for starving men, and the cause of my children, my fellow parishioner parents, and the confessors seeking some guidelines as to how to begin a counterrevolution in their own liturgically-ravaged dioceses is far from a petty one. Let us, as I have argued in these pages before, give credit where credit is due, and encouragement to benevolence whatever its provenance and extent.

What I am arguing against here is becoming dizzy with what really is but a restricted success, completely satisfied with what are, indeed, crumbs and not a banquet, and the mistaking of a refugee camp for Shangri-la. Despite everything, our oases partake much more of a Sinai than a paradise of milk and honey, and pharaoh's armies are still in our hot pursuit to boot. We must realize that however grateful we should be for what we have been given (after having fought vigorously for years to get it!), that even this will not be secure until the bleak ecclesiastical landscape around us turns brighter in all regards. Every rocking of the ecclesiastical boat, with the positive attention of making its passengers realize that it is sinking; every suggestion for moving from traditionalism in One Diocese to its worldwide victory; every scheme for reconciliation of the Society of St. Pius X with Rome or the erection of an Apostolic Administration, should be confronted and tested by us with a spirit that is both hopeful and prudent at one and the same time. Let us indeed use this Lenten and Easter season to express our satisfaction with what has been accomplished so far. But let us also exploit it to prepare ourselves for a renewed militancy, and a courage and humor sufficient to last us until we finally reach the Promised Land.

16

Michael Davies and the Movement[†]

ONE AND INSEPARABLE

ONE OF MY FIRST ASSIGNMENTS WHEN beginning my studies in England as a twenty-one-year-old in 1972 was a paper on Catholic life in Britain. Being involved with the Traditionalist Movement in the United States since 1970, I wanted to know what my fellow travelers on the European side of the Atlantic were up to anyway, so I launched into the project with enthusiasm. Attendance at a Traditional Mass at Westminster Cathedral gave me my first chance to explore their world. When Mass was over, a large crowd gathered in the plaza outside the doors. I plunged with my questions into one particularly lively group. "Don't talk to us," they told me. "Talk to Michael Davies. If anyone knows the Movement, he does. He is the Movement. He's the traditionalist's Traditionalist."

That's where my Michael Davies experience began. It continued over thirty-two subsequent years, nurtured by repeated encounters at London Conferences, Roman Forum lectures in New York, twelve Summer Symposia of the Dietrich von Hildebrand Institute on Lake Garda, Una Voce meetings in Rome, the occasional pilgrimage to Chartres, discussions in his office at the top of his home in Bromley, and innumerable dinners and visits to pubs. And through all that time and all those experiences the original judgment of my London crowd was amply confirmed. There was no need to travel the whole world to learn about the Movement. Here it was, in microcosm, reflected in the life and activity of one highly amusing Welshman, who also had the added benefit of amusing my children with too much candy, their first sips of scotch, and readings of entertaining British imperialist poetry.

Michael's very real Faith reminds me of that of Ludwig von Pastor. Von Pastor, historian of the popes, had to devote much of his writing to a recording of ecclesiastical nightmares, brought on by everything from miscalculation to high crimes and misdemeanors.

† First published in *The Remnant*, October 15, 2004.

But he was savvy without being cynical. Hence, he could revel in undisguised happiness at a canonization ceremony in St. Peter's Square, overjoyed that the real holiness of the Mystical Body of Christ had once again been given a chance to manifest itself. Similarly, Michael, whose life's labor was dictated by the need to recount the worst tale of woe in Church History, radiated Faith to all who knew him. My wife and I noticed this on the last day of the Chartres pilgrimage in 1994, at the moment when the cathedral definitely came into sight. His face was lit by that same undisguised joy in God, the gift of life, the promise of eternal happiness, and the magnificent opportunity of seeing the glory of Christ's Church reflected in the testimony of the mass of men paying homage to the Lord of History around him. And this, after several days of "hangman's humor," comically (but sadly) commenting on the horrors of the desert through which the Bride of Christ was presently wandering. No one left Michael's presence blithely thinking that we would experience ecclesiastical peace in our time. But no one left Michael's presence without the profound hope that Faith would see us through this disaster, and that Catholic Truth would conquer in the end. If a beer or two during a sleepless rainy night on the road to Chartres helped to maintain our spirits alongside a mountain of prayer, well that was part of a loving God's aid to His faithful servants also.

Michael was ultimately a very peaceful man and a very understanding critic. He did not like quarrels for quarrels' sake. Nor did he excommunicate anyone who did not excommunicate him. Hence, he was willing to work with all groups that would work with him and test every opportunity that arose to restore quiet and order to traditionalists in particular and to the Roman Catholic Church in general. I know that this won him a certain censure, short or long lasting, from a variety of different segments of the common Movement. One may measure the validity of Michael's generosity and hopefulness as he pleases; they came, as did everything in his labors, from a truly Catholic agony over the current state of Holy Church and a passion to find a way out of her misery. The man was not happy about one thing only: that he was obliged to record a history of unparalleled collapse. There were no works from Michael Davies' hands without the shedding, internally, of an ocean's worth of horrified tears.

How do we really say anything definitive about a great man just a few days after his death, when the importance of his passing has not yet been fully digested? How do we do this when the great man in question was also our friend and a profound personal influence over our thoughts and spiritual life and work as Catholic activists—in my own case, for thirty-two long years? The effort has to be tentative and somewhat clumsy at its very best.

Our dear friend needs Faith no longer. He is now among those who are supremely conscious of the Truth. As far as we can know, however, Michael is still in need of our prayers. We have to work to get him out of Purgatory, as quickly as possible, with all the Faith, Hope, and Charity that we can muster. We owe it to him, for everything that he did to shape that Faith, Hope, and Charity in our own lives in the first place. I do not wish to say anything theologically incorrect, especially where Michael is concerned, but I am certain that a host of other Catholic Heroes, with St. John Fisher at the top of the list, are up there pulling for him alongside us. Goodbye for now Michael, we will pray for you regularly in the Mass that you did so much to defend and exalt; the Mass That Cannot Die.

17
Dr. Eric de Saventhem and Christian Nobility†

HOWEVER PAINFUL IT MAY BE TO REMIND ourselves that we have lost two outstanding International Federation Presidents in the space of one twelve-month period, both love and respect for Dr. Eric de Saventhem's powerful example demand that his passing be given a sorrowful pride of place in these pages. The basic details of his life need not be retold here, extraordinary though they were, and so illustrative of the unique problems faced by Catholics in a violent and anti-religious age. Many Una Voce members are already as familiar with his personal saga and achievements as they are with those of Michael Davies. Let us therefore seize this sad occasion to undertake something which I believe to be much more appropriate to Dr. de Saventhem's long-term significance; of much greater utility to his extended Una Voce family than a mere chronological account of his labors can provide: an extended meditation upon the concept of Christian nobility and our late President's embodiment of its chief characteristics.

What is nobility? Perhaps few terms have been as brutally cheapened in our revolutionary era as this exalted one has been. Most people today equate nobility solely with the idea of an upper class based upon riches, and riches generally earned in rather crass and vulgar crowd-pleasing ways. Noblesse oblige is often measured solely in terms of how much cash the "nobleman" in question gives away to the community at large. What comes to my mind constantly in this regard are graduation ceremonies where the precise sums which honorary degree recipients have donated to buy their "noble" academic status are read out loud by some shameless university official.

For most of the human experience, however, nobility has had little openly or directly to do with even honorably won wealth and

† First published in the *Una Voce America Newsletter*, Spring 2005.

its laudable dispersal. Strictly speaking, a nobleman, at his origins, has historically been nothing other than "a known quantity." He has been someone who "is clearly what he is" and can always be counted upon to represent the specific standards he has espoused both reliably and gloriously. A nobleman passes on those standards for others to live up to and, hopefully, to surpass. The brilliance of his achievement weighs most intimately and forcefully upon his immediate family, giving it a certain edge in the struggle to follow in its "known quantities" path, but, conversely, a much more intense shame to live down if it does not. Still, the greater the nobleman and his glory, the more his model urges itself as a standard for the whole of society to emulate, and the more its failures parallel, in depth, any scandals aroused by his delinquent family.

Historical nobility has also been closely associated with a life of painful exertion which, rather than necessarily ending in peaceful enjoyment of one's goods, may actually involve their total rejection. Life-long strain, self-donation, respect of previous examples of stubborn persistence and denial, and even willing acceptance and abandonment to death are central to the achievement of the noble soldiers, athletes, family heads, and statesmen depicted for us in the works of Homer, Pindar, Solon the Lawgiver, and our other Greek and Roman forefathers.

But struggle, sacrifice, and hero worship can be terribly flawed if the standard that is pursued and the known quantities who are honored are ultimately false and shallow in character. This was why Plato recast the image of the nobleman on the model of Socrates, the ideal individual who understood that life was a pilgrimage from darkness to the light of Truth, and that only when and if this Truth were discovered, could its spread to others require unconditional self-sacrifice. This was why Church Fathers like St. Gregory of Nyssa, who greatly admired the Platonic quest, nevertheless saw the need to complete it by extending it into the realm of the supernatural, fixing our final attention upon the Divine Nobleman, Christ—the Way, the Truth, and the Life, as well as the Good Shepherd who sacrifices Himself for His sheep. Plato's nobleman was more exalted than his earlier counterpart, since he no longer merely gave wholehearted testimony to any standard whatsoever, but to a true one and a true one alone. The Christian nobleman was more illustrious still, because he abandoned himself completely to an imitation of that Word Incarnate who transforms and ineffably elevates all nature in service to the Living God.

Building a Christian nobility has always been a difficult task. Human individuals, even those open to the medicine we call grace, can readily fall prey to the shallow and lying seductions of a creation flawed by sin; to a scandalous, hypocritical, surface adherence to what should be an all-consuming Imitation of Christ. Given the wicked temptations accompanying warfare, and the peculiar circumstances of early medieval history, efforts to construct that nobility were first aimed at the whole body of western soldiery. Saints and statesmen sought mightily to turn this *malitia* (evil force) away from unscrupulous visions of glory and focus it upon creation of a militia Christi, composed of committed crusading knights who fought only other combatants and solely on behalf of the weak in demonstrably just warfare. So effective were Catholic labors in this realm, that it became possible to use the image of the Christian knight as a model for the ennoblement of men and women in other spheres of life as well. This is why a St. Francis of Assisi could take over military imagery and use it to stir men on to ascetic and missionary battles; a St. Dominic to the clash of the intellectual against heresy.

Personally, this is also why every time I think of the Christian nobleman, I have in mind the famous sixteenth century woodcut of Albrecht Dürer. Here one sees a rather gnarled armored knight on horseback, traveling to the Heavenly Jerusalem, which is set on a hill in the background distance. The forest through which he passes is a frightening one, filled with all manner of threats including singularly macabre ones which perhaps represent his own fantastic temptations. Nevertheless, single minded in commitment to reaching his goal, he rides steadfastly onwards. He will not deviate from his path no matter how bizarre or intense the obstacles to it. Nor will he grow overly alarmed by them. He is calm throughout the nightmare. Here is a man who suggests courage and can command without arrogance; a commander one can follow and obey without self-abasement and fawning. The authority behind his personal confidence and that which he inspires in others comes from God and not from himself.

Dr. de Saventhem, as far as I am concerned, was precisely the kind of complete nobleman, natural and Christian, outlined above. Guiding his already innately steadfast, reliable spirit was an intellect which had been superbly trained for and aimed at the quest for understanding Truth in Plato's sense of the hunt. His Socratic abilities were sharpened in a particular way by that linguistic knowledge which allows a man to grasp the Truth aesthetically and personally, in all of its multiform complexity and unending beauty. Piloting his sharpened and aesthetically awakened intellect was a soul dedicated to prayer and the regimen provided by a profound sacramental life. How could this embodiment of Catholic nobility not then ride forth and lock in battle with an unreceptive and uncomprehending era? How could he not contest with all of his energy an age that refused to cultivate the one methodology that could truly and completely ennoble it—adoration, abandonment, and imitation of Christ? How could a man with his appreciation of the Eucharist not especially combat this self-destructive, man-centered, vulgarizing refusal when recognizing it in a false liturgical reform? How could he not strain and suffer and donate his fortune and his health to such a cause, calling upon the memory of past Christian noble heroes to sustain him in years of unrewarded struggle?

The gifts of the Holy Spirit to a Christian knight, as well as to every ordinary believer on his way to a similar ennoblement, involve both wisdom and calm, wrapped in one harmonious package. I don't think that anyone who enlisted under Dr. de Saventhem's command and heard his orders could possibly deny that he, especially, offered the crystal-clear realism of a wise man combined with the patience and far-sightedness of a believer who recognizes the strange ways in which God works His Will. Unwavering in his loyalty to the indefectible Bride of Christ, he nevertheless knew that she was wandering off onto one of the worst of the all too many unfortunate detours she has taken on her trouble-filled pilgrimage to God; unstinting in his criticism of her loss of sanity, he was unmovable in a measured and even-tempered way, with the sure conviction that this madness, too, would sometime pass way; bound irrevocably to the one unchanging code of the orthodox Faith, he could easily discern the same noble Catholic spirit in a myriad of quite different outward envelopes, including that represented by his handpicked successor, Michael Davies.

Dr. de Saventhem was a man who both confirmed and yet gave the lie to William Butler Yeats' famous poem, The Second Coming.

Yes, one might be tempted to say upon hearing him speak, things are falling apart. The center does not hold. Mere anarchy has been loosed upon the world. Some rough beast indeed slouches towards Bethlehem to be born. And yet here, to give the lie to Yeats' lamentation, was this true nobleman, this Optimate, this best among the best, who nevertheless did possess all conviction, and was, simultaneously, full of passionate intensity of the right kind. Here was a Catholic known quantity if ever there was one, and when and where we bewildered novices needed him.

Families and communities possessing a noble vision and noble heroes often try to give them still greater splendor by stretching their roots further into their past than anything but legend warrants. Thus, the Romans depicted their self-sacrificing mission of law and order as one stemming from the early days of the Republic, and the medievals transformed their first barbaric ancestors into fully formed Christian knights. Useful as such legends can be to create standards for future generations to follow, it is better to have real flesh and blood models of nobility to pressure us into action. This fact was drilled into my consciousness some years ago when my wife and I visited an Italian prince's castle and were taken to say his little daughter's evening prayers in the family chapel: in front of the tombs of the immediate family saints.

Our Una Voce Family has just such a historical model in Dr. Eric de Saventhem, his life, and his mission. Our long-time leader is the true founder of our noble apostolate; of our noble line. If we wish the society around us to take what our heroic president had to say and do seriously, then we, like the immediate family of any other nobleman, have more of a responsibility than anyone else to follow him, emulate him, and, if possible, surpass him in his achievements. If we, like other noble lines, aided by the charism of our founders, do not shoulder our burden in carrying on their work, then the scandal will be ours and we will be judged more harshly accordingly.

Holy Virgin and all you saints of God, pray for our dear, departed Dr. Eric de Saventhem. May his soul and all the souls of the faithfully departed Christian knights rest in peace. May their example inspire us in the battles yet to come.

18

"The State of Tradition" in the United States[†]

INTERVIEW WITH JOHN RAO, PHD

DR. RAO IS FOUNDER OF THE ROMAN Forum and Dietrich von Hildebrand Institute in New York. He is also a frequent contributor to *The Remnant*, *Latin Mass Magazine*, and SeattleCatholic.com. He has been actively supporting the Traditional Latin Mass in New York for many years by his writing, teaching, serving as acolyte at St. Agnes on 43rd Street, and encouraging many people. He graciously responded to our interview questionnaire.

Let us first define (for the purposes of this article) Tradition. By Tradition, we mean those principles, whether devotional, liturgical, or cultural, which apply to the Roman Catholic Church and which were in existence prior to the changes brought about after the Second Vatican Council, and which now have been restored either by the laity, by a priest or bishop, or by the Vatican. At the pinnacle of Tradition under this definition is the Mass according to the Missal of St. Pius V and all the devotions, rubrics, and Catholic cultural elements surrounding this Missal. This would naturally include the Church's sacred music tradition in Gregorian chant and sacred polyphony among many other things.

1. With this definition in mind, how would you assess the state of Tradition in the US today? What have you witnessed that leads you to your conclusions?

This depends on what one is comparing things in 2005 against. Compared to 1975, the situation is much better. Compared to 2000, somewhat static, though that should change due to the new Pope. I judge this purely on the basis of the weariness of activists whom I know who have simply been waiting for something, anything,

† First published in the *Una Voce Columbus*, August 2005.

to happen. Also, I think that Tradition in the United States is hampered by political and social factors that are untraditional and have a tremendous influence over orthodox Catholics. These limit their ability to respond fully to the Traditional life.

2. *Please provide statistics from your parish, priestly order, diocese, etc. on the growth or decline of Tradition particularly in the past twenty years. Personal anecdotes are welcome.*

In the last twenty years, we have gone from no official permitted Masses to at least five Sunday and Holy Day Masses in the Archdiocese of New York. We still have problems with the Triduum and Confirmation, but very few [problems of permission] with marriages and funerals.

3. *The laity, since the changes brought about after Vatican II, has become less aware of Tradition or simply does not know Church History and teaching regarding Tradition. What are you doing/what can the Church in the US do to improve knowledge of Tradition, its validity and great value?*

I run the Roman Forum, which provides systematic teaching in Catholic Culture, both in Italy in the summer and in New York City during the academic year. More of this has to be done, both on the private level and for seminaries, where historical training is usually abominable.

4. *How do you deal with Americans who were abused or shunned because of their questioning of changes during the turbulent 70s or, how do you defend Tradition against Americans who promote the changes and fight to keep Tradition away from the Church? What good has come from your confrontations?*

I find it almost impossible to talk with older people who have become alienated from the Church, either for conservative or liberal reasons. We just live on two different planets. My parents, for example, both near 90, have a hard time understanding a Traditionalist position, and have even forgotten what the old Church that they lived in for fifty years was all about.

5. *There are many factions of Tradition in the US today including some that are seen as outside of Holy Mother Church. Have there*

been efforts among them that you consider positive and helpful for Tradition?

Here, too, I find many people frozen in their positions and suspicious of one another. I try to avoid confrontations with SSPX friends.

6. *The survival of the Traditional Movement in America depends on the Catholic youth. Is the youth catching on? What evidence can you give?*

Youthful priests and students have been a great source of hope. There are very many young priests and seminarians who are eager to support the Traditional Movement and say the Traditional Mass. As for students, I can safely say that all of the serious students whom I have taught immediately understand why I am a Traditionalist. Recently, I gave a lecture for the graduate student organization at Catholic University of America. I was stunned by how many of them are traditionalists or traditionalist supporters.

7. *Even the Editors of Karl Keating's* This Rock *had to agree that traditionalist families are quite possibly the future of the Church in America (June 2000). Do you agree? What evidence can you give?*

Traditionalist families face many problems in the realm of education and basic economic survival. We homeschool and have found it possible to do so without too many difficulties on the primary level because of all of the facilities open to us here in the center of Manhattan. I know many people who are trying to homeschool but simply do not have the interest or talent for doing so, and are letting their children's education suffer in consequence. I know many who are positively contemptuous of many aspects of education as well. Our biggest problem is economic survival in a world that pays no heed to Catholic social teaching. One is forced to be an absent parent simply to pay for the continued existence of the family. My parents and those of my wife, both of whom had decent-sized families, never had to strain themselves in the same way that we and other traditional families do in order to pay the rent and feed the kids. I don't know where this will eventually take us, except into a kind of serfdom.

19

The New Millennium and Traditionalists[†]

REFLECTIONS OF A PURGED UNA VOCE AMERICA PRESIDENT

I later heard Brother Otho say, in talking about our time among the Mauritanians, that a mistake only then becomes an error if one stubbornly persists in it.

(Ernst Jünger, *Auf den Marmorklippen*, Ullstein, 2001, p. 26)

ENTERING THE PROMISED LAND?

Remember all the enthusiasm over the arrival of the latest batch of a thousand years? Many people—the highest authority of the Church prominent among them—simply could not contain their exhilaration at the thought of the signs and wonders that would accompany the change of the numbers 1-9-9-9 to 2-0-0-0. The year 2001, would, of course, have been the correct date to anticipate, but that spoil-sport digit "one" interfered too sloppily with the purity represented by three, splendid, chubby little zeros in a single, uninterrupted row to be acceptable. So 2000 was the moment anticipated for the definitive arrival of a future brighter than any past.

Ah, for just a brief return to those heady days, when some of my otherwise reserved acquaintances from Opus Dei had answering machines whose messages ended with a rousing "forward to the millennium!" Oh, for but a partial revival of the uncontrollable enthusiasm of Thomas Friedman, optimist laureate for *The New York Times*, when that one cloud on the horizon, the possible world wide computer glitch, failed to materialize! For him, this failure stunningly confirmed the advent of a luminous age of international peace and cooperation. His first column of the year 2000 was a veritable paean to emerging planetary solidarity. It

† First published in *The Remnant*, December 25, 2005.

fancifully depicted the way in which the inhabitants of each city already safely delivered from the terror of midnight chaos stood by their television screens rooting for those a time zone behind them to safely break on through to the other side.

Well, here we all are, five years into the Promised Land. And are you *Remnant* readers enjoying your new millennium? I dare say that you are not. In fact, I wager that you, like me, are finding that it has all the potential for soon making the justly detested twentieth century appear actually to have been days of wine and roses. Perhaps it was the next millennium everyone was expecting? Do you have the patience and health of Methuselah to wait around long enough to find out?

But let us not indulge in numerology any longer. The unpleasantness of the current situation was obviously not the fault of the indifferent date "2000" as such either. The basic contours of our complex and frightening new environment were, as is usual in history, outlined quite some time before. By the 1950s, Third World issues announced the approach of a future which would disrupt efforts to fit all of life's conflicts neatly into the context officially approved of by the two Great Powers.

Just ten years later, the Soviet Union, shaken by the failed adventurism of the Khrushchev Era, had frozen its structures and policies in time, condemning itself to bankruptcy, cynicism, and, ultimately, western libertinism and its attendant new diseases. "You're next," a cardinal from eastern Europe told a friend of mine already sixteen years ago, in 1989, understanding, as he did, that the demise of the East Bloc would inevitably be followed by a trouble-filled disintegration of its American dominated western counterpart.

Still, just as the revolutionary events of 1789–1794 made the developments of the previous two centuries infinitely more real to the public at large, the vertiginous experiences of the last five years have brought home for anyone with eyes to see the fact that "the times, they are a-changin." Consider the data for yourselves. Jets in the World Trade Center. Fatherland Security. A "Hundred Years War" in the Middle East. The collapse of NATO. A demographic revolution rendering the theories of John Locke and the Founding Fathers as inexplicable to the new populations of Europe and the United States as Hinayana Buddhism to Cardinal Merry del Val. The Chinese economic juggernaut. Indian domination of state and business telephone complaint bureaus. Budget deficits that would send the most radical spendthrift into voluntary credit counseling, promoted and encouraged by conservative Republicans. Inundations from the sea, earthquakes from below, and, most recently, sick birds from above, stimulating the fear that Chicken Little himself may be the carrier of the aviary infection falling ever westward from out of the Asian skies.

The post World War Two era is indeed totally and irrevocably dead. Irony of ironies, there is even a German pope on hand to say its funeral prayers. But with its demise has come much more: the arrival of the final stage of the Enlightenment. That movement's underlying message has always been creation's independence from its God, and man's need to secure the triumph of his fallen natural will. What distinguishes these latter days of the Enlightenment in America is the recognition that the victory of unbridled will is most effectively attained not through direct, open, Nazi-like commitment to its cause, but indirectly, under the rubric of pursuing democracy and pluralist freedom. This is precisely what is reflected in the work of the bizarre combination of Straussians, neo-cons, oil men, supporters of Greater Israel, and other assorted ideologues and men on the make who dominate our country today. Such adulators of raw strength possess a rhetorical machine sweetening the depiction of their activities that makes Goebbels (Hitler's minister of propaganda) look like a pathetic loser at kindergarten propaganda class. Moreover, they have at their fingertips a financial power and industrial and technological ability useful for squeezing and destroying anything standing in their way which is exponentially greater than that wielded by any tyrant ever known to history.

So confident of success is this true Axis of Evil that some of its supporters find it hard, even now, to keep the masquerade of democracy and pluralism going. Hence, their often rather surprisingly open talk about the obsolescence of those concepts of "human nature" and "natural law" which somewhat limit their depredations. Given the chance to break all substantive opposition coming from people motivated by higher ideals, they would drop their outwardly noble rhetorical cover definitively and forever. But as matters now stand, this opposition continues to exist. Christian themes are still alive enough to have the power even to make some unconscious members of the Axis of Evil feel guilty and sense the need to justify themselves with reference to permanent truths and morality. Co-option of the remaining Christian resistance, therefore, continues to be the order of the day. Which leads me straight to the main question before us: how is the process of co-option going? And what impact does it have on the Traditionalist Movement?

THE "MAURITANIANS"

Let me begin to answer that query by noting that, historically, large numbers of people confronted by bewildering change backed by willful men have responded to it by going on vacation to Never Never Land. Once they have arrived there, they have denied that anything new and dangerous has actually entered into their lives at all. Many ancient Greeks, Romans, and Near Easterners took this holiday of denial, stunned as they were by the innovations accompanying the multicultural empires shaping their world beginning with the conquests of Alexander the Great (336–323 B. C.) and continuing down to the victory of Christianity.

In order to obtain permission for Never Never Land games, however, the visitors to these varied playgrounds had to collaborate with the existing system and its rulers on those matters that really guided their practical lives. Forget about simply avoiding anything which might give offense to the big shots. Personal security required that they enthusiastically praise the divinity of the establishment oppressing them. And this they readily did: over and over again. Collaboration for the truly powerful might entail the shouldering of active obligations to the great monarchs of the age before rushing home to the more pleasant task of cultivating impotence. Collaboration, for the weak, might mean just working, paying taxes, and never transgressing the sacred wall separating private fantasy from social and political reality. Most collaborators kept the wheels of the regime machinery going because they did not wish to risk their necks by openly opposing it; some since they had become so used to its gears that they took them for granted as an unquestionable given, maintaining ties with their own oppressed traditions through pure inertia. A few of those who collaborated were fully co-opted by their masters. They became fervent propagandists for the new order, even hoping to be accepted into its inner circles.

But not everyone confronted by bewildering, force-backed change has gone down the escapist-collaborationist path. A respectable number have reacted to such transformations by militantly taking up arms against them, and this outside of those legitimate structures of their societies which have cowardly or unthinkingly opted for an accommodating posture.

Both the attraction and problems of this confrontational response are brilliantly analyzed by Ernst Jünger (1895–1998), one of the most important German writers of the twentieth century, a man who converted to Roman Catholicism in the last years of his life. His analysis appears in what I consider to be his best work, *On the Marble Cliffs* (*Auf den Marmorklippen*, 1939), which takes us, allegorically, from the horrific change and confusion following the First World War to that which could be expected to accompany a second such conflict. Here, Jünger tells us of the activities of the distinctly irregular band of "Mauritanians," part Crusading Order, part anarchic, untamed horde, which provided an appealing outlet for men seeking solid camaraderie and unapologetic militant action in the midst of collapse and chaos. So understandably alluring is the Mauritanian Order that the unnamed protagonist of the novel and his brother Otho rode out on their horses to fight the many-headed demons of the age alongside them.

Jünger admits, however, that the peculiar "time out of time" spent with this sympathetic fraternal host was not without its risks. Mauritanian irregularity encouraged an atmosphere in which major delusions regarding the past and the nature of the current chaos could be nourished, as well as apocalyptic fears or impossibly utopian hopes for the future. The Order's wild exuberance could invite new problems which would not be recognized as such until they had become ingrained and exceedingly difficult to uproot.

Most dangerously, its potential for intellectually and strategically anarchic action might unwittingly contribute to the victory of the *Oberförster*, the novel's Hitler-like figure, who did act regularly according to a strategic plan, and who saw both the disorder of his day as well as the wild reaction to it as a golden opportunity for the devastation of all civilized life.

It is worth reading *On the Marble Cliffs* merely for Jünger's prophetic description of what exactly the consequences of the *Oberförster*'s victory would be. The protagonist and his brother stopped active participation with the Mauritanian Order before any of its possible mistakes could lead them to unintended disaster, but they never thought that their period militating alongside it was wasted. Neither did they condemn its members for remaining inside, still exposed to its potential flaws. "I later heard Brother Otho say about our time with the Mauritanians," Jünger has him say, "that a mistake only then becomes an error if one stubbornly persists in it."

IN REACTION

Most of our contemporaries show all the signs of reacting to the big, bad new millennium and its Axis of Evil by indulging in escapism and collaborationism—a totally understandable response, given the almost unbearable economic and social situation in which they are placed if they resist. Moreover, they have long habituated themselves to the escapist collaborationism dictated by American Pluralism. This has never tired of encouraging limited, meaningless expressions of freedom inside Never Never Land ghettoes, so long as the poor souls who prance about in them leap and cavort to the tune sung by the strong on matters that really count—and write a poem or two to the glories of the system humiliating them for good measure.

Americans have long learned to appreciate the unparalleled freedom they possess to focus obsessively on secondary matters. And it is undeniably true that they can dedicate themselves to the memorization and even open recitation of the names of the Patriarchs of Antioch and Alexandria in the quiet of their own living rooms without fear of police intrusion. All that has changed since 2000 on this front is that they have to make the whole world safe for neo-conservative exploitation and frat boy torture in order to retain their rights to be monumentally inconsequential.

What is truly upsetting in such game-playing is that Roman Catholics are right up there in the front lines, escaping and collaborating alongside the best of them while Nemesis continues his inexorable advance. As usual, some of those who collaborate do so out of fear—in America, fear of missing a golden opportunity for success and "falling behind." Again, it is more than understandable that they do so today, since it has been made practically impossible for anyone to avoid "falling behind" without plunging into an economic game that claims the attention of both body and soul every single waking hour.

Once more, some collaborate because of an unreflective acceptance of the new rules of the game. Such people maintain ties with their Catholic traditions purely out of a well-meaning inertia. Collaboration, in both cases, means that the bulk of the average believing Catholic's day is spent living and being forced to adulate a flat, naturalist, God-defying, self-asserting modern life which only the really strong can effectively (and perversely) "enjoy." This naturalist reality is denied by him upon returning home to live in a private Christendom in no way harmful to the masters of the new millennium. Here, one can sing pious hymns and touch the covers of old Catholic texts bought from nostalgic book clubs. Here, one can read articles in conservative newspapers and journals about past saints, whose whole lives unabashedly condemn his collaborationist subservience to the temporarily forgotten outside world.

Catalogues from bright and shiny new Catholic schools and universities are available to him in Never Never Land. The institutions described therein promise to save the next generation from perdition while they train it to function either in a world that no longer exists or one that is actively engaged in dismantling the remaining pitiful remnants of its Christian heritage. They ensure that Catholic youth will graduate either as cogs for the lowest levels of the global economic machine or as experts in voting for, implementing, and praising the program of their willful capitalist and imperialist masters. The Catholic activism in which their alumni will engage will be of the acceptably harmless variety. Such activists will jot down endless comments in crisp new notebooks at the umpteenth impotent conference leading to nothing other than a post seminar dinner party. The day after celebrating their action, they will return to flipping their burgers or presiding over investments destroying another age-old culture. Now there's a return for the modern Never Never Land investor!

Moreover, just as in the Hellenistic Era following Alexander the Great's conquests, some of these Catholic collaborators are openly co-opted, become cheerleaders for the new order, and marvel at God's blessing over the entire enterprise. The Novaks, Weigels, Neuhauses, and Acton Institutes of collapsing Christendom rival one another in inventing ever new flips on the theme of why tossing the whole of Catholic Social Teaching out the window is traditional; why embracing a socio-economic modernism shut tight to transformation in Christ is the only truly Christian enterprise worth considering. By all means say your Catholic prayers in your homes and in your churches, they urge us. But be sure to include among them one that begs that the outside world remains safely in the hands of men and laws who brook no interference with their prerogatives. "Don't tread on me!" is their preferred hymn for the Feast of Christ the King.

Others among our new millennium contemporaries have, of course, taken the Mauritanian pathway of irregular resistance to unpalatable change. Most of the Roman Catholics who are among the Mauritanians actually entered down that route of opposition forty years earlier, in the wake of the conciliar disaster. I am thinking of all those traditionalist men and women who, in the midst of the debacle devastating legitimate religious institutions since the 1960s, sought refuge in a myriad of different militant, activist associations. In such groups, they were able to wrap their arms fervently round some identifiable remnant of the Catholic shipwreck. There, like the Mauritanians from *On the Marble Cliffs*, they discovered true comradeship. There, they regained their psychological footing and found a chance to conduct a clear and unapologetic battle against a corruption of both the Church and the secular world which they knew was destined to grow ever more deep. But there they also exposed themselves to the possible mistakes which, stubbornly adhered to, could become errors unintentionally aiding the advance of the *Oberförster*. Some have gone off the deep end in consequence. The majority, I would argue, really have not.

UNA VOCE AMERICA

All these subjects have been much on my mind lately due to a very great personal disappointment: my recent dismissal from the presidency of Una Voce America. Quite frankly, neither I nor many of the individual chapters of Una Voce has any way of knowing all the motives behind this purge, which was effected by liquidating the position of president entirely and replacing it with a chairman for whom a national search is now being conducted. One has to be part of the Board of Directors to have access to the information needed to understand it fully; it is not, by statute, a decision to be made by democratic vote.

I have tried logically to piece together the reasons for my disgrace from bits of discussions over the past years, and now feel pretty certain that my articles in *The Remnant* critical of the pontificate of John Paul II played a crucial role in it. It may be that my anti-Americanist politics dictated the verdict as well. Bursts of excitement over one or the other strategy to follow could also have entered into it. In any case, I was, I believe, perceived as being a radical wild card who posed a threat to serious negotiations with the Church authorities in the United States and the Vatican; a Mauritanian whose mistakes threatened to become a dangerous error harmful to traditionalism in America as a whole. If I am wrong about this, I apologize. If I am not, I owe some defense of myself to the many people who have asked me what it is that happened. I decided that the best way to offer such a defense was in the context of a broad reflection on the reality of the situation facing the Traditionalist Movement in America today, and what I think needs to be done to respond to it.

When I first entered that movement, in the early 1970s, those of us who were neither collaborating with the establishment nor militating in the ranks of the Mauritanians found themselves in limbo. Our limbo was also shaken by a full-blown crisis. Dietrich von Hildebrand, the Roman Forum, and Walter Matt were in the first stages of splitting off from *The Wanderer* and Catholics United for the Faith (CUF). The von Hildebrand alliance was ready to take its critique of the ecclesiastical disaster wherever it might lead in order that its argument would be true to the record and completely coherent. It knew that the pope was really the pope and the bishops really the legitimate bishops, but it did not exempt from criticism any prelate whom it thought to be contributing to the growing nightmare.

The Wanderer was only willing to rake bishops over the coals. It was insistent upon the need to praise the wisdom of a Paul VI who, on the one hand, was actively engaged in egging those prelates on to madness, and, on the other, in caving into their still wilder calls for wider destruction.

CUF was outraged even by attacks upon the bishops, quoting St. Pius X to defend the thesis that it was not the laity's lowly place to criticize the authorities whom it might have thought were placed in their positions precisely to protect ordinary believers. Presumably this meant that the English laity would have had to shield from criticism the legitimately recognized Archbishop Cranmer of Canterbury while he subverted and protestantized the Church in England under Henry VIII.

If the advice of *The Wanderer* and CUF had been followed, there would have been no further attack on *Pope John's Council*, the *Mass of Paul VI*, or *Cranmer's Godly Order* as a model for the modern weakening of the theology of the Mass. We would simply have had to make the best of them. There would then have been no chance to stand tall before our children when they inevitably asked us if we had spoken out on obvious problems when they emerged, when it was hard to do so. We would have been forced to answer that we had waited until the danger had passed and we were such harmless little flies in a completely changed universe that we could even be invited to reserve a Catholic Social Doctrine table at fundraisers for tastefully liberal or conservative causes for the amusement of our betters.

The non-Mauritanian faction would have joined all the other escapist-collaborationist groups in history. It would have left the Hans Küngs of the world alone to be welcomed into the presence of the Pope with only a Mauritanian Bishop Fellay to present an alternate view of modernity reflecting much our own. It would have ignored the lesson of Church History that reforms of bad situations come in mysterious and complex ways, and not always through smiling and being good little boys while the authorities fawn before the powers that be. Any reading of the writings of St. Bridget or the opponents of the late Renaissance church underlines that lesson quite clearly. "Criticize everything that you think needs to be criticized," the late Dr. William Marra told me when I first got involved in this movement. "When you fight," he added, "do not excommunicate anyone who does not excommunicate you first. And even then, check over and over again to see if he really means it or is still willing to talk to you."

That seemed to me to be good advice then and it seems to me to be good advice now.

What I have always liked about Una Voce is precisely the fact that it was part of this non-Mauritanian method. It worked inside the regular Church structure and yet "rode" closely and sympathetically alongside the Mauritanians, excommunicating neither, critical of both, but, in its heart of hearts, cognizant of the fact that the latter were its true blood brothers. Una Voce's "insider" approach required negotiations with legitimate authorities committed to "renewal." But it undertook these discussions out of the noble desire to get from the authorities what they must, in justice, give back to the Catholic world, and to do so before their flirtation with the outside modernist world led to a full-scale co-option by it.

Its sympathy for the Indult came from the immediate help that *Ecclesia Dei* gave to some traditionalist communities to prosper, and the hope that it offered for future expansion. Una Voce's continued friendship for the Catholic Mauritanians was due to a number of things: appreciation of just how much it was indebted to Msgr. Lefebvre for keeping the Traditional Mass alive in the first place; realization that the continued survival of the movement was tied to their existence as a vibrant pressure group; and recognition of the fact that many—perhaps most—traditionalists still had little alternative but to turn to their services and protection or suffer unbearable spiritual pain. If it criticized the Mauritanians, it was the friendly criticism of blood brothers who were eager to end the crisis before irregular vigilante action produced any of its possible bad fruits. There was some sort of yin-yang relationship at work here. Was this investigated fully in all its canonical and rational nooks and crannies? No. It was probably impossible to undertake such an inquiry in an era in which everything was in constant, bizarre flux anyway. In fact, given the extent of the crisis, it would have been very difficult to know in specific instances who was taking the right tack in dealing with the legitimate authorities: the Mauritanians or the non-Mauritanians. There are numerous similar situations in the long history of the Church where "good guys" and "bad guys" ended by both being recognized as having assured a happy conclusion to a major problem.

I have never had occasion to associate Una Voce with a different kind of policy. Moreover, it never dawned on me that stating my views on broad ecclesiastical and socio-political matters—and identifying myself only as a private scholar while doing so—might be conceived of as being incompatible with my position as President of Una Voce America. It seemed to me that I was merely following models that were clearly there right before my eyes. Did anyone think that we actually loved the reforms of Pope John, Pope Paul, and Pope John Paul? Could anyone possibly think that we should not honor the sufferings of the Mauritanians, or that we should treat them like lepers and untouchables?

But perhaps it was the character of the criticism, aimed, as it was, at a reigning pontiff, which was deemed unacceptable? Certainly, I did not and I do not take giving such criticism lightly. I know that I am eager to find every excuse for praising the current Pope and encouraging him to do as pontiff what he urged as being good while Cardinal Ratzinger. The Una Voce which I love is obliged to deal with all sorts of people, and I, too, agree that no one should go out of his way unnecessarily to offend them. In fact, my own experience has taught me that some prelates and curial officials who seem to be enemies at first glance may turn out to be nothing but conduits for officially unpleasant policies. Personally, they can show themselves to be open to argument or even already sympathetic to our cause. I agree with Una Voce America in its dislike of making stinging personal attacks on prelates who promote one or two unfortunate decisions. I share its recommendation of a prudent silence regarding a former enemy who looks like he is on the verge of coming round to the traditionalist view and need not therefore mercilessly be bashed about the head.

Still, I cannot, for the life of me, see how backing away from substantive criticism of honestly perceived long-term dangers is in any way useful, even if this means attacking the highest authority in the Church. The whole pontificate of John Paul II was based on disastrous policies which rendered even its admittedly good actions, such as the granting of the Indult, merely bits of icing on an impossible to digest cake. To treat it otherwise would be tantamount to giving oneself a lobotomy. Such a retreat from reality would demand a self-censorship producing hopelessly illogical arguments which could then easily be refuted by one's opponents. It would encourage an escape from the complete reality of the situation to which we are exposed, the winning of Pyrrhic "victories" filled full of holes, and, most seriously, the danger of real co-option by and conversion to the world view of the masters of the new millennium. And, unfortunately, all these problems seemed to me to be growing ever stronger as the late pontiff's end neared, and adulation cut off more and more possibility of sound thinking. It appeared to me that all of this was being used by our opponents to serve as a perilous springboard to further radicalization under the next pontificate and its as yet unknown pope.

Calls for a humble, self-critical petitioning of a Pope Benedict who always treated us with understanding while Cardinal Ratzinger strikes me as proper and just. Calls to a similar petitioning of many bishops and curial officials whose chief interests are non-theological staffing and financial problems makes equal sense to me. Being civil to the civil should, I think, guide any man's order of the day. But self-censorship undertaken to please those members of the post-conciliar establishment who simultaneously demand that we praise their openness to free, rational discourse would be an intolerable and laughable undertaking, especially when one sees how tempted such men are to kowtow to the strongest expressions of irrational, anti-Christian contempt and pressure.

Why keep our mouths shut and even go so far as to accuse ourselves of failure to be "open" when confronting people who have been unfailingly and publicly contemptuous of our leaders? Who have dealt with us as though we were uneducated, uninformed boors? Who have charged us with being "fellow travelers on the path of Luther," while treating the real Luther as though he were actually a friend? Who have demanded our support for the 1965 missal as proof of our possessing even half a brain? Who have held up as models for us to follow weird religious orders which have fallen apart amidst public scandal? And who do not show the slightest bit of regret for their uncalled-for behavior? To what end would we do such a thing? To get advice destined to encourage our self-destruction? To ensure our own co-option more efficiently? To earn a reputation for callous feeling for the men and women who have suffered so badly for so very many years?

If the price of being considered acceptable at the court of men who wish we did not even exist is to treat them as more important to us than loyalty to the truth or friendship for our Mauritanian blood brothers, then the unseemliness of it all would be just too much to bear. Such an approach would best be left to other less squeamish hands. Better to pray one's rosary on his own and wait for victory through a miracle of God alone.

CONCLUSION

There is absolutely no way that I myself can keep quiet regarding my conviction that the new millennium awaited with such enthusiasm by the numerologists is rapidly shaping up—certainly in this country—to be the age of the *Oberförster*. That *Oberförster* is not the Hitler-like figure of Jünger, but an *Oberförster* Union of all forces dedicated to the victory of naturalist willfulness. This alliance has shown an inimitable ability to co-opt its enemies, Catholics foremost among them, apparently because so many of us are eager to believe in its fraudulent rhetorical commitment to patriotism and freedom and human dignity. The *Oberförster* Union has no problem permitting Catholics to spout off orthodox doctrine as much as they wish, allowing them regular Traditional Masses, and even sending its many rather unconscious members along to attend them. All that Catholics have to do to ensure the maintenance of these privileges is to abandon the entire vision of the Kingship of Christ over men and society; to become historically and sociologically meaningless. Unfortunately, if the *Oberförster* Union were then to go down to defeat, it would drag this strange sort of Anglican traditionalist Church into the mud with it. For all of its enemies would have come to think that being Catholic was the same thing as being one with the *Oberförsters*—or, at the very best, court jesters for their entertainment.

Mistakes are part of fallen human life, and I am always mulling over in my mind whether or not I have been guilty of printed mistakes of substance or prudence or simple lack of charity. I do not think I have been guilty of enough of them to represent an error in the sense that Jünger describes it. I do believe, however, that it would be such an error for us not to face up, in our diverse spheres of activity, to the reality of just how much the new American millennium demands the dismantling of the whole structure of the Catholic life; that it would be an awful flaw not to discuss fully and unashamedly how this reality relates to a complete and coherent defense of the Traditional Mass; that it would be a great blunder not to distinguish accurately among our negotiating partners so as to keep at arm's length those who would love to co-opt us; that it would be offensive not to recognize our friends whoever they may be—especially Mauritanians whom we may still, nevertheless, feel obliged to critique.

Traditionalists, non-Mauritanians and Mauritanians alike, have got to keep their eyes open and on the final prize of salvation if we are to survive and win victory in this dangerous new millennium of ours. This awakened state must involve a regular self-questioning and self-assessment whose basic framework is not particularly difficult to imagine. Are we really working in a Christian manner or have we tossed charity to the winds and become bitter, spiritless beings? Do we wish to see our enemies crushed or converted? Are we honestly seeking to restore unity within the one true Church of Christ, under the one true successor of St. Peter, Pope Benedict XVI, with its one true Orthodox Catholic Faith? Or have we become obsessed with building an empire out of our own organizations, their leaders, and their narrower causes? Are the allies that we have made in our work of negotiation or militancy intellectually and spiritually justifiable ones, or has their influence caused us to alter our Faith and our understanding of the character and extent of the supernatural guidance that it offers? Are we aware of the whole battlefield on which the struggle that we are in must be fought, or have we limited it to the one escapist, Never Never Land part of it which is to our liking? Is the Enlightenment our God or is Christ?

If we find that we are making mistakes, then we have to spit them out like pieces of tainted meat and move on. We don't want them to get worse. "I later heard Brother Otho say, in talking about our time among the Mauritanians, that a mistake only then becomes an error if one stubbornly persists in it."

20

The Fight for the Traditional Mass[†]

VOCAL, VARIED & COORDINATED

OUR HOLY FATHER, POPE BENEDICT XVI, has made numerous comments, both in public and in private, indicating his openness to the concerns of Catholics committed to the Traditional Roman Rite of Mass. Church modernizers, badly divided as they may be over many other issues, will most certainly remain firmly unified in efforts to prevent papal action redressing traditionalist grievances regarding the liturgy. Those among them of more moderate temperament will counsel traditionalists to keep their silence in this springtime of the new pontificate and simply wait patiently for something good to happen. Meanwhile, their more ferocious colleagues will work harder than ever, openly and behind the scenes, to ensure that liturgical disaster continues unabated. They will do so directly, by pursuing the logic of destructive "reform," and indirectly, by seeking to divert papal attention to other matters, including an intensification and expansion of the ecumenical movement. If my judgment on this situation is correct, I would urge the following course of action upon all traditionalists loyal to the See of Peter:

An ever more vocal and extensive presentation of our demand for the Traditional Mass. This should be expressed in a manner that is friendly to the Holy Father, given his expressions of friendliness to us. Nevertheless, it should be thunderous and unambiguous, and stress our unshakeable conviction that the loss of the Traditional Mass has been an unmitigated calamity for the Church and for the cause of civilization as a whole. Moreover, our critique should be addressed to all the relevant Roman authorities, including those which continuously complain that their hands are tied and that they can do nothing on our behalf. Let them feel as though they must find a way to cut through the cords that bind them. Our opponents never tire of such activities. Our silence now, at this

† Unpublished article.

opportune moment, will merely be construed as consent to our further humiliation. I would begin vocal action by December, after we have judged the results of possible curial changes in November.

A truly serious, organized campaign of round-the-clock public prayer and procession begging God for justice for the Traditional Mass. At best, this would be done in Rome as well, and in such a way that it comes to the attention of the Holy Father himself;

Admission of the reality of our manifold differences as traditionalists, and agreement to a temporary, strategically-valuable end to criticism of the varied methods adopted by each segment of the traditionalist camp in its labors for the Liturgy. Our enemies will work in this fashion in their common effort to defeat the cause of the Traditional Mass. We should imitate them. Let those with a diplomatic temperament be diplomats, and those with a taste and a talent for polemics polemicize; let anyone working with the Indult work with the Indult; let the Society of Pius X pursue its goals and negotiate with Rome as it itself sees fit. Allow each to advance along its own favored line of march and leave the rest to Providence. If possible, this policy of "no enemies on the Rite" might even advance from a strategy of mutual toleration to one involving regular, mutual consultation for the sake of the cause of final liturgical victory; to the creation of a kind of Traditionalist League, whose leaders remains in close contact with one another.

Everything that I have said is predicated upon a peculiar moment in time and the personal statements and personality of the new pontiff. Changed conditions could, admittedly, require changed tactics. For now, let us approach a friendly pontiff in a friendly way, let our voice be heard more vigorously than ever before, and let our various comrades go about their diversely-organized hunts for liturgical justice without reproach from us.

21

The Waiting Game†

THE TWENTY-FIRST AND ELEVENTH CENTURIES COMPARED

WAITING GAMES, WHETHER THEY involve wondering when a delayed airplane flight will actually take off, or speculating if a long-desired *motu proprio* will ever see the light of day, are never a particularly entertaining pastime for normal people. They seem especially unsuited to Eastertide, a season intended for rejoicing in the fulfillment of the divine message rather than writhing in uncertainties and frustrations regarding its earthly misfortunes.

It may well be the case that our undeniably good-willed pope will have ended the current Traditionalist Waiting Game with respect to the liturgy by the time the present article is published—i.e., before Eastertide, 2007 is over. But even if he does so, I still think that we *Tridentini* who have suffered from so much ambiguity and disappointed hopes over the past forty years, and have continued to cherish the Papacy and Rome through all the heartbreak just the same, ought to explore the many twists and turns that the miserable Waiting Game can take just a wee bit longer. Even in this season of joy.

One interesting means of doing so is by taking a brief glance one thousand years backwards, to the sorrows and hopes of our pro-Roman, pro-papal Catholic ancestors during Eastertide, 1007. They, too, were troubled and unsatisfied participants in a Waiting Game. Their experience reminds us that nothing is easy; that valid aspirations can sometimes take a very long time to fulfill; that the agents fulfilling human hopes can be surprising ones; that the seeming end of one problem may bring many new anxieties and disappointments in its train; that, as the saying goes, if it is man who proposes, one must always remember that God disposes, and that He does so as He sees fit. Such a short historical investigation can help us mightily to put our own woes in a perspective

† First published in *The Remnant*, April 15, 2007.

conducive to the spiritual calm that the season—and the Catholic spirit in general—ought always to assure.

Eastertide, 1007 was not a happy time for Rome, the Papacy and their friends. Yes, it is true that many details are lacking in our knowledge of the whole of that particular calendar year. Moreover, Pope John XVIII (1004–1009) may himself have possessed a number of good qualities contributing to the one or two ecclesiastical successes reported during his reign. Nevertheless, Eastertide, 1007 was part of a less than optimum slice of time wracked with plague, renewed Saracen activity and contest over the kingship of Italy between St. Henry II of Germany (1002–1024) and an ambitious nobleman named Arduin of Ivrea. Much more importantly still, at least from our standpoint, Eastertide, 1007 was part of a decade of Roman Church humiliation brought about by papal subservience to the strong-arm tactics wielded with depressing effectiveness by the neighborhood Crescentii clan: a local gang inspired by a self-serving, parochial vision of the role of the Papacy in the life of Christendom.

And worse was yet to come. The Crescentii managed to bully one more decent Pope, Sergius IV (1009–1112), into basic helplessness. Yes, they finally lost their grip after 1012, due to several untimely family deaths, an all too brazen attempt to bulldoze their own candidate onto the throne without even the semblance of an election, and the loss of prestige coming from their backing of a couple of unsuccessful antipopes. But their place as masters of the Seven Hills was taken by the Theophylact Family, the Counts of nearby Tusculum. These Tusculani, as they are generally styled, had enjoyed such a domineering position once before, and had sometimes even exercised it with more respectability than their debased competitors. Unfortunately, they were soon to provide one of the worst of the occupants of the papal office, Benedict IX. Probably only twenty years old at his accession, Benedict sat three distinct times on the throne of St. Peter (1032–1044, 1045 and 1047–1048), due not only to political pressures, but to a corruption so great as to permit him literally to sell his own position and then try to steal it back after pocketing the dough. Rome in 1007 might still retain her prestige to good purpose in far-off Christian lands, but her closer inspection by the Easter crowds both of that year and the following decades could not help but make them realize that in many respects she *stank zum Himmel*.

One man who bewailed how little Rome and the Papacy in Eastertide, 1007 lived up to the hopes placed in them by their friends from abroad was St. Odilo, Abbot of Cluny (c. 994–1048). This great monastic reformer, very much active on the international stage, had just recently himself been a witness to and played his role in a grand dream of a Roman imperial revival which had had as one of its major aims the liberation of the Papacy from mundane neighborhood squabbles and the re-dedication of the Holy See to its proper, worldwide spiritual goals. Anyone among the Easter crowds of 1007 who was interested in first-hand testimony to that extraordinary vision and its exalted hopes would have been obliged to probe someone like St. Odilo to learn of its character. Three of its more central inspirers and agents—the Emperor Otto III (983–1002), Pope Gregory V (996–999) and Pope Sylvester II (999–1003)—had by then all passed on to the other world, while a fourth, Bishop Leo of Vercelli (d. 1026), had his hands full simply trying to survive.

Otto III, half German and half Byzantine, was the key figure in the entire exalted enterprise. King of Germany from the age of three, his premature death at twenty-two cut off his plans for a marriage which might have helped him fend off his constant temptation by sins of the flesh. It left him heirless as well. Personal problems aside, he possessed both an undeniable piety and a top-notch classical education, both of which gave him the chance to put his superior military training to work on behalf of a broad, meaningful understanding of the nature of Christendom and where it ought to be headed.

It was his visit to Rome in 996, at the age of 16, in answer to the call of Pope John XV (985–996) for help against the Crescentii brood, which turned out to be the greatest formative experience of Otto's life. Accompanied by many of the great Church leaders of the day, most importantly, Gerbert of Aurillac (950–1003)—master scholar, Abbot of Bobbio and sometime Archbishop of Rheims—the King's march looked more like a religious procession than a regal train. At its head was the Holy Lance, presumed to be that of Constantine the Great, containing a nail from the Cross of Christ.

In Italy, the young king met a number of charismatic figures who further confirmed his already strong sense of political-religious mission; men like St. Romualdo (950–1027), founder of Camaldoli, and St. Adalbert of Prague (956–997). The former was a hermit/

monk who understood how to translate zeal for sanctity into an effective tool for quieting the social disorder unleashed by the restless counts, vassals and other assorted hoodlums of the day. The latter, adored by Otto as a model of both humility and love for the Church, was destined to end his life as a martyr while on mission in the north of Europe.

Finding Pope John XV dead on his arrival, and the Papacy the slave of local factionalism, the King installed his young cousin Bruno on the papal throne as Gregory V. Gregory then presided over Otto's imperial coronation at St. Peter's on May 21, 996, where the overwhelmed King-Emperor was cloaked with a robe and a crown portraying the magnificence of the cosmos, evoking the Old and New Testament, and placing his reign within the context of the Divine Plan and at the service of the greater glory of God.

Otto now understood fully the mission that his passion and education had shaped him to fulfill: he had a responsibility to secure the order of an all too fragile Christendom, and to do so by simultaneously exalting Christ's Church, with her visible center in Rome. As the document through which he appointed his chaplain and enthusiastic supporter Leo as Bishop of Vercelli later indicated, the Emperor's task was one of making certain "that the Church of God remain free and safe; that she prosper throughout our Empire . . . that the power of the Roman People be extended and the State re-established, so that we might merit from living in this world honorably and thus fly more honorably from the prison of the life. . . . "†

Returning to Germany, our Emperor-on-Mission was soon to learn that the swamp of Roman politics was deeper than he may originally have guessed. The Crescentii, aided and abetted by an eastern imperial authority in Constantinople irritated by this youthful competitor for Roman glory, quickly exploited Otto's absence from town. They tossed Gregory V out of Rome and placed the young man's former Greek tutor and disloyal friend, John Philagathos, on the throne of St. Peter as the Antipope John XVI (997–998).

Otto and his many scholarly, reformer friends now saw that their work of revival required a lot more muscle behind it to make it stick. A new and fully armed procession set forth to Italy at the end of

† Pierre Riché, *Les Grandeurs de l'an mille* (Paris: Bartillat, 1999), 289, my free translation.

997, with men like Gerbert of Aurillac, the above-mentioned Leo (soon to be) of Vercelli, the great Bishop Bernward of Hildesheim (960–1022) and St. Odilo of Cluny on hand to emphasize the ultimately spiritual aim of this temporarily clenched, German fist. Rome was reached in 998 and the head of the Crescentii Clan, who held out for three months at the Castel Sant'Angelo, finally captured and decapitated. Antipope John was disgraced, rather brutally punished and imprisoned. Gregory V regained his throne. The re-entry of Pope and Emperor into St. Peter's, and their joint responsibility for rule, reform and the growth of the Roman State and Church were celebrated in a prayer-hymn written by Bishop Leo:

> *Refrain*: Christ hear our prayers; cast your glance upon your city of Rome; in your goodness renew the Romans, awaken the forces of Rome, permit Rome to revive under the Empire of Otto III.
>
> I. We salute you, our Pope; health to you, very worthy Gregory. Along with the august Otto, your apostle Peter welcomes you; you ascend to something sublime. Humble yourself.
>
> II. Leaving the house of the Bride [the Church of Rome] you re-enter it as the [spiritual] Bridegroom, and you recover the gifts of your venerable father [the Apostle, Peter].
>
> III. You are Peter; you ordain the praises of Peter; you renew the rights of Rome; you restore Rome to Rome, so that Otto may become the glory of the Empire.
>
> IV. May Otto succeed in all things, may he who took you from Gaul and led you to Rome always prosper; God has made him great and has raised up your arm.
>
> V. You are the mouth of the churches; you are the master of all in the holy mysteries; you are the bond of the people; you judge the various causes, you free the captive souls.
>
> VI. Otto, rule yourself; be attentive and vigilant, you who according to the Apostle have charge of the bodies of men; it is for the punishment of sinners that you bear an invincible sword.
>
> VII. Ancient Antioch venerates you in all things; ancient Alexander runs anxiously towards you; all the Churches of the world are to be found in your furrow.

VIII. Babylon of Iron, Golden Greece fear the great Otto and serve him, their spines bent; he who has liberated the King of Kings [the Pope] commands as Emperor the whole world.

IX. Rejoice, noble Pope; you honor the first of thrones [the Papacy] with the majesty of your name; you raise up the second [the Empire]. . . .

X. Rejoice, Pope, rejoice Caesar; let the Church exult with happiness, let the joy be great in Rome, let the imperial palace rejoice. Under the power of Caesar, the Pope reforms the age.

XI. O, you two luminaries throughout the lands, illuminate the churches, put darkness to flight. May the one [the Emperor] prosper by the sword, may the other [the Pope] give resonance to his word.

XII. Lord Pope, raise to its feet what lay on the ground [the Papacy]; consider the gift of God; God has made you great, and the help of Peter is your support; keep the memory of the bonds and your glory.‡

Our young missionary, the better to fulfill his responsibilities, both natural and supernatural, decided to take up permanent residence on the Palatine Hill, the home of the old Roman Emperors. There, he began to adopt Byzantine imperial customs, to seek himself a bride from his imperial "colleague," and to preside, together with Pope and Bishops as a "Thirteenth Apostle" at reforming Synods throughout Italy. When another temporary absence from the city led to a revival of the old, parochial, Roman shenanigans, and even perhaps the poisoning of Pope Gregory V, the Emperor's determination to renew the age grew greater still. No fears for apocalypse in the year 1000 for him! (As, in fact, as Riche makes abundantly clear, there were no such fears among Christians in general). Otto named his great scholar friend and fellow visionary, Gerbert, as his cousin's successor. Gerbert took the name of Sylvester II, apparently to emphasize his desire to cooperate loyally with the new Constantine, just as the first Sylvester had worked in tandem with Constantine the Great. An Ottonian document of January, 1001, probably prepared by Leo of Vercelli, once again clearly spelled out the imperial commitment to extricating the

‡ Riché, *Les Grandeurs de l'an mille*, 257–258.

Papacy from the sewer of Roman politics, while, interestingly enough, also denouncing the exaggerated papal political ambitions outlined in the fraudulent Pseudo-Donation of Constantine:

> Otto, slave of the Apostles and according to the will of the Saviour God, august Emperor of the Romans. We proclaim Rome capital of the world. We recognize that the Roman Church is the mother of all the churches, but also that the carelessness and incompetence of her pontiffs have for a long time now tarnished the titles of her brightness. In fact, these pontiffs have not only sold and alienated through certain dishonest practices the possessions of St. Peter outside of the city, but—and we do not affirm this without sorrow—the goods that they possessed from our own imperial city. With still greater license, they allowed these goods to pass into common use at the price of gold; they despoiled St. Peter, they despoiled St. Paul and their altars themselves. Instead of restoration they have always sowed confusion. In disdain of pontifical precepts and disdaining the Roman Church herself, certain popes so pushed their arrogance as to confuse the greater part of our Empire with their own apostolic power. Without caring for what they lost through their fault, without preoccupying themselves with that which their personal vanity caused them to waste, they replaced their own squandered goods . . . by turning towards (exploitation) of foreign ones—that is to say ours and those of our Empire. [Hence] the lies forged by them, by means of which the Cardinal-Deacon John (surnamed Mutilated Fingers) drafted in gilded letters a Privilege which he fallaciously rooted very deep in the past and placed under the name of the great Constantine.[§]

Otto appears to have been the primary captain of the revived ship of Church and State, a man who took his role as Thirteenth Apostle quite literally. Lest one think that his role was questioned by the great spiritual leaders of the day, St. Odilo's testimony is there to correct him. So enamored of Otto and his work was the reform Abbot that he penned the following poem exulting in the extent of the Emperor's glory, giving no hint of fear of where it might possibly lead:

> Let the Slav groan and the Hungarian grind his teeth.
> Let the Greek be struck with bewilderment.

§ Ibid., 272–273.

Let the Saracen be troubled and take flight.
Let the Africans pay tribute and Spain seek aid.
Let Burgundy venerate and cherish the Emperor and Aquitaine run joyously to meet him.
Let all Gaul say: "Who has heard of such things?"
And the Italian People, arms raised, will cry out: "By the power of God, this is the only son of Caesar, Otto the Great."¶

By 1002, however, the grand vision of *renovatio* was finished. In the year 1000, while Otto was away on a magnificent political-religious missionary expedition which took him as far away as present day Poland, and through which he also tightened the bonds linking Hungary with the family of western Christian nations, revolt brewed back in the peninsula. The Emperor returned, only to find the malaise spreading to Rome by the beginning of 1001. Even though soon quelled, the experience of being so easily trapped on the Palatine Hill made it clear that the Eternal City was unsafe for Otto and his imperial-reformer entourage. The poignancy of the disappointment is captured by the speech to his rebellious subjects that Bernward of Hildesheim puts in Otto's mouth on the third day of the siege:

> Listen to the words of your father, pay attention to them, meditate upon them carefully in your hearts. You are no longer my Romans. Because of you I left my fatherland, my family; through love for you I neglected my Saxons, all the Germans, those of my own blood. I have led you into the farthest regions of our Empire, into places where your ancestors, when they submitted the world to their power, never placed their feet. And why have I done this, if not to extend your glory to the ends of the world? I have adopted you as my children, I have preferred you to all others. Because I have raised you up from your fate, because of you, I say, I have aroused jealousy and hatred against myself. And you, in exchange for all this, you have rejected your father; you have caused many of my intimate friends to perish by a cruel death; you have rejected me. But you *cannot* reject me since I would never allow anyone to remove from my heart those whom I paternally embrace.**

Emperor and Pope fled to Ravenna. There they consulted some

¶ Riché, *Les Grandeurs de l'an mille*, 303.
** Ibid., 304–305.

of their closest supporters, Odilo of Cluny, Leo of Vercelli and St. Romualdo among them. The latter warned against any attempt to return to Rome as tantamount to an act of suicide. Otto ignored the great founder of Camaldoli, moved back southwards and reached the very outskirts of the Eternal City... only to die from what was perhaps a recurrence of malarial fever. St. Bruno of Querfurt (970–1009), Apostle to the Prussians and beneficiary of Otto's missionary vision, describes the end for us on January 24, 1002:

> At a moment that he did not expect, death fully armed came to find him... The very firm decision that he expressed to convert [from his fleshly falls from grace] in the presence of all of the Great Men of the Empire, the sincere confession that he made of his faults, all that wiped out the sins of his youth... In shedding great tears, which made all those assisting cry as well, he asked for the relics of the saints, among which was a large piece of the life-giving Cross... He received with a fear mixed with joy the body and blood of the Lord. Moreover, from the beginning of that serious illness, he had wanted to receive each day the Holy Eucharist, because it is upon this that eternal life entirely depends. Even at the moment of death, he did not lose any of his faculties and it was with a sweet sigh that, aided by the mercy of the Saviour, in whom he had always hoped, he expired.... Those who remained present said that the dying man gave up his soul with so much sweetness that he appeared similar to a sleeping man who was breathing.[††]

"Cry world, cry Rome, and let the Church lament," Leo of Vercelli sang in a poem capturing the misery of all of Otto's friends. "Let the chants in Rome fall quiet. Let sorrow scream out to the palace, since, through the absence of Caesar, trouble extends across the world"[‡‡].

The men of Eastertide, 1007 would have known that this announcement of great trouble was no exaggeration. Sylvester II experienced it without delay. Returning to the Eternal City, he saw the Crescentii fortunes immediately rise. The pope had the good luck to die just one year later, 63 years old, still a noble figure, but broken by the Waiting Game—the wait for a revival of the Papacy and Rome. His second and Crescentii-tormented

---

†† Riché, *Les Grandeurs de l'an mille*, 307–308.

‡‡ Ibid., 308.

successor, Sergius IV, who knew him well, wrote the following epitaph for his tomb at the Lateran:

> When, at the sound of the trumpet, the Lord shall come, this spot in the world will produce the remains of that Sylvester who is buried here, he whom the very wise Virgin [Wisdom herself] rendered famous in the world at large, and the grandeurs of Rome made the head of that world. Emerging out of France, Gerbert first earned the See of the people of Rheims, the Primal See of that country. Then he earned the governance of the noble Church of Ravenna, and became powerful. At the end of a year, he obtained Rome and changed his name to become the new pastor of the entire world. The Caesar, Otto III, to whom he was always devoted and faithful, loved him much and offered him that See. The one and the other honored their age through their brilliant virtue of wisdom. The entire age rejoiced and all evil was broken by them. Sylvester occupied the Roman See according to the example of the Gate-Keeper of Heaven, and it was the third time that he had been conferred a pastoral charge. One luster after having received the See of Peter he quit the world through death. The world was chilled with horror, peace disappeared, and the triumphant Church shook and forgot its calm.[§§]

Would that the shock had been a short one! But, alas, as noted above, the period of mourning for the failure of Otto's dream was not the end of the tale. There were many Roman and Papal and Catholic woes to come before the situation improved significantly. Believers already used to seeing decent pontiffs reduced to puppets of the local clans had yet to deal with the thrice-disgraced Benedict IX, brutally attacked by St. Peter Damian in the latter's aptly named *Liber Gomorrhianus* as a demon from hell in the disguise of a priest, and by a future successor, Blessed Victor III, as utterly unspeakable.

We Catholics of Eastertide, 2007 live in a time when the Papacy and the Eternal Rome it represents have also been dragged through the mud and continue to be reviled; a time when they have again been subjected to manipulation by petty, parochial interests. These parochial interests are not precisely those of clans like the Crescentii and Tusculani, even though there are plenty of specific individuals who can be identified as playing their part in the

§§ Ibid., 310.

work of papal and Roman enslavement. Rather, today's parochial interests are those of the petty vision of naturalist, Enlightenment ideology, dominant in our society for over two hundred years, whose many and varied vocal supporters all insist that men and institutions must bend unceasingly to the spirit of one's time and place. Such bending prevents anyone succumbing to it from soaring above his immediate material surroundings in order to understand the meaning of the universe from the perspective of the eternal Creator and Redeemer God. This guarantees a burial rather than a mere bending—a burial in a materialist mud that grows ever thicker and more debased with the progressive loss of memory of past Catholic intellectual and spiritual illumination and achievement. Until the day of total liberation from such living euthanasia nothing of lasting significance can be accomplished by those who are its victims. The best that the men and institutions who have been buried alive by it can achieve is to offer a lasting testimony to the futility of basing thought and action on anything which is changeable and cheap.

We Catholics of Eastertide, 2007, like St. Odilo one thousand years earlier, can also look back to a time not so very long ago when wondrous things were being done to fight for just the sort of liberation from debasing naturalism which could set the ecclesiastical house in holy order. This was the era which began with Pope Gregory XVI and ended under the reign of the man who, in an uplifted world, would by now long have been known as Blessed Pius XII. In those happy years, the Catholic spirit indeed did soar above the barbed wire enclosure in which Enlightenment naturalism and its parochial supporters wished to imprison it. Papal Rome did then work for the ages, precisely because it was electrified by a love for the Incarnation and the Mystical Body; by an awareness of their impact on political and social life which disdained media hype and the demands of immediate consumer relevance. It was only when a subjection of this soaring vision to the Free Supermarket of Ideas and Consumption took place that our current problems began, and the Waiting Game became our daily companion.

Perhaps, as noted above, our present version of the Waiting Game will have ended by the date this article is published. But even if this proves to be the case—as St. Odilo and other activist Catholics of Eastertide, 1007 who lived well into the miserable decades to come could tell us—that would not mean that we would be done with it forever; that our difficulties would immediately and definitively disappear. The enemy is strong and wily. His temptations are just that—tempting, and powerfully so. A victory on one front could be followed still by defeats on many others. An intelligent and well-intentioned pope might see his will thwarted by ideologues and scoundrels. In sum, there simply is no guarantee of an absolutely certain, stable, Catholic triumph until the end of time.

The *unum necessarium* for traditionalist Catholics in Eastertide, 2007 is to maintain that permanent spirit of Christian joy and hope which the season ought to encourage. There are certainly good historical reasons for doing so. Some of the disappointed believers in the mission of the Papacy and Rome of Eastertide, 1007 who had waited so long for revival, and thought that they would witness it as a result of the reigns of Otto III, Gregory V and Sylvester II, survived long enough to experience practical earthly proof that broad hopes can eventually overcome enormous obstacles and become realities. They survived to see a long-lasting reform of Head and Members. By 1049, a new King-Emperor, Henry III, had placed an even more vigorous crusading pope, St. Leo IX, on the throne of St. Peter. This pontiff took charge of the movement for Christian revival. The Papacy was extracted from the parochial mud. Christendom was guided to practical fulfillment of an exalted vision of transformation in Christ; one that still continues to exercise its influence in traditional circles today.

But it proved to be a different kind of reform movement which took shape, one that was more conscious of current feudal political realities and highly doubtful of the viability of an imperial revival of the kind envisaged by Otto; one which, while grateful for the aid given to it by the Germano-Roman State, decided that the Church needed more independence than it was ultimately willing to allow her. The Emperor St. Henry II (1002–1024) focused on improving the situation in the north of Europe, knowing that the resources available to him were limited. Clunaic monks found that even some Crescentii-type hoodlum-noblemen could be turned into crusading soldiers for the cause of a holier Church and society. Pope St. Gregory VII (1076–1085) vigorously rejected the subordinate role accepted by Sylvester II. Always committed to the crucial importance of joint Church-State labors for the construction of

Christendom, this second wave of the reform movement placed its most profound hopes for Catholic growth and perfection in the struggle for personal sanctity and sense of responsibility not just of Emperor and Pope, but of everyone without exception. For, in the final analysis, only the liberation of all of us from the tunnel vision of materialism and sin; only the willingness of all of us to see the world from the perspective of the Creator and Redeemer God, can build the society for which the eleventh century victims of the Waiting Game suffered.

When our own Waiting Game comes to a more secure finish—probably after a heap of new and mighty battles—papal Rome will once again take charge of the task of transforming all things in Christ. When it does it, it will call upon its supporters to judge the familiar world around them, whose customs and unquestioned presuppositions reflect two hundred fifty years of Enlightenment debasement, with the same passion for rooting life in the full Catholic Tradition that motivated eleventh century reformers. All of us will then find ourselves expected to make adjustments which might now surprise us. We will discover that many things that we today take for granted as perfectly compatible with Church teaching are terribly and essentially flawed, the American system chief among them. Flaws will be uncovered even in what appeared to us just recently to be a Catholic Golden Age, and these will also have to be addressed and corrected.

Will we be up to this task of adjustment? I certainly hope so. But I personally think that the task of stepping back and reassessing the proper path to building Christendom was easier for eleventh century men whose hearts and spirits were already lifted to higher goals by the exalted though flawed vision of an Emperor Otto rather than for twentieth century peoples shaped by the cheap lies of a sloganeering civilization that cannot look farther into the future than the next meaningless election.

22

Feet, Fathers and Catholic Fraternity†

"PRIDE," MY YOUNG LADY FRIEND SAID TO me as New Year's Day, 1972 gathered steam, a wide wry smile on her lovely face "You have hoisted yourself on a petard of pride." A quite deadly and all too just response indeed to my sophomoric bragging that it was already one hour past midnight, and that I had not yet committed a single act that was even venially sinful.

The memory of this chastisement of frivolous pride at the hands of someone whom I was eager to please came back to me with a big, unexpected bang on the 2007 Chartres Pilgrimage (a Pilgrimage, by the way, whose miserable weather Michael Matt viciously accused me of conjuring up with a recent article of mine lamenting the wretched physical and psychological toll that heavy rain would take on all of the chapter participants, myself at the top of the list).

In any case, there I was on Saturday, the morning of our departure, once again puffed up with low class pride, this time inspired by the knowledge that I, without the slightest shadow of a doubt, would have no difficulty walking the old familiar route whatsoever. Not only had I gone down that path before, but I had a recollection of veritably waltzing along it in 2006. Moreover, this season's inevitably leisurely stroll would be even easier, given the use of new, state-of-the-art, waterproof shoes which I had been convinced to purchase by a seemingly omniscient and persuasive salesman back in Manhattan. How ridiculous of *The Remnant*, my wife and the ghosts of generations of hikers and soldiers long gone to their eternal boots to warn me that I ought, perhaps, to have bought my footwear not a week but months earlier than Pentecost! And that maybe I should have broken the shoes in thoroughly before attempting a seventy-two-mile trek with them on.

"Are you sure you are going to make it in those?," Fr. Paul MacDonald, our chaplain, asked me with his usual pastoral solicitude, clearly insinuating that my state-of-the art equipment was not all that the foolish merchant and his bamboozled customer cracked it

† First published in *The Remnant*, June 30, 2007.

up to be. Madness, I assured myself again, dismissing his doubts. I am a Traditionalist, hear me roar! Bite my dust! Breaking in shoes was a task for rookies; not for a veteran who knew that accepting a ride on the Wimp Wagon to an early rendezvous at the bivouac with the weaker representatives of the species was an absolutely unthinkable proposition.

Alas, my Fall from pompous arrogance came quickly. At the end of the first day, after the ascent of what the American chapter popularly calls Cardiac Hill, my feet had degenerated into two burning, abrasive, raging, pestilential stumps. In fact, they had become a Platonic Idea of Pain; a podiatrist's gold mine. By the afternoon of Pentecost Sunday, I could not, for the first time in my life, move without agony, and I watched in reptilian humiliation as eight- and eighty-five-year-olds scampered off into the rainforest for another six hours or so of prancing towards Chartres as though they were about to take a spin around the ballroom at the Ritz.

My only chance of pilgrim's progress by this point lay in making a mad dash to my luggage, which sat in our hotel, ready to receive those who really merited rest—the following day, that is to say. There, in those bags, could be found the battered but broken-in pair of sneakers which had done such yeoman service for me in years past. Another badly wounded hiker somehow managed to commandeer a ride into the city, a young girl claiming to suffer from mononucleosis joined us, and off we trundled. On arrival, twenty hours earlier than expected, I shoved my state-of-the-art shoes contemptuously into the bedroom rubbish bin, put on the old faithfuls, lumbered up, ate, took a snooze and prepared to meet our group back in the piney woods the next morning at the crack of dawn.

Unending cracks of thunder, gusts of wind and cascades of chilly rain delayed that crack of dawn until 8:00 A. M., when I was dumped by the Notre Dame de Chrétienté shuttle service on a country road at the start of the column of pilgrims. There I stood, greeting chapter after chapter, until that of Our Lady of Guadalupe, placed on Monday near the end of the line of march, finally appeared. It was during this wait that the wry smile on the face of my long forgotten New Year's date re-emerged before my eyes with picture postcard clarity. Surely, I shuddered, I would now see that same sneer on all my fellow pilgrims' faces. "Hear you roar? Bite your dust, eh?," they would snicker. "Slept in Chartres, did you, O Creature of a Day? Do you know what it was like for real penitents in the bivouac last night?" At that point they would certainly hold up their broken-in shoes, Dessatin-stained feet and How to Prepare for the Pilgrimage literature, shaking them at me all in unison. An impenetrable angelic force field would be generated around them. I would be left outside where there is nothing but lamentation and gnashing of teeth. My reputation as a counterrevolutionary Catholic activist would be buried, forever, deep underneath the northern French blood and mud.

But none of this proved to be true. In fact, thinking that it would be so was merely pride's last gasp effort to keep me in its grip, focusing my attention on myself, on my merits and demerits, rather than the higher reality around me. For the "Marchers for God" were in no way concerned about inflicting punishment. Their minds and hearts, whether consciously or unconsciously, were fixed not on the feet of the faithful—neither mine nor theirs—but on loftier themes more worthy of the Fathers of the Church.

I bring up this patristic argument because the welcome of every chapter along the line of march to all of those many, many persons joining or rejoining them now, for reasons good and bad, at the last moment, on Monday, with the final goal in sight, reminded me of a magnificent passage from one of the greatest of the Greek Fathers, St. John Chrysostom. This passage, read in Eastern Catholic Churches on Holy Saturday, conveys a sense of overwhelming joy over the imminent arrival of the Easter Feast. I do not have the text in front of me now, but from what I remember, it invites all those present at the Divine Liturgy to lift up their hearts and rejoice in the ineffable hope offered to believers by the historical fact of the Resurrection. What counts, as always, St. John tells the Holy Saturday worshippers, is the willingness to make a serious commitment to Christ and His message. Those who made such a commitment long ago, and fasted the entirety of Lent, should now allow the joy of Easter to fill them with intense Christian love and happiness. But so should believers who had begun to observe the penitential season only halfway through its forty days, and even everyone who had joined in seriously only at this eleventh hour, during the ceremonies of the Vigil itself.

St. John had many themes in mind in this passage, but the one that struck me most in the context of my experience on Pentecost Monday was that involving his concern for the Catholic fraternal spirit. Our hope, this great Father was stressing, comes only from our belief in and union with our Blessed Saviour and His Easter victory. Our eyes must be aimed, above all else, at Christ and the Redemption that He won for us. If they are, then the spirit of that joy which He wishes to give freely to everyone cannot help but take possession of our minds and hearts. Our attention then will drift away from a petty calculation of our specific merits and those (probably, in our estimation, considerably less) of our neighbours in order to redirect itself towards the infinitely more significant reality of the common offer of grace and eternal life with God; to the source of this gift Himself. We will then realize that all of us can gain what the Word Incarnate offers only in Him and through the Mystical Body that He brought into being; that our salvation comes from membership in one fraternal union, whose basic operating procedure requires that its participants work as freely for one another's benefit as Christ worked for them. We will then understand that it is the duty of those among us who are Lenten stalwarts, "veterans in Christ," to welcome and encourage the rookies, the last-minute penitents, and anyone who has fallen and yet picked himself up to walk down the path of righteousness inside the Mystical Body once again. We will then see that, through the mystery of grace, the strong can even learn certain lessons from the weak and the confused who have regained their footing in Christ; lessons which may help them to avoid imitating the errors of the repentant wayward ones, and perhaps uncover previously unknown flaws in their own seemingly sterling behavior as well.

It was this focus on Christ and the forgetfulness of self so conducive to creating a spirit of fraternity which propelled the thousands of Catholics united under the patronage of Notre Dame de Chrétienté to undertake their physically punishing three-day pilgrimage, and help one another to do so successfully, in the first place. And it was this same spirit of fraternity that allowed the pilgrims who had walked the whole distance joyfully to welcome and encourage their fellow Catholics who rejoined them—or perhaps had only begun their penitential journey—on that happy morning.

The immediate stimulus to Pentecost Monday's outburst of welcoming, fraternal joy was, of course, the sight of that visible hymn to God which is the Cathedral of Chartres herself, an artistic song and sermon analogous to and perhaps even more effective than the written one of the golden-tongued Patriarch of Constantinople. Pride, feet and chastisement of failure were under these circumstances so low on the hierarchy of values of the chapters marching towards Christ in His church as to fall entirely off their radar screen. We were reaching the goal together, stronger and weaker alike, united in our love and submission to our one Saviour and His one Holy, Roman, Catholic and Apostolic Church.

Our Lady of Guadalupe chapter left Chartres and its beneficent stimulus early on Tuesday morning. But far from fading into nostalgic memory, that same Christ-centered, welcoming, joyful fraternal spirit continued to manifest itself for the remaining days of our Remnant pilgrimage. In doing so, it underlined the truth that men and women who abandon themselves to Christ indeed do learn how to put the different natural aspects of life into a proper "hierarchy of values," and how to use them in a way that helps to sustain their Faith and ultimately allow all their unique distinctions and accomplishments to shine forth in vivid high relief. If you want to meet individuals, join the Traditionalist Movement! I encountered some pilgrims within our little microcosm of Christendom-in-a-bus whose love of life and God revealed personalities which could bulldoze their way through a contemporary cocktail party crowd filled with victims of our cheap, pointless, mess-of-pottage civilization; which could reduce to rubble its argument that it is modernity which promotes individuality and creativity.

Fortunately, a plethora of natural stimuli to lift our hearts and minds to Christ, His Mystical Body and everything that flows from them for fraternal union and individual perfection did not disappear with our merry band's farewell to the great cathedral on a hill. How could it? For the whole of that hierarchically-structured medieval Christendom to which the Kingdom of the Franks gave birth, with its cornucopia of illustrations that nature is meant to be an enormous *sursum corda* and mirror of God, lay before us on the rest of our journey. A formidable lot those Franks of old truly were, to allow their traces still to be followed in our own debased age! Immensely self-confident, but highly conscious of their need to bend to the teachings of the True Faith and to find practical ways to put its message into daily use throughout the entirety of the realm, the Frankish spirit is clearly outlined in the Prologue (763 A. D.) to Pippin's revised version of the Salic Law. This was the basic "constitution" of the so-called "Salty" Franks, of which a relevant excerpt is given below:

> The illustrious people of the Franks was established by God himself; courageous in war, steadfast in peace, serious of intention, noble of stature, brilliant white of complexion and of exceptional beauty; daring, swift and brash. It was converted to the Catholic Faith; while it was still barbarian, it was free of all heresy. It sought the key of knowledge under divine guidance, desiring justice in its behaviour and cultivating piety. It was then that those who were the chiefs of this people long ago dictated the Salic law...
>
> Long live Christ who loves the Franks! May he protect their reign; may he fill their leaders with the light of his grace; may he watch over their army; may he accord them the rampart of Faith; may he grant them the joys of peace and the happiness of those who rule over their age... After professing their Faith and receiving Baptism, these Franks enshrined in gold and silver the bodies of the saints and martyrs whom the Romans had burned with fire, mutilated with the sword, and delivered to the teeth of ferocious beasts. †

Supernatural stimuli to Catholic fraternity were also in no way lacking to us, above all through the presence of the Traditional Mass as our constant companion, our master and our intimate friend alike. But justice demands recognition of the fact that our fraternal spirit was immensely aided in a supernatural manner also by the ministrations of our own golden-tongued preacher. For let it not be thought that our chaplain is only a man of proven expertise in proper pilgrimage footwear! He is, above all else, distinguished by his deep knowledge of and love for the theology of the Mystical Body of Christ, which he knows how to impart with eloquence, with wit and with pastoral effectiveness.

Fr. MacDonald's own brilliant grasp of these questions comes, to a large degree, from his familiarity with the writings of a magnificent Catholic teacher of the nineteenth century, Cardinal Louis-Édouard Pie (1815–1880), Bishop of Poitiers and a man whom every Catholic intellectual and activist ought thoroughly to study. Cardinal Pie, friend of Blessed Pius IX and one of the

---

† Pierre Riché, *The Carolingians: A Family Who Forged Europe*, trans. Michael Idomir Allen (Philadelphia: University of Pennsylvania Press, 1993), 83.

inspirations for that pontiff's *Syllabus of Errors,* was a first-class representative of a movement of nineteenth and early twentieth century Catholic thought which explored the building blocks of true fraternity and the nature of that which destroys it better than any since the time of the Church Fathers. This school, whose ideas are reflected in all the great encyclicals, emphasized the same points as noted above, but with telling reference to our own particular modern historical situation.

Cardinal Pie and his colleagues drove home the message that lasting fraternity and fraternal love can only come from individuals "getting out of themselves," looking for the objective Truth beyond them, and allowing that Truth to shape them through communities which could support lasting fraternal love and charity. They saw that individuals cannot achieve this goal on their own. The communities that could and would guide men and women were mostly natural ones dealing with truths that can be learned from reason and nature, institutions like the family and the state, though many others besides. Still, it was, they explained, primarily by submitting to the Truth and Grace of the Creator and Redeemer of nature, taught and offered by His Church, that natural truths and the institutions embodying them could fully know how to avoid false enthusiasms and learn how they are supposed to guide individuals to their ultimate goal, which is eternal life with God.

The immediate stimulus for such thinkers was their shocked awareness that knowledge of such a need to move beyond the self and regain a sense of individual complementarity with society had been generally lost, even in Catholic circles, due to eighteenth century Enlightenment naturalism. This had worked to take the props out from under real fraternal love and self-awareness. It has done so by seeking to "liberate" the individual from objective Truth and the social cradle which helps mightily to rock him to God. Enlightenment naturalism claimed that each person on his own could find his way to cooperative behaviour with his neighbour, perfection and "salvation," whatever this might mean. But all it really succeeded in doing was to give to individuals a fraternity based on the willful dictates of the strong; one that dragged all men and women into an illicit contract with irrational enthusiasms and vices; one that was contemptuous of the true distinctions and needs of human persons; one that was unstable and short lived to the extreme.

Fr. MacDonald began his patristic-nineteenth century formation of our merry little penitential band into a well-trained fraternal battalion in the army of the Church Militant in Sacre Coeur on Montmartre in Paris. From his initial sermon at his first Mass onwards he set our eyes firmly on Christ and the effects that He and His Church could have on us as a group and as individuals. Moreover, he insisted, that effect did not have to be limited merely to the exciting period of our Pilgrimage in France. No pagan-like fatalism, he argued, destined us to fall from Christ and the spirit of fraternity guiding us to use nature and grace to move ever closer to eternal life with God once we returned from the Kingdom of the Franks and disembarked at JFK.

Allow me to dwell just a bit longer on this point: our ability and desperate need to maintain a patristic/counterrevolutionary spirit of focus on Christ, the Catholic fraternity emerging from it, and the welcome and encouragement that must be given to those who join in the Lenten Season, the march to Chartres and the overall Pilgrimage to God "at the last moment." It is important for Remnant readers to do so at this particular hour in history, because, *motu proprio* or not, I am deeply convinced that the cause of the Traditional Mass is going to grow ever stronger, and the spirit of the conciliar Church ever more fractious and suicidal, with the passing of each day. As this happens, new recruits are inevitably going to be attracted to the Mass of the Ages—if not the majority of Catholics, who will, perhaps, never come over to our side unless commanded to do so, at least that minority of individuals which can, given circumstances, begin to think and prove itself susceptible to change for the better on its own.

Our Lady of Guadalupe Chapter saw some signs of what I believe will continue to take place in the future while on our post-pilgrimage tour of southern France this year. For one thing, certainly in comparison with my own experiences in the past, gaining permission to say a Traditional Mass seemed to me to be much easier than ever before. In the single case where an obstacle appeared, it lasted but a moment, with a messenger sent to invite our chaplain to celebrate at the most important church in town. Our visit to the apparition site and church in Cotignac involved encountering a nun who had made the Chartres Pilgrimage, knew of *The Remnant*, and kept the *Latin Mass Magazine* in her convent. It also entailed being joined for lunch after Mass by Oratorian priests in what became a veritable Catholic agape. With one hand digging into a magnificent paella, the other holding a glass of rich local wine, and my eyes feasting on the mountain scenery of Provençe, I had a long chat with the Oratorian superior, who spoke very knowingly and favourably of the Fraternity of St. Peter, and who said goodbye to all of us with seemingly genuine sorrow on his face. Nothing like this happened to me in the 1970s, 1980s, and 1990s. Why, it was one of the few times in my life that I felt as though I were part of—dare I say it?—the mainstream!

Now I admit that some of those who might seek to join the line of march of us veteran pilgrims for the Traditional Mass as the eleventh hour approaches might not be quite honourable in their intentions. If the *motu proprio* is released, and then depending on exactly what it may say, there are certainly going to be efforts made by some fifth columnists to "tame the traditionalist beast" by planting modern "viruses" inside the traditional liturgy and creating a myriad of new jurisdictional problems for the religious orders which have been established to keep it alive. The best defense against such possible wolves in sheep's clothing and their maneuvers is, as always, an insistence upon maintenance of a firm line regarding the integrity of the Rite and a refusal to accept its being mixed in with elements from the *Novus Ordo*.

That being said, however, it still remains the case that the large majority of the eleventh-hour pilgrims are inevitably going to be people who are confused as well as attracted, and at times hard to sort out from men and women who could be suspected of entertaining unacceptable intentions once they have insinuated themselves inside the Trad Camp. Eyes focused on Christ, firm in doctrine and commitment to the liturgy, a spirit of Catholic fraternity will nevertheless demand that we not circle the wagons and make it difficult for latecomers and even people whom we consider to have been proponents of errors in the past to enter the compound if they sincerely wish to do so. A spirit of welcome and encouragement has to be ours once more. For if we sneer at them, holding up the traditionalist equivalent of our broken-in shoes and forty years of literature emphasizing our anger at their previous record rather than our delight at their conversion, we will have totally lost the insight of St. John Chrysostom and the message of the Chartres Pilgrims. We would, in our own way, be like those British Christians who refused to help St. Augustine of Canterbury with the mission to the Angles and Saxons because they were too hardened against an enemy who had done them so much harm in the past to wish for them anything other than eternal damnation in the present. And in doing so, we would lose an opportunity to look at ourselves again to see if there are any hidden flaws against Christ and our brethren that we have up till now failed to detect and correct. To paraphrase Daniel Webster, Catholic firmness and fraternity, now and forever, one and inseparable. There is no sense in our enjoying the fruits of our Catholic fraternity, manifesting their superiority to the cheapness of the products of the civilization around us, and then, having perhaps aroused a desire to exchange a mess of pottage for ambrosia and nectar, denying access to the banquet hall because it is too late to join the club. All the doors to the Mystical Body have to be swung wide open until the last gasp of each individual truth seeker.

This year, our trip through the Kingdom of the Franks took us into its Aquitainian and Provençal fringes; areas much more closely tied with the ancient Roman past and much less touched by the barbarian incursions than the regions north of the Loire. All of the places that we visited, from Carcassonne through to Arles and even Nice (more known as a resort than a center of Catholic culture) benefited from the firm hand of the Catholic Franks, with a message that only those of us inducted into the jointly social and individual doctrine of the Mystical Body could really truly understand. This year's journey was the best of the three that I have taken with *The Remnant*, because of the fact that our movements were limited and there was more time to digest and enjoy the places visited. I certainly would wish that aspect of the Pilgrimage to be repeated in years to come.

Nevertheless, I wish also that it could be combined together with gaining the message to be taught to us by the Catholic spirit inhabiting the full vastness of the Kingdom of the Franks. This is, after all, a realm which spread not only over the area of present day France—what continued to be referred to as The Kingdom during the Middle Ages—but also that of present day Belgium, Holland, Germany, Switzerland, Austria, the Czech Republic, Slovenia, Croatia and most of Italy and Sicily—the lands of the medieval Holy Roman Empire. The Empire, remember, was also the heir of the Kingdom of the Franks. Some of these spots have been explored by the post-pilgrimage tour, but there are others whose natural-supernatural Catholic "message" needs yet to be heard. I would love for the merry band to see Trier, to go to Wuerzburg, to Fulda, to Bamberg, to Regensburg, to Monreale and Palermo, all of them magnificent centers of Catholic glory, along with those of most Christian France.

And while we are at it, why stop there? Whatever the Prologue to the Salic Law might say, that formidable lot which built up Christian order in the past is far broader in ethnic background than the comely Franks might have wanted to admit. We have been provided with a far-flung group of friends who have a sack filled with Catholic treasures to teach a fraternal band eager to rest their tired feet and take in another kind of lesson after that taught by the physical one of the path to Chartres. We have Greece to explore, the islands of the Aegean and the coastline of Asia Minor with its cities redolent of accounts from the Acts of the Apostles, not to speak of the great Marian shrine at Ephesus. All that which is Catholic and truly Orthodox belongs to us and ought to be embraced and enjoyed. What an *embarras de choix*!

Now, how Michael Matt would accomplish getting us comfortably from Chartres to Athens I have no idea. Still, he brought us to the Kingdom of the Franks in the first place. He got the golden-tongued Fr. MacDonald to join us. He showed me how to smear grease between my pilgrim toes. He put together a group that welcomed me back into its ranks with open arms after my unwarranted display of self-sufficiency. He seems capable of accomplishing anything in this realm!

But even if he opted for just the three-day hike and seven days in Chartres I would go back again. Whatever the choice for the future may be, I have signed on for the duration. Personally, I need all the Catholic fraternity and all the natural and supernatural stimuli to lift up my heart and mind to God that I can get. The modern world, with its cynical message, creeps up all too insidiously into one's life to neglect them.

23
The Soul Man[†]

"One plunges in and then sees what happens."
(Napoleon, on battles—
and *motu proprio* implementation)

SANTA MARIA MAGGIORE AND CRAVEGGIA are two splendid towns in the Valle Vigezzo, which lies on the northeastern Alpine edge of the Italian region of Piedmont. Merely getting to these rather hidden jewels is an unadulterated delight. One boards the little *trenino* which departs from the central station of the charming border city of Domodossola and begins a forty-minute climb to Eden, each twist and turn of its tiny track offering new and unexpectedly spectacular mountain vistas.

After being deposited in Santa Maria, the lower location, the visitor needs only five minutes to wander down the road to find the Hotel Oscella. Here, splendid rooms, a large, lovely garden and grand nineteenth century aristocratic flair are all offered to him for the paltry sum of thirty-five Euros a head. From this fine hotel he can then begin his promenade throughout Santa Maria, his climb to the neighboring, much higher town of Craveggia, and his inevitable questioning as to why the communities of the Valle Vigezzo are so different from other mountain places in close proximity to them.

What would give rise to such questioning? For one thing, the very old parish church of the Assumption in Santa Maria Maggiore, which was rebuilt almost entirely in the early eighteenth century. This structure seems much larger and richer in decoration than the population and local economy of such a site would ever have warranted. Then there is the fact that a number of the local villas, especially in Craveggia, remind one more of chateaux country in the Loire than of chalets in the Italian-speaking Alps.

Luckily, these architectural mysteries were soon clarified for me by my guide, a dear friend from Gallarate, an industrial and

† First published in *The Remnant*, August 15, 2007.

commercial center near Milan's Malpensa Airport, quite different from the Valle Vigezzo, at least in physical appearance. Maria Grazia has a second apartment in Craveggia. This flat, given the French atmosphere of parts of the town, has an appropriately *Boheme*-like character. From its windows a view opens out on both the mountains as well as the innumerable and quite unique chimneys of the entire area. It is the perfect spot in which to read and meditate upon the history of the valley, its present problems, and its potential future contribution to the revival of Catholic civilization, all of which my friend has done in great and discerning detail.

Maria Grazia explained to me how the inhabitants of the region, most of whom eked out a living from cow-herding, were forced to migrate for at least part of each year to try to supplement their meager incomes. Two men who left were Giovanni Paolo Feminis (1666–1736) and Giovanni Maria Farina (1685–1766), the inventors and popularizers of what is perhaps the world's most famous fragrance: *eau de cologne*. Having made a fortune out of this attractive scent, Feminis in particular decided to spend a good part of his noble gains in beautifying the Valle Vigezzo, with the parish church of Santa Maria Maggiore as a special beneficiary of his largesse—hence one reason for its unusual size and wealth of adornment.

Others who departed the valley did so as chimney sweeps, their favorite destination being the Kingdom of France. In 1612 a young assistant of one of these migrants is said to have climbed up a chimney in the royal palace and then down a second unexpected passageway into another hearth, where he overheard traitors plotting the assassination of the young Louis XIII. The boy told his employer, who passed on the information to the Queen Mother. A grateful Marie de Medici and her spared son offered the chimney sweep a well-deserved reward of his choice. His noble Catholic social spirit pushed him to ask for a favor which would help his impoverished neighbors back in the Valle Vigezzo as well as himself. Would it not be possible for all those forced to abandon his homeland for work in France to do so without legal obstacles and nuisance taxes on either their labor or any products they had to sell?

Indeed it was, and this was the making of the fortune of many of the clever, courageous lads from the region, some of whom were gifted artists rather than merchants or chimney sweeps. Since these new migrants seem to have shared the altruistic spirit of their benefactor, they, too, spent a good deal of their money decorating churches and helping out others back at home. Moreover, despite maintaining their main residences in France, they retained their personal ties with the valley, constructing the above-mentioned chateaux-like villas to house them on regular visits from Paris. Some of their descendants still come to their homeland for weddings today. Some even lie in local cemeteries to await the Resurrection of the Dead and the Final Judgment.

Santa Maria Maggiore and Craveggia had no special history as resort towns until after the Second World War. It was then that ex-partisans who had hidden out in this region between 1943–1945 began to bring their families here to escape the summer heat of the Lombard plain. The Valle Vigezzo grew popular in yet wider circles. With popularity came the call for modern Change. And, as the purveyors of modern liberty repeatedly instruct us, Change's wishes must receive a favorable response. When Change moves into town all free men are obliged to hustle to fulfill his every desire.

What Change brought to the valley was the disease of soullessness. Nothing unusual about that! For, as anyone with eyes to see can readily attest, the price of Change, as defined by the high priests of modernity, is the ever more comprehensive sacrifice of all that gives life serious, fulfilling, spiritual meaning. For Change and the modern conception of freedom and progress lying behind it require commitment to what the French writer Celine called "death on the installment plan"; the encouragement of a life-long yearning for euthanasia; a self-destruction that begins with the slow but steady murder of the soul of men and the communities in which they are meant to prosper and perfect themselves.

Now, admittedly, casual day-trippers would probably not sense the growth of the tumor of soullessness in the region. Neither would unrestrained free market economists. After all, would it not seem to them that everything there is in absolutely pristine physical condition? Maria Grazia, who began summering in this zone in the 1950s, would certainly not deny that truth. Money has recently poured in as never before. Houses have been solidly restored; gardens embellished; restaurants established with finer foods and wines; events and entertainments organized on a much grander scale. Yes, the outward signs of the valley's entrepreneurial achievement are totally undeniable.

Still, its soul is dying and the real life of its communities along with it. The locals are moving to condominia outside of town; the cow herds seem to have shrunk down to one symbolic beast grazing near the community center; the old Italian-Parisian families are seeking buyers for their chateaux; houses and businesses are being bought up and restored by strangers, who come here only a short time each year and who bring with them the tinsel vision which already dominates their own cities rather than the substantive seventeenth century French cultural vigor of previous part-time residents. What is being created is a place which is "all for show"; a Disneyland version of the Valle Vigezzo. The tourists to whom this caters can buy tickets to visit its outward splendor, which is untouched and even improved somewhat. What they cannot do is form the "soul" and spirit that would enable them to participate in what remains of the normal life of the valley and maintain its vitality into the future.

Surely most of us have witnessed the progress of this spiritual tumor in an otherwise healthy-looking body under other circumstances. Avila, in Spain, always came to my mind when I thought of the phenomenon in years past. The first time I saw the city of St. Theresa it was rather shabby, but throbbing nonetheless with the life of ordinary people working, praying and enjoying themselves until all hours of the night. A second trip, decades later, introduced me to an Avila which had been magnificently restored by wealthy investors from Madrid, whose rare visits left the center a residential ghost town. Trendy shops sold useless modern trinkets instead of baby clothes and curtain rods. Offices housed weird organizations playing on the city's mystical traditions, now turned into something new age like and spooky. My disappointment lessened when I heard a band playing and singing traditional Spanish music with great technical skill. It shot up when my wife pointed out to me that all the players were Chinese. The locals, as in Santa Maria Maggiore, had moved, lock, stock and barrel outside the city walls. Inside those walls lay the false promise of five-star hotels and the reality of creeping spiritual decay.

Change that demands this kind of commitment to "death on the installment plan" has nothing to do with any rational acceptance of the economic realities of a new millennium. Rather, it reflects a conscious choice of a way of life based on an incomplete and therefore inhuman vision of existence; an understanding of man and society founded upon that fundamental, hideous contradiction which has taken root in the West since the time of Luther: the idea that we are building a glorious new world of freedom while we simultaneously and slavishly submit to every command of our supposedly irresistible, grasping, depraved, material nature. It is the conscious choice of this anti-spiritual *weltanschauung* which emboldens its proponents to depict perfectly viable societies and economies serving men and women whose healthy bodies and souls work together as though they were doomed remnants of a nostalgic romanticism; to crush them; and to replace them with their soulless alternatives. Moreover, it is the endless propaganda that has accompanied this fatalistic philosophical and political vision of "liberating" materialist Change that has broken the resistance of people who would love to preserve the souls of their cities and countries and their children, but who have nevertheless lost all sense of how to do so.

The Change Gang has behind it a five-hundred-year history of successfully browbeating individuals and societies into following its guidelines. Still, no one in the Valle Vigezzo or anywhere else around the globe is unalterably obliged to commit himself to the death on the installment plan that it peddles. People here and elsewhere must be taught to fight for their right to a full, human, physical and spiritual life once again. This is where the Soul Man comes onto the scene, and it was chiefly to meet him and to see what he has done that my friend Maria Grazia wanted me to come to visit the region.

I hope that forty-four-year-old Don Alberto Secci, a native of the Valle Vigezzo, a former curate in Craveggia and now pastor of the town of Santa Maria Maggiore, forgives me for using this term from my tacky rock-n-roll past to identify him. Nevertheless, I believe that the words "Soul Man" accurately fit him. For what this energetic priest of the Archdiocese of Torino is doing is to show his parishioners the way back to the life of the spirit, both for themselves as individuals as well as for their magnificent mountain communities. Moreover, I am convinced that what he is doing is pregnant with incalculable consequences, and a model for Catholics in the United States as well as in Italy.

Don Secci has local help in his spiritual labors, and from two important sources. The closest at hand is one of the greatest pastors of the Catholic Reformation era, a man whose influence is still felt all over northern Italy: St. Charles Borromeo. A relic of this saint was given to the parish church of Santa Maria Maggiore and the Valle Vigezzo by his relative, Cardinal Federico Borromeo, on the 8th of April, 1627. Secondly, Don Secci can count on the assistance that comes from a famous sanctuary in the nearby village of Re. This is often referred to by people as the Sanctuary of the Lady of the Blood, due to the twenty-day bleeding of an image of the Madonna struck by a stone hurled at this painting by a disgruntled, losing gambler in 1494. The Madonna's sanctuary is a heavily visited one. People pray at the altar where St. Charles's relic lies. Both are therefore natural weapons in the pastor's efforts to reunite his people and his community with the souls that they are losing.

But Don Secci has certainly added his own special contribution to the reinvigoration of the Valle Vigezzo's spirit. He has done so by running what is probably the only full, traditional, diocesan parish in Italy. For long before anyone began dreaming of the publication of a *motu proprio*, he had offered his parishioners all their Sunday and weekday Masses according to the 1962 missal. And his work has borne serious and continuing fruit.

I saw this with my own eyes, on Monday, July 23, placing myself towards the back of the church so that I could get an idea of the response of the worshippers who were present at the morning Mass. The weekday crowd was large, mostly women, as would be normal in Italy. Everyone took an active part in the liturgy and knew the Latin responses thoroughly. A couple, obviously outsiders, came in after I did and sat in the pew behind me. "If only all Masses were like this," the man commented to his wife, "then the other churches wouldn't be as empty as they are." Mass ended and a line of parishioners formed outside the sacristy to consult with the pastor. "It's like this every day," Maria Grazia informed me as we joined it.

Our turn finally came and I quickly realized that Don Secci was one of those men whom I felt as though I had known and fought alongside all my life. Aside from his personal warmth and welcome, this was obviously due to the fact that we were clearly both on exactly the same wavelength. Here was a priest who fully understood the spirit of the Traditional Liturgy, who had studied the whole nefarious tale of the historical assault upon it, who was familiar with the work done by men like Michael Davies to defend and restore it, and who grasped the need to labor together with a myriad of different groups to take full advantage of the blessing given to our cause by Pope Benedict XVI's document. Here, also, was a priest who saw that the *motu proprio* is a new and happy "Pandora's Box," destined to awaken the Catholic population more and more to the full riches of the whole of the Tradition and the transformation of all things in Christ that that Tradition promises to men and nations who accept it. Both of us agreed that there is no way that exposure to the graces, the beauty and the historical depth of the Traditional Mass will not cause ever larger numbers of Catholics to ask questions about the entire, long-term crisis of Faith and Christendom; whence this crisis emerged; who is historically responsible for starting and then aggravating it. Both of us agreed that freedom for the Traditional Mass is but the first step towards making Catholics aware that the answers to their problems lie with the fullness of life promised by the Mystical Body—not with that death on the installment plan hawked by the con men of modernity from Martin Luther through John Locke to the materialists of the soulless Disneyland culture robbing the Valle Vigezzo and the rest of the Christian West of their birthright.

Don Secci is a humble man, and he gave me permission to write this article about him only if I thought it would be useful to prod people to follow his example. That example is twofold. On the one hand it is an example of how to begin the task of putting men and societies back in touch with their souls: by taking Napoleon's comment about battle strategy and applying it to our own situation. For this diocesan priest and pastor of Santa Maria Maggiore just "plunged in and waited to see what would happen" when he decided to turn his parish Tridentine. He is still around to relate the tale. On the other hand, Don Secci's example is also that of a marriage of his courageous plunge with an enormously charitable spirit. He does not snarl at people for their mistakes with the liturgy, He does not drive the neophytes and the simply curious away from his church with the suspect and derisive spirit that I have all too often seen many traditionalists display towards newcomers. Don Secci welcomes men and women whom he knows will need his guidance and may even turn away from the Truth a few times before grasping the whole of the picture that he has begun to paint for them.

The men and the products of the Valle Vigezzo have always tramped along the highway to the outside world. I want the courageous and charitable example of the Soul Man of Santa Maria Maggiore to migrate as the chimney sweeps and the artists and the inventors of the fragrances of the past centuries migrated away from this mountain hideaway. Wherever it does so spread, people will forget about prudence, plunge into the work of Tradition and simply "see what happens" in consequence. Priests will walk out to their altars one morning and just open up the pages of the 1962 missal and go. Mothers will approach their local pastors, as my wife did the other day, and inform them that their sons know how to serve the Traditional Mass whenever they are ready to take the plunge themselves. The missals *will* open, and without petitions to unfriendly bishops and meetings with their Buddhist-minded Worship Committees. Graces will flow. Unexpected questions about the fullness of the Faith will be asked anew. Unfounded modern dogmas will begin to be exposed for the lies that they are. Fatalistic changes will be seen to be paper tigers and pompous hoo-ha. For the spirit of the Soul Man is one that recognizes that the *motu proprio* has created a new starting point for the West as a whole. It is a spirit that points the way back beyond "just" the Mass to a new courage, a new charity, a new evangelization and a New Christendom in which death on the installment plan has no future role to play whatsoever.

24

The Freed Mass, the Formless Society and the Second Front[†]

LAST MONTH, STANDING IN FRONT OF THE Church of St. Agnes in New York City, I ran into a fellow traditionalist to whom I expressed my joy over the *motu proprio*. "Well, if *you* are hopeful about it," she responded, "then it *really* must mean something!"

That comment upset me a great deal, because I always believed that the Church—as the Bride of Christ—would eventually come back to her senses regarding the liturgy. When I look over my past writings, I see that I have regularly argued that Catholics, justly outraged and horrified by contemporary evils though they were, should nevertheless maintain their calm and patience amidst all the turmoil. For the lesson of previous historical crises seemed to be that ecclesiastical disasters generally were set right, and that hopes for a change for the better were sometimes even rewarded during the lifetime of those who had witnessed the beginnings of a particular nightmare.

So why my acquaintance's surprise that I thought that something good had actually happened? Who knows? Perhaps that shock came from an unjustifiable equation of my truly deep alarm over the dangers emanating from our political and social order with hopelessness regarding the internal constitution and vigor of Catholicism. This equation would not be unusual, given the fact that for many of our fellow believers, doubts about the beneficence of our way of life is tantamount to lack of faith in the divine promise given by Christ to His Church.

Thankfully, Catholicism and the spirit behind the American system are not consubstantial. And it is precisely because I place such profound hopes in the former that I wish to drive home the utter hopelessness of faith in the latter. As far as I am concerned, the encouragement of alarm regarding the guiding principles of

---

[†] First published in *The Remnant*, September 15, 2007.

our political and social realm is the *sine qua non* for allowing the great promise of the *motu proprio* to have its full impact.

Allow me for just a moment to explore this future promise, moving beyond the *old* hopes that Pope Benedict's document satisfied in order to identify some sound new ones. I think that I can do this with reasonable conviction. For what we were given in *Summorum Pontificum* was more than "just" freedom for the Mass. What we obtained was more than a "mere" recognition of the justice that was owed to that Traditional Liturgy after its unprecedented savaging. What we were blessed with in this document was the beginning of a return to a historically identifiable, truly pastoral language boding well for the recovery of the full Catholic vision of the need to restore all things in Christ.

The Church abandoned her familiar linguistic territory to move into a strange rhetorical jungle in the 1960s. She entered it as an amateur and seriously misled explorer, destined to be pounced upon and manipulated by the savage inhabitants who knew their way around the place and how to wield its tongue effectively. This rhetorical jungle is an Hegelian zoo where the True, the Good, and the Beautiful are said to be in constant flux, destined for redefinition by the irresistible demands of the ever-changing democratic spirit of the times. But the perennially fluid spirit of those times, disguised as democratic through repetition of glib mantras by time-serving Word Merchants in search of big-time bucks, has always, in reality, meant whatever the strongest individual and group fantasies and self-interests have decided the popular will ought to be.

In entering this rhetorical Heart of Darkness the Church invited Apocalypse Now Everything that was most essential to her supernatural and historical reality could be declared "surpassed" by the requirements of a new age with a "higher consciousness"—i.e., the latest desires of the ideology-and-money-driven powers-that-be. The discarding of any given doctrine and custom logically brought with it the need for crushing other related ones. All of the traditional arguments that could be logically and theologically mobilized to defend the embattled patrimony were condemned by the new, esoteric rhetoric as meaningless and absurd, since the structure of familiar rational and theological discourse had also been "surpassed" along the same Hegelian lines. A "fresh" dialectic was now the norm, one that a sane Catholic mind could not understand and master, since it ran totally counter to the teaching of philosophical realism, traditional theology, historical experience and the testimony of one's very eyes and ears. If a normal believer did try to use this distorted logic and speech, he became trapped in confusions and in contradictions, opening himself up to the ridicule of the experts in jungle argumentation. Anyone seeking a historical example of the bewilderment and madness such a predicament can cause should look to the pathetic mumblings of King Louis XVI, forced to defend his actions as a monarch and as a Catholic in the hostile idiom of a Rousseau, a Danton and a Robespierre. The horror, the horror, indeed.

But the *motu proprio*'s focus on spiritual and legal respect for Tradition has once again placed the pastoral rhetoric of the Church back in recognizable Catholic and, one ought to emphasize, classical Socratic territory. It has pulled the basic speech of the Body of Christ out of the rhetorical Heart of Darkness. It has had the audacity to speak of history and of real sociological evidence—such as the number of young people attending the Traditional Mass. It has had the courage to place justice above the arbitrary and hypocritical will of the strong and their smooth-talking, spirit-interpreting agents. If I can make an analogy, it has once again deployed the Catholic past behind the people and the pope, so that all may face the real problems of life as one unified force—just as the Traditional Mass places congregation behind the priest in one unified act of worship of the Triune God.

Yes, there is a bit of "invented history" in the *motu proprio*'s discussion of the reason for our forty years' wandering in the desert. From what I remember, Paul VI did not merely fail to anticipate the strength of attachment to the Traditional Mass. Rather, he was enthusiastically committed to a liturgical revolution which he knew and expressly indicated would offend pious people. He himself supported a vision of history whose very essence would require unending future changes to suit new manifestations of the insatiable "spirit of the times." Full respect for the historical record—something one can find in Michael Davies' books on the subject—would not only require noting such truths. It would also demand admission of the fact that even if the old rite were never legally abrogated, the authorities did everything in their power to make the laity believe that it had been, and that those who did not accept this reality were disobedient obscurantists.

Still, these are the games that institutions, including divine institutions with a human side, regularly play. The rediscovery by the Church of her proper pathway after a vacation in Never Never Land is generally a messy, halting, and not fully honest affair. It almost never takes place in one, clean, action-packed, cinema-like scene. Very frequently, embarrassment and prudence lead her to seek to save appearances by ignoring or misrepresenting what really happened during past nightmares that she sincerely winces over now and wishes to forget. An article that I wrote several years ago for *Seattle Catholic* explored this psychological state in some detail in relation to the overcoming of the horrors of the Great Western Schism.

Historical game-playing, painful though it can be, is a minor blemish on the flesh of *Summorum Pontificum* compared to the significance of its return to traditional forms and familiar words in its pastoral language. The potential number of glorious consequences stemming from such a remarkable and courageous recovery of a rhetoric pronounced irrevocably dead by the powerful of this world is great. Under the guidance of this form of speech, Catholics could find themselves logically led not from one fanciful and destructive change to another, but from the rehabilitation of one rooted and helpful tradition to the next. This could have the magnificent effect of exposing the jungle rhetoricians who have dominated the Church for the past forty years, now forced to deal once again with a rhetoric based on tradition, history and realism, for the bullies and manipulators of "the democratic spirit of the times" that they really are. It could transform them into pathetic figures stumbling to justify their Hegelian thoughts and actions in a realm whose *lingua franca* was once more an understandable Catholic idiom. And it could result, eventually, in the full clarification of the historical record, with the analysis of men like Michael Davies shown to be correct and finally given their proper place of honor.

Yes, all this could take effect, quite naturally, *if the Church could be left to her own devices*. Unfortunately, this valley of tears is *not* the best of all possible worlds, and, as a result, the Church will *not* be left to work out her future relying on her own internal strengths. She has to contend with the impact on her life of an outside political and social order whose dominant spirit is intensely hostile to her very survival (much less her revival); an environment which the tradition the Church is now engaged in recovering teaches her must itself be transformed in Christ.

Allow me to specify the problem with the dominant spirit of that outside world by first calling attention to a magnificent gathering that I attended at the Church of Our Saviour in New York City on September 9. A number of groups and individuals were involved in preparing this event, including the Society of St. Hugh of Cluny, dedicated to implementation of the *motu proprio*, the superb Saint Gregory Society of New Haven, which has done so much for the cause of good church music for many years already, and one of the sharpest traditionalists in the whole of the movement, Mr. Stuart Chessman. It began with a Solemn High Traditional Mass, which made me think what the joy over the Resurrection of the Dead might be like, given that I saw in attendance practically everyone whom I have known to be involved in the struggle for the liturgy over the past forty years. Following the Mass, Fr. Uwe Michael Lang, author of *Turning Towards the Lord*, a scholarly discussion of orientation in worship, gave a brief and deeply insightful presentation on *Summorum Pontificum*. He did this in the context of introducing Mr. Martin Mosebach, a highly-renowned German man of letters, whose defense of the Traditional Liturgy, *Heresy of Formlessness*,† has just recently won his nation's highest literary award. Mr. Mosebach then read selections from his book and answered questions from the packed audience in the church undercroft.

The evils—the heresy—of a committed, evangelical formlessness in the liturgy is Mr. Mosebach's chief theme, and one which he develops in an extremely readable and extraordinarily valuable manner. Formlessness can never assure the proper worship of God. Form and beauty, Mr. Mosebach explains, are not suspect, aesthetic "extras" in establishing man's correct relationship to his Creator. They are an essential element in identifying and maintaining that relationship, and pointing the way to a myriad of other theological and natural truths while doing so. Hence, Mr.

† Available in a new edition by Angelico Press.

Mosebach's delight in the return of the Traditional Mass, which reveals such a profound respect for form and beauty developed organically through the ages.

Our political and social order thrives on formlessness and sees in any attempt to establish forms and norms with claims to transcendent and universal significance a dagger aimed at its heart. Formlessness is at the very essence of that fanatical pluralism whose gospel of liberty and toleration places endless searching and endless flux above civilization and culture building of all kinds. Some of our pluralist masters actually believe in the value of this formless emptiness. Some give lip service to it because of the fact that its "doctrineless doctrines" serve their self-interests, keeping at bay that interference with their materialist, property-accumulating enterprises which form, meaning, morality and culture building authorities have always brought along with them.

Formless pluralism, joyfully open to the acceptance of everything except that which has real substantive structure and content, knows that Catholicism is its chief enemy—John Locke, one of its most important founders, said as much already at the beginning of the eighteenth century. While the false but potent religion of Islam does also present this empty beast a problem today, a revived Roman Catholicism must always remain its most formidable and fearful foe. Hence its need to nip any Catholic rediscovery and recommitment to the fullness of its forms and its faith in the proverbial bud. Hence its mobilization of all of the myths and the images that it has successfully used over the years of its dominance in order to try to frighten people away from the "evil" consequences of a Catholicism with real bite. Hence, to take but one obvious example, the equation of the return of the Traditional Mass with antisemitism, Hitler, the Second World War, genocide and probably high cholesterol as well.

If nothing drastic happens politically or socially, the formless pluralist world outside will probably not take drastic action to halt the forward advance of the form-filled Traditional Mass. It does not take the incalculable effect of grace seriously. It does not focus its attention on possible changes in the hearts of spiritually and intellectually curious individuals. It knows that most Catholics, under normal conditions, are as co-opted by the system and tired out from the increasing work demanded of them to survive within it. It knows that so long as some sort of stability remains, many of those who might be attracted to the Traditional Mass would be content with what could be labeled Romano-Anglicanism, a clubhouse Catholicism, happy with its possession of a decent liturgy, but unmoved by the idea of transforming all things in Christ. That prognostication seems to be borne out by the arguments and behavior of Catholic libertarians and conservatives, for whom the formless emptiness of the political and social order, at least with respect to economics and warfare, appear to be sacred.

But what if the situation changes drastically from one moment to the next? Due to yet another disastrous war or an economic collapse? History abounds with illustrations of such things happening practically overnight. No one in Paris, Berlin, London and Vienna on July 28, 1914 imagined that he would be sleeping in a tent praying madly for his life a couple of weeks later. Under such conditions, the appeal of the different, form-and-substance-filled Traditional Mass and the idea of Christ as king of man and society might very easily grow as swiftly as militant Islam has done. Masses of men and women, and not just astute individuals would then be touched by the Gospel message. At that point our desperate, evangelical, pluralist masters would rapidly display their true colors more viciously, and their willingness to use violent means to render the promise of the *motu proprio* for the full restoration of the Catholic vision meaningless would become crystal clear. So would their ability to count on help from disgruntled Catholic rhetoricians from the Heart of Darkness.

Michael Davies' hopes for help from Cardinal Ratzinger seem to me to have been amply justified by the facts. Further hope for the cause of the Church is also valid. Still, the tradition of that Church in which we place our legitimate hope tells us that we must treat the political and social conditions in which she carries out her mission seriously. If the spirit behind those conditions is a bad one; if it emasculates Catholic action under "normal" circumstances and seeks to crush it entirely under desperate ones, hopes placed in its beneficence are a recipe for disaster.

Victory on the liturgical front must be followed up by intensification of the hunt for victory on a Second Front; the Front fighting for political and social transformation in Christ. Does battle on this Second Front seem practically impossible at the moment?

Well, then, why not try, at least, to make a theoretical, personal break with subservience to and praise of formless pluralism as an idea? Momentary practical impotence does not require embrace and active collaboration with the enemy. And an intellectual and spiritual break with a "doctrineless doctrine" that hates and kills the Catholic vision makes a more powerful and irritating statement to its supporters than one might think. Once you experience what happens when your preferential option for a form-filled order of things becomes known to the people around you you will see exactly what I mean.

25

The View From Rocco's†

ON STRENGTH, POPES, AND HOLY WEEK CRISES

JITO, THE LOCAL JAPANESE MARTIAL ARTS instructor, popped into Rocco's the other day. I had not seen him for so long that I had even forgotten his name. Smaller than the late Emperor Hirohito in height, and more jovial than a satisfied kabuki buff coming back from an evening jaunt in the Floating World of Tokugawa Edo, he would never stir fear in the heart of the unsuspecting observer. In reality, however, this man with the look of a perpetually pliant victim is as strong as seventy samurai. Madame Butterfly could certainly have used his services against the American Consul who betrayed her.

Joe, at the espresso machine, was justly raking the banking world and subprime mortgages over the coals when Jito arrived, but the latter quickly changed the subject by showing the both of us how easily he could flick one of the waitresses into the air and knock the little lady out cold. Luckily, he was able to make his formidable abilities crystal clear without actually taking them to their logical and painful extreme. What the Full Jito might mean, if unleashed against an open foe who had given him cause for offense, can easily be deduced from most Kurosawa films. In any case, exposure to the good chap's externally humble demeanor and hidden superhuman vigor seduced me into the following Walter-Mitty-like fantasy.

The movers and shakers of modernity generally perceive us believers to be a flock of pathetic losers, subservient to their will and incapable of roughing up a frazzled flea, much less a whole socio-political system. On the other hand, it serves their propaganda purposes well to continue to speak of us as though we possess an incredible power to crush them. In other words, our role, in their eyes, is to remain smiling, impotent punching bags while nevertheless permitting ourselves to be depicted to the world at large as a batch of mindless, insatiable, aggressive, inquisitorial Genghis Khans.

† First published in *The Remnant*, February 15, 2008.

I began to imagine what it would be like if we suddenly threw a curve ball at the high and mighty of the anti-Christian naturalist West; if we unexpectedly threw away the prepared script, abandoned our agreed-upon role as long-suffering milquetoasts, and let loose our inner-Jito, flipping and flopping them from one end of Rocco's to the other; in short, if we momentarily transformed the enemy's mythical lamentations regarding our almost non-existent influence from ridiculous legend into hard fact.

Being a historian, my chosen candidates for abuse were only dead troublemakers. Then, just as I thought that I had found the perfect deceased victim for my fantasy, Chris Ferrara came along to tell me that there was a living and timely one right under my eyes: Abe Foxman and his many, many allies across the globe. And just as I thought that I had identified the best meek-looking Catholic-turned-Jito, Chris informed me that that role was actually being played by no one less than Pope Benedict XVI himself, through his controversial change of the Good Friday bidding prayer concerning the Jews.

Now, obviously, many traditionalists have contested Chris's claim. For them, Pope Benedict is a weak man who merely sold-out to pressure and the irresistible temptations of his own liberal past. But whose assessment is correct? Theirs? Or Chris's? I would like to offer my own thoughts on this matter in the only way that I am competent to do so, by means of meditating upon a historical comparison.

That comparison also involves a Holy Week ceremony, one that used to be an integral part of Holy Thursday in Rome; one that had vast repercussions in the field of Church-State relations and therefore was a public "happening" of the first order throughout Christendom. This dramatic Holy Thursday event was the yearly publication of the papal bull, *In Coena Domini*. Allow me to begin discussion of the document in question by taking from the *Catholic Encyclopedia* of 1911 a brief description of its character, along with a reference to a popular interpretation of its dogmatic importance:

> [*In Coena Domini* was] a papal Bull, so called from the feast on which it was annually published in Rome, viz., the feast of the Lord's Supper, or Maundy Thursday. The ceremony took place in the loggia of St. Peter's in the presence of the pope, the College of Cardinals, and the Roman Court. The Bull was

read first in Latin by an auditor of the Sacred Roman Rota, and then in Italian by a cardinal-deacon. When the reading was over the pope flung a lighted waxen torch into the piazza beneath. The Bull contained a collection of censures of excommunication against the perpetrators of various offences, absolution from which was reserved to the pope.... There was a clause in the older editions of the Bull, ordering all patriarchs, archbishops, and bishops to see to its regular publication in their spheres of jurisdiction, but this was not carried out.... In spite of the opposition of princes it was known to the faithful through diocesan rituals, provincial chapters of monks, and the promulgation of jubilees. Confessors were often ordered to have a copy of it in their possession.... In the controversies that arose at the time of the Vatican Council about papal infallibility, the Bull *In Coena Domini* was dragged to the front, and Janus [a noted opponent of the dogma] said of it that if any Bull bears the stamp of an ex cathedra decision it must surely be this one, which was confirmed again and again by so many popes. Loaded down though they were with the titles "Most Christian" and "Most Catholic," the traditional rulers of Christendom, whether of monarchical Austria, France, Spain and Portugal or republican Venice, openly spewed venom against *In Coena Domini*. After all, the transgressions chastised therein—chastisements requiring special papal intervention for forgiveness—were to a large degree those repeatedly committed by the governments under their control. By the latter half of the eighteenth century, and some twenty years before the French Revolution, these rulers felt strong enough to demand the abolition of the grand Holy Thursday bull entirely, along with its powerful statement regarding Christian moral influence over political and social life. They were egged on to do so by the Jansenist and Enlightenment-inspired ministers of state, bishops, and cardinals who almost everywhere advised them. These same men were relentlessly pressing them forward to a general assault on the entire Catholic order, most especially upon the Society of Jesus, which best represented the need to dedicate all of nature to the greater glory of God.

Standing in the way of such secularization was Carlo della Torre di Rezzonico, Pope Clement XIII (1758–1769), and his Secretary of State, Cardinal Luigi Torrigiani. Matters came to a head when Clement, outraged over actions of the government of

Parma regularly condemned by *In Coena Domini*, sent that state's sovereign, Duke Ferdinand, a monitorium on January 30, 1768. This warned him that he had incurred the Holy Thursday bull's threat of excommunication. A storm of abuse was then unleashed from all over Europe, led by men like Louis XV's chief minister, the Duc de Choiseul, who called the pope "a complete ninny," and Torrigiani "a first-class fool" (cited in Ludwig von Pastor, *History of the Popes*, Volume 37, 271). It led not only to retaliation in the form of the occupation of Papal territories in Italy and Avignon, but also to European-wide assaults on both the monitorium and its Holy Thursday parent:

> Almost all the Catholic Governments forbade the circulation of the monitorium in their States. Despite the nuncio's energetic efforts to persuade Louis XV to have the Brief published, the Paris Parlement, instigated by Choiseul, banned it on February 26th, 1768. It was only the Minister's cool-headedness that prevented the order being given for its public burning by the executioner. On March 13th the Parmesan Government, adopting the opinion given by the royal Giunta, issued a decree by which the failure to surrender the monitorium incurred the penalty suffered by rebels and traitors. On March 16th, 1768, the Council of Castile published against the Pope's admonitory letter a royal ordinance to which were attached the opinions of the two Fiscals, Campomanes and Moñino, with their harsh invectives against Rome. An edict of the King of Naples, of June 4th, 1768, ordered the surrender of the *papel de Roma*, as the Brief was contemptuously dubbed, and the Bull *In Coena Domini*, threatening anyone who retained them with the penalty for high treason. Similarly, on April 30th, the Portuguese Government ordered the collection of every copy of the monitorium and declared that anyone who distributed, copied or retained it was a traitor.... On August 9th, 1768, Count Firmian, the Imperial [Hapsburg] Lieutenant, addressed a circular letter to all the Bishops in Lombardy, forbidding the publication in future of the Bull *In Coena Domini*.†

These Homeland Security measures were accompanied by a protest presented to the Holy See in the name of all of the Bourbon princes. The Duc de Choiseul saw that protest as a means of

† Pastor, *History of the Popes*, 37:277, 287

demonstrating to the Papacy who it was that really called the shots in Christendom, and how little the petty opposition of one reigning pontiff truly mattered. For him, the next conclave would be the chance for progressive Europe to have a suppliant, modern pope:

> The French Minister insisted above everything on the necessity of the Kings of France, Spain, and Naples taking joint action against Clement XIII. In a memorandum to the Pope the representatives of these three Powers were to express their amazement that he should have published, without previous negotiation or warning, a decree against the Duke of Parma which was in itself both insulting and unjust, since it apparently inflicted excommunication on him for a purely secular matter. Family interest did not allow the rules of the House of Bourbon to overlook this insult. They therefore found themselves compelled to demand, with the means placed in their hands by God, formal satisfaction for the insulted party. The Holy See must formally and publicly countermand the Brief. If the Pope did not comply with the request within a week, the three monarchs would recall their envoys from Rome and expel the Papal nuncios from their States. In the event of a refusal, which was anticipated, relations with Rome were to be broken off for the remainder of the pontificate. Business would be carried on, "but we will deal with the Court of Rome in such a way that we will be the masters of the next conclave, and the most pressing task of the next Pope will be to make good the stupidities of his predecessor".‡
>
> For the Bourbon Powers the coming election was not primarily a question of personalities. What was desired was not the election of this or that Cardinal but a complete change in the policy of the Holy See, no matter who was chosen. "It would be a danger to religion and the centre of unity," wrote Choiseul to Bernis on April 10th, 1769, "if the throne of St. Peter was occupied by a Pope with the principles of Clement XIII and with a Minister such as Torrigiani. It is not everyone who thinks as I do on this matter, and the fanatical opponents of the Roman Curia, who in my opinion are as much to be feared as the Jesuits, regret Torrigiani's departure and would have liked Clement XIII to have reigned another ten years, for, had this happened, a schism or even the destruction of the temporal supremacy of the Pope

‡ Ibid., 274–275.

would have been more likely. There is no question but that the Pope must be a man who understands the spirit of the Courts and of our age, which is entirely different from that of the last century. He must be a man who while maintaining the dignity and the appearance of power tries to adapt himself to circumstances.... One is entitled to expect that the rule of the next Pope will inaugurate a memorable epoch in Catholicism. But if he follows the old Roman principles there is no hope for it"[§].

Pope Clement was a straightforward and strong man. He responded to this highly offensive power play with great dignity and fortitude, giving the lie to the claim that secular rather than spiritual concerns underlay his actions while doing so:

> The Pope skimmed through the memorial presented by the French representative, Aubeterre, and told him he would neither withdraw nor alter the Brief, for he could not do so with a good conscience. It was only at the prompting of his conscience that he had published the monitorium. The threat of reprisals he treated with contempt. The same reply was given by Clement XIII to the Spanish envoy, with the observation that he would rather die than betray the rights of the Apostolic See and burden his conscience with a heavy load for which he would have to account at the judgment seat of God. He was not afraid of reprisals. The monarchs might take as many as they wished; they would meet with no resistance, for he had neither weapons nor soldiers with which to oppose them. Even if he did have them, he would not use them against Catholic princes and sons of the Church. The only weapons he had were prayer and the Cross of Christ, in which he put all his trust[¶].

Nevertheless, the monarchies in question proved that they did indeed hold the balance of power in their hands. They made good on their menace to manipulate the next conclave, which took place only one year after the Parma incident. Giovanni Vincenzo Antonio-Ganganelli, who took the name Clement XIV (1769–1774), was elected pontiff and in no way disappointed them. His first Holy Thursday came and went without the traditional *In Coena Domini* ceremony, and this was followed within the next few years by its total public renunciation. Time-serving clerics were thrilled

§ Ibid., 38:27.

¶ Ibid., 37:278–279.

by the change in attitude on the part of the powers-that-be once their non-negotiable demands had been granted:

> Clement XIV had already failed to make any mention of the Bull in his announcement of the jubilee of 1769. On April 5th, 1770, the Spanish ambassador, Azpuru, was able to report that he had learnt from a reliable source that it would not be published on Maundy Thursday. A week later he confirmed this news. The Pope had yielded to the pressure put on him by the enlightened Ministers of the Courts. Many regarded this policy as a false one and as a heavy blow to the prestige of the Holy See. Dissatisfaction was shown by the Cardinals, who had not been consulted, joy by the "enlighteners," who, as, for instance, the Voltairian Azara, declared it a triumph of good sense to do away with "this monstrous Bull, a work of darkness and a treaty with the Devil." But men of Azara's type were still not satisfied, for, they held, even though the Bull was not published, the excommunications still went on; it must be formally revoked once for all. In the following years too the reading of the Bull was omitted. The Pope told Cardinal Orsini that he had never understood how, in contrast with the discipline of the first centuries of Christianity, such a custom could have taken shape, and on Maundy Thursday of all days—a view which was hardly the result of deep study. In 1774 he ordained that it was no longer to be cited.
>
> As if by way of reward for Clement XIV's highly conciliatory attitude, Conti [the nuncio to Portugal, one of the worst persecutors of the Church] was to be received in as grand a manner as possible. The nuncio described in a self-satisfied way the great marks of honour with which he was welcomed. On crossing the frontier he was met, not by a small detachment of troops, as was his predecessor, but by a complete regiment. The king had placed his own galley at his disposal for the crossing of the Tagus, and his state coach was waiting for him on the other side.[**]

Clement XIV went on to satisfy the great Catholic powers in other regards, his most famous kowtow to the new world order being the completion of the inhuman destruction of the Society of Jesus already begun on the national level. Meditation upon his responsibility for its demise, almost contemporaneous with the

** Ibid., 38:114–116.

Holy Thursday Sell-Out, sent him into a deep depression that poisoned the final days of his life.

> Francesco Sanseverino, Bishop of Alife, said that the Pope's behavior was becoming unbearable to those around him and that this was due possibly to mental as well as physical suffering. There can be no doubt that Clement XIV's deep-seated mental and spiritual depression was connected with the reproaches he brought against himself for having suppressed the Society of Jesus. A classic witness in support of this is the well-informed Cordara, whose evidence is all the more important inasmuch as he always did his best to justify every act of the Pope's. "The Pope," he said, "was haunted by the ghost of the dead Society of Jesus, again and again he remembered the damage its suppression had wrought on the Church, the dishonour this unfortunate decision had brought to his name, the hatred it had engendered. He pondered on the loss to the Apostolic See of a safeguard and support, on how Christ's field had lost a picked band of workers; he thought of the scandal caused to the faithful, of the triumphant joy of the heretics, and of the great bewilderment of Christians throughout the world. This distressing thought so racked him day and night that sometimes he would babble in sheer grief and seemed to be beside himself. Often in the night he thought he heard the bronze bell of the Jesuits, though no one had rung it."††

No one ought to be surprised as to why I chose this particular historical example concerning the abandonment of the Holy Thursday ceremony to pit against the issue of the change of the Good Friday prayer. Both, *mutatis mutandis*, involve the application of enormous political pressure on behalf of a combination of self-interested desires and the victory of an anti-Catholic worldview. What mattered in the eighteenth century were the ambitions of dynasties and republics dominated by secularizing power worshippers who had abandoned their faith. What matters in the present juncture is not liturgical change as such (I do not see this in any way as an "opening" for the destruction of the Traditional Liturgy), or fear for the end of religious dialogue. What matters today is the political demand that the one Church that *really* counts in the elite's mind when it thinks of religion at all accept a pluralism

†† Ibid., 38:525.

involving divinization of the desires of *secularized* Jews and the *raison d'état* of the state of Israel.

Pope Benedict XVI's change of the Good Friday prayer, under these circumstances, could never be ascribed to a weakness like that of Clement XIV. As Chris has well demonstrated, that prayer has been strengthened rather than weakened. The Pope has in no way responded to the wishes of the Choiseuls of our day. Benedict has instead once again shown that he is a defender and a rebuilder of Christendom rather than its undertaker.

It is, of course, understandable that traditionalists might ask whether the Pope could not have been more like a Clement XIII. Such a demeanor would have entailed a straightforward dignified rejection of all political pressure and a reaffirmation of the Good Friday prayer as it was. Certainly my whole spirit pulls me down the Clement XIII direction. Like most of my fellow traditionalists I react badly against changes of any sort—especially in an environment where change for change's sake has been the cause of such broad ecclesiastical destruction and personal spiritual pain. Nevertheless, two considerations must, I think, be taken into account before lamenting Benedict's failure to go the Rezzonico route.

One of these is practical, and practical in a very sobering way. Clement XIII failed. He failed, to a large degree, because when he ordered the Catholic army to charge he looked behind him and found that the troops simply were not there. I cannot overemphasize just how much the Church of his day—the College of Cardinals, the national episcopacies, the clergy, and the influential laity—was shot through with "Fifth Columnists" who had no interest in *In Coena Domini* and the victory of Christ the King. Similarly, I cannot overemphasize just how much the Church of our day would not follow Pope Benedict where he would have to go if he really put up a full public struggle against pluralism, the demands of secularized Jews and the desires of the State of Israel. Were he to do so, conservative Catholics and even many members of the traditionalist camp itself would suddenly forget their fears concerning ecumenism and the liturgy and denounce him and his supporters as agents of terrorism and Islamic aggression.

My other consideration follows along the lines laid out by Chris Ferrara. Maybe we are so influenced by our times that we "deconstruct" people's actions all too much and fail to understand them for what they really are. Perhaps the pope does clearly understand that we have arrived at an extraordinary historical turning point—in some ways brought on by the failed utopian visions of his predecessors—requiring solid extraordinary actions on his part. Maybe when he speaks of hope for salvation rather than the damnation of the vast majority of mankind in an encyclical that was, after all, on hope, he really wanted to encourage practice of the Faith and not spread heresy. And maybe when he rewrote the Good Friday prayer he did so in a devout "ivory tower," unconcerned with both traditionalists as well as pluralist political hatchet men, and actually focused on what the intercession is supposed to be all about—the salvation of the Jews and what would best achieve it.

In the final analysis, I, like Chris, think we still have good reason to support a man who has been good to us. We traditionalists have justifiably spent a great deal of time and effort explaining why Pope Pius XII acted the way that he did underneath the political pressures that he faced. If we honestly feel that Benedict has modified this prayer under similar kinds of pressure, we could try to understand him and his possible recognition, as noted above, that he does not really have command over that many Catholic battalions in a war that would target pluralism and Israel.

Things could change. As far as I am concerned, however, at least at this moment, our meek pontiff has shown that he is capable of inflicting at least a Half Jito on the enemies of Christ. When the troops—traditionalists included—grasp the fullness of the battle we have to fight, maybe he will inflict them with the Full Treatment. I tend to believe that that day will come. It is naive to think that we will see "peace in our time."

26

A View From Rocco's[†]

THE LIBIDO FOR THE THESIS AND THE TRADITIONALIST CHALLENGE

"BABY BOOMERS AND GENERATION X CAN really come together through their respective commitments to the New Frontier and the promise of Change." I cannot vouch for the exact words, but that certainly was the gist of the sentence that I read in the newspaper abandoned on the table directly behind my *Stammtisch* at Rocco's by a hurried breakfast client last week. The sentiments expressed were obviously those of an excited supporter of Barack Obama.

I have no particular desire to pick on the senator from Illinois—certainly not for the benefit either of a woman who would do her level best to destroy the homeschooling movement or a man who would send its graduates off to die in a Hundred Years' War for the maintenance of the Imperium. Nevertheless, a sentence whose every component part illustrates our age's obsession with sloganeering does beg for some sort of comment. This is especially true given the challenge that it poses for traditionalists.

There really is not that much one has to say about the above phrase in and of itself. "Baby Boomers," "Generation X," "coming together," "New Frontier," and "promise of Change" with a capital "C" are all purely invented terms. They do not refer to anything that exists in the real world of everyday experience, like a cat or even a slice of pizza. What they reflect are merely the dreams and desires of those people who have brought them into being and who manipulate them for their own ideological or mundane self-interested purposes. More interesting to me than the malleable words themselves is the fact that they involve the boring repetition of fatuous statements that we have already heard enunciated many, many times before, and that such pap can still be taken at face value even by otherwise serious men and women.

---

† First published in *The Remnant*, March 15, 2008.

A number of factors contribute to the success of this endlessly recurring "much ado about nothing." The one that I want to focus upon in this article is a passion which can easily be defined as *the libido for the thesis*. This is a vice which must first be introduced with reference to the dangerous teachings of Georg Wilhelm Friedrich Hegel (1770–1831) regarding the meaning of history and the role of *thesis*, *antithesis* and *synthesis* therein.

Catholics and Socratics have many reasons to be annoyed with Hegel and Hegelianism. From his chairs at the universities in Jena, Heidelberg, and Berlin this rather arrogant professor worked to muddy hopelessly the concepts of God and nature, as well as to end the beneficent reign of Aristotelian Logic over the human mind. Moreover, he completed the obfuscation of philosophical German so skillfully begun by Immanuel Kant. If anyone ever called for a banana peel to slip on, so as to avenge through laughter those many students whom he intellectually tormented, this man does. "*Hegel ist Nebel*," my Sudeten supervisor at Oxford warned me in 1973—"Hegel is fog." And normal people generally want fog to be dispelled.

My concern at the moment is chiefly with the foggy support that Hegel's theory of history gives to the libido for the thesis and, through its ravages, to the maintenance of the eternal return of bankrupt contemporary sloganeering. Allow me briefly to refresh *Remnant* readers' memories concerning the precise character of Hegel's historical vision before driving this dismal point home.

For Hegel, history is ultimately ruled by a highly complicated "idea," endlessly debated by his followers, which is nevertheless related by him (and them) to the realization of freedom in history. This idea is given practical reality and matured through the ages by means of the struggle of various liberty-bearing concepts, themselves assisted in the flesh-and-blood world by different physical forces (states, classes, parties, etc.) that help Freedom with a capital "F" to perfect its full meaning and promise.

Hegel also argues that this ascent of Mt. Freedom is accomplished according to a very precise plan. It is scaled at each distinct moment in time with the crucial aid of one of the abovementioned liberty-bearing concepts—known during its potent though temporary "day in the sun" as the *thesis*—and supported in its intellectual task by the temporarily most powerful physical entity in contemporary society. For many in Hegel's circle, the liberty-bearing concept of their age was the idea of a commonwealth governed by law codes protecting individual free men's lives and property—what the Germans call a *Rechtstaat*. Such disciples claimed that the most effective builder of their contemporary *Rechtstaat* was a Hohenzollern Prussia whose will to power had been demonstrated since the latter part of the seventeenth century. Of course in their minds Prussia had also earned its dominant role by shouldering the ineffable privilege of paying their master's university salary.

Still, Hegel insisted, any given age's thesis had to face enemies. The most serious of these foes shaped the era's temporary, dominant opposing principle—the *antithesis*. The antithesis was itself aided in its labor by a new up-and-coming physical entity giving its message practical clout. There was no need to agonize over such a clash, however, since the antithesis also inevitably worked to ripen freedom's meaning and bring it to term.

Even more encouraging for the cause of the final perfection of freedom was the fact that each period's unavoidable struggle of thesis and antithesis gave birth to a *synthesis* which in turn served as a fresh starting point—a fresh thesis—working mightily for the elevation of man to the Omega Point—also, needless to say, in tandem with yet another practical standard-bearer in the socio-political realm.

Now one little problem has always prevented my acceptance of the seemingly plausible and admittedly rather tempting Hegelian vision of history. That problem is a simple one. All I have ever encountered—at least when examining the supposedly vibrant, evolving field of modern thought and behavior—is reiteration of one and the same unchanging thesis. That thesis brooks no antithesis and synthesis to move it onward and upward in the scaling of Mount Freedom. Moreover, while passing itself off as rational and dynamic, it seems intent willfully to state its axioms and then to use the political and social power allied with it to kill everything truly intelligent, critical, and full of life and hope for man and society.

This unchanging thesis is not the convoluted Hegelian concept of the realization of freedom in history. Rather, it is that ubiquitous naturalism of the Enlightenment which stands behind the modern notion of liberty as well as the modern notion of everything else, from alpha to omega. Enlightenment naturalism is embraced by its supporters not with scientific calm but with irrational passion; namely, with a pronounced and quite jealous *libido for the thesis*—for *this* thesis, and *for nothing but this thesis*. Criticism of the thesis is totally unthinkable. "In Germany," socialists used to joke before the First World War, "there will be no revolution, because in Germany all revolution is strictly forbidden." Catholics could readily make a similar jest in our time. "In 2008," we might say, "there is no opposition to the thesis of Enlightenment naturalism because all such opposition is strictly forbidden."

The libido for the thesis sternly limits the acceptable intellectual struggle of our age to a pseudo-conflict among blood brothers, all of whom accept the Enlightenment's underlying principle of nature's independence from God as an unquestionable given. Whether from diabolical possession, madness, ignorance, or the blindness brought on by narrow self-interested motive, these blood brothers make a good show of going for one another's throats, even while lacking all solid intellectual reason for the pointless punch-outs that have characterized our time.

A classic example of their boring boxing match is the "battle" between dictatorial communism and liberal-democratic capitalism, both of which are children of the very same naturalist Enlightenment, and neither of which offers any substantive room for the transforming grace of Christ. Only a painfully crippled imagination and a libido for the thesis would lead a supporter of Adam Smith to think that "hearts that are restless until they rest in God" can find the peace that they seek in the simple substitution of a more bloating brand of naturalism for another one less successful in its efforts to stuff the body to repletion. He is the equivalent of a deli owner who enthusiastically offers a man an unchanging, life-long substitution of big Swiss Cheese sandwiches on baguettes for puny ones made out of tasteless, floppy white bread as the final, existential answer to all life's problems. Better, admittedly, but still qualitatively more of the same. Man simply does not and can never live by nature alone.

What happens to a true antithesis in this yawn-inducing environment? If possible, those driven by the libido for the thesis simply pass over what a real antithesis has to say in silence, in the hope that it will go away without having to shuffle the intellectual cards it lays on the table. But if silence does not work, what the *libidini* generally do is to attribute to the standard bearers of a serious opposition totally unrecognizable caricatures of the ideas that they actually espouse. The purpose of this distortion is not merely to ridicule thinkers who are free from the libido for their thesis, but also to dismiss them as obscurantists too stupid to understand that their (misrepresented) thinking has been discarded in the progress of the intellect and history to perfection. After all, who could possibly oppose Enlightenment naturalism other than primitives eager to wash their laundry on riverbanks and to hurl the cheap beads hanging round their necks in pointless reactionary rage against the machines which have come to liberate them?

This kind of caricature is regularly used to mock traditionalist socio-political thinkers. Does one write an article on the topic of government and clearly identify the grave difficulties connected with the adulation of past monarchies—while also noting that they reemerge again today with a vengeance in the divinization of the American system? Such assertions are much too nuanced for victims of the libido for the thesis to deal with soberly! Discussion of the tiniest pipsqueak of an argument pointing out the fallibility of our own Enlightenment naturalist-shaped regime must at all costs be avoided. Real issues are thus obscured, and the traditionalist author slandered as an anachronistic proponent of a freedom-hating Absolutism that *he* actually despises and *they* all too clearly worship. Does the traditionalist indicate that he has absolutely no intrinsic problem with private property and free enterprise, but merely thinks that other factors have to be taken into account in economic policy as well? Too nuanced, too dangerous for one-dimensional *libidini* tastes! Anyone suggesting that individual freedom be viewed in a social and supernatural context must be painted either as a Stalinist or a Luddite who wishes to till the soil with tree branches and live off of nothing but witchetty grubs.

Since no room is permitted by the libido for the thesis for the true antithesis to naturalism—namely, a full Catholic vision that argues for the need to respect *both* natural *and* supernatural influence over daily life—there is no space given for any possible *synthesis* either. By synthesis, what I mean here is the chance for the real insights to which any new age can indeed give birth to enter into an *honest* dialogue with the whole of our historical past and theological-philosophical heritage in order to refine and deepen an understanding of the one eternal Truth. Such a synthesis has come about in centuries gone by, and could, if seriously permitted, perhaps occur again.

Allow me to take but one immediate practical example from the current election campaign of *possible* synthesis and the stop sign placed in its path by the libido for the thesis. Many Catholics in the months gone by have expressed a tremendous sympathy for Ron Paul. This made perfect sense to me. His fight versus the Iraq War has been unswerving and inspiring. The modern American state, like all modern states, operates according to numerous evil principles that an anti-statist like Ron Paul has been correct and courageous in opposing. Some of his insights might be helpful to Catholics. But the libido for the thesis has led many of his libertarian supporters to tell us that applauding Ron Paul's stance on issues like the war is merely a first step to our necessary acceptance of his whole Murray Rothbard/Ludwig von Mises world view, itself but a variant of Enlightenment naturalism. Antithesis? Synthesis? Forget it! *Sola Enlightenment* rules the roost. All that the pseudo-battle between different warring proponents of the same basic position seems to lead to is this: an intensification of each faction's libido for the victory of its particular version of their shared underlying thesis when the boring pendulum swings temporarily back into its camp from that of one of its naturalist blood brothers.

Admittedly, there is no room for anything but the thesis at the *end* of the Hegelian vision, however this is interpreted. History, at that point, would have achieved its meaning and all intellectual struggle would correspondingly have ceased. What makes the dominant libido for the thesis particularly galling is that almost no one from among its supporters would argue that history has actually come to that conclusion just yet. Yes, Stalin did so, for a moment, in the 1950s, and Fukuyama, also temporarily, in the 1990s. But the others? I do not hear them openly saying such a thing. And yet this does not prevent the *libidini* from treating the supporters of a real antithesis—the Catholic vision—as though they have nothing serious they possibly can say; as though we have in fact finally reached our eternal intellectual and socio-political

Everest; as though there is nothing further left for believers to do but enjoy the view from Mount Enlightenment; as though Catholic freedom means nothing other than the privilege to choose among different vantage points from which to gawk at the same drab, unchanging naturalist vista.

We are now finally in a position to answer the question as to why the recurring arguments of bankrupt political rhetoric continue to exercise their seemingly unshakeable influence over the world around us. They do so for two reasons, the first of which is that the strong men who dominate modernity and have shown that they will do whatever is necessary to maintain their control over it have either consciously or unconsciously understood that the libido for the Enlightenment naturalist thesis is helpful to them. It gives them the appearance of a *natural right* to do whatever they wish to do, just as it establishes what seems to be a *natural law* demanding our unquestioning acquiescence to their dominion.

Furthermore, the masters of modernity (once again, either consciously or unconsciously) have also grasped just how valuable Hegelianism is as a weapon in their depressing project. Hegelianism's glorification of what is most powerful at any given moment in history as the best expression of mankind's ever youthful, evolving progress towards freedom, allows those with the biggest clubs in their hands to masquerade as the ever-changing, ever-beneficent paladins of the cause of liberty; a liberty which actually liberates them and them alone, but to the detriment of *all* of us, victims and "victors" alike. Moreover, Hegelian dismissal of the messages of past history and the voice of the powerless as hopelessly "surpassed" (one of the favorite words of this unfortunate school of thought) by the teachings of the present and the dictates of the strong has a two-fold consequence. It prevents the "losers" from recognizing the fraudulent repetitiveness of the vision of developing freedom, and it prohibits all exposure to the substantive truths espoused by the "surpassed" camp. Man's political education is reduced to a "consciousness-raising" designed to train him to find meaning in sloganeering and sloganeering alone.

Clearly, this has worked. Hence, the second reason for the success of such bankrupt rhetoric is that ordinary people simply no longer understand any other kind of political language. They are incapable of grasping a political statement in terms other than the empty phrases cited at the beginning of this article, even though in the depths of their souls they feel an ever more ominous malaise. Modern man longs to believe that the latest sloganeering will finally fulfill its empty promises. And he is still so distracted from even the slightest serious glance at the "surpassed" historical record that he can never digest a basic fact of life crucial to his social well being: that this rhetoric is and always will be the tool of the willful strong in their unending work of veiling Truth and oppressing the weak.

The editors of *La Civilta Cattolica*, wounded by the same libido for the same thesis in the 1850s, were so baffled by the misconstruction of their arguments against it that they often wondered out loud whether they were writing in Sanskrit rather than Italian or French. They repeatedly expressed bewilderment over what else they might do to get their substantive Catholic message across. But there was nothing more that they could do, at least on the purely intellectual level. There simply was no rational way of breaking out of the dialogue bouncing back and forth between the different variants of that unchanging Enlightenment naturalist position which was—and still is now—the sole conversation tolerated by the *libidini*. What they had to deal with—and we continue to face today as well—is primarily a psychological disturbance. The disease of minds and spirits reflected in the libido for the thesis calls for Catholic soul-doctoring even more than the Catholic intellectual discussion which we must, of course, nevertheless still nurture, in order to treat and cure effectively.

Hence, my final, short, but very important point: the challenge posed to traditionalist Catholics by this dreadful malady. Yes, as noted above, we believers *do* possess a real intellectual antithesis to the Enlightenment naturalist thesis. This *must* be presented to our contemporaries so that they can reject the hideous errors and evils of *modernity*. And, yes, we also have the supernatural and natural tools for effective soul-doctoring at our fingertips, if only we would take them up and use them—*all of them*.

In order to present our real antithesis and perform our effective soul doctoring properly, however, we must remember one crucial truth—that we are *Catholics* before anything else—*catholiques avant tout*, as our counterrevolutionary forbears said in the nineteenth century. This means that we must never allow anything to stand in the way of our learning everything that Catholicism teaches and everything that it encourages and works with, including whatever happens to be *merely modern* rather than a reflection of the spirit of modernity.

That desire to be *catholiques avant tout* in turn entails rejecting the temptation to transform the word *traditionalist* into a slogan, repetition of which relieves us of the effort to discover whether we actually are learning and acting in line with the fullness of our heritage or not. Certainly we traditionalist Catholics have never intended to do such a thing. Still, we are not granted miraculous defense against the snares of the devil simply by uttering the word "traditionalist" over and over again, as though it were an infallible weapon against them. The libido for the thesis can strike us just as easily as it can strike anyone else. If it were to do so, traditionalism would not mean what is Catholic; the word Catholic would be manipulated to fit whatever we have developed a passion for desiring traditionalism to signify. Should such a thing come to pass, we would become nothing but another force in the naturalist camp, passing off what we *strongly will* to be Catholic—whether it actually is so or not.

I can see that it is now time for me to leave the cafe. One of the waiters is fiddling around with the electricity and I have no desire to blow up before the next issue of *The Remnant* is published. Besides, I have to go to the dentist. After that, even our troubled modern world will temporarily appear to me to be prelapsarian in its beauty. I will celebrate by not looking at any newspapers in the cafe for at least a week to come, leaving Barack, Hillary, and John to spout off their rhetorical hoo-ha without me.

27
Interview with Cornell Society for a Good Time
(2008)

Question: In your experience as a professor, what historical insight or set of historical facts have you generally found to be most surprising to your students, educated as they have largely been by teachers ignorant of, or hostile to, the Catholic Faith and a Catholic understanding of history?

Quite frankly, most of the students whom I have taught over the past twenty-nine years at St. John's University have never expressed surprise or, for that matter, any opinion whatsoever regarding the material that I have presented to them. The most enlightening (and depressing) thing that I can tell you in this regard is that, even despite their terror concerning grades in my courses, almost all of my students completely ignore the pro-Catholic, record-straight-setting information I give them, and recite the dominant errors and mantras aimed against the Faith on tests. As far as I can determine, this is in no way due to deeply-rooted conviction on their part. Rather, it merely indicates the power of the propaganda fed them from practically every social channel since early youth. They simply cannot expel the erroneous and hostile words from their heads, just as I cannot purge the theme songs of situation comedies on television (like "Car 54") remembered from my own youth.

The answer to your question is much easier with respect to more interested public audiences. The biggest surprise for them is that Catholic History exposes one to a critique of the Anglo-American socio-political system and Liberal (i.e., when speaking of the United States, Conservative) Capitalism. By far the biggest problem I have in my broader teaching capacity is that of convincing people that it is possible to criticize the American system, just as it is possible to criticize every other system in the history of the universe. The mere whisper of a criticism usually brings back the absurd response that I must, therefore, be a supporter of an anti-Catholic Divine Right Monarchism à la James I of Britain.

Actually, the only people whom I know who have a Divine Right vision of a political order are those who think that everything the United States wants and does is blessed by God and *ipso facto* Catholic. Unfortunately, many conservative and Traditionalist Catholics fit into this category of Americanists.

Question: If you were given the chance to provide one lecture's worth of historical material to every graduating college student, what would you think most profitable for them?

This, for me, is an easy one to answer. I would lecture on Werner Jaeger's studies of Greek Paideia and its relationship with the new Christian dispensation, combining this with a discussion of Emile Mersch's book, *The Whole Christ*. Such a lecture would enable me to speak of all the themes I consider to be most important for understanding life as a whole and human history: the fact that the message of the Incarnation demands that Catholic Christianity work with every solid natural insight in history, "transforming them in Christ" for the benefit of the salvation of the individual; the fact, also, that the individual is a social being, and cannot be saved outside of natural and supernatural society, in all its immense diversity.

Question: As a matter of practical politics, would you consider a campaign for reducing the size and scope of the US government, or a campaign to alter the philosophy animating the government, as a strategy more likely to succeed in bringing about a more Catholic political life in America? What single change, to put it more broadly, should a Catholic first pursue in the public ordering of American life?

The primary work of a Catholic *qua* Catholic is to work to return the Church to doctrinal and pastoral sanity. There is little of ultimate significance that we can do until the Papacy in particular is firmly on our side and the Church authorities in general do not undercut our efforts, once again, to "transform all things in Christ."

Having said that, I would not want to discourage people who feel called to political activity to undertake such work. To my mind, however, decreasing or increasing the scope of governmental activity is secondary to a sense of what proper government is in the first place. There are aspects of life in America in which I think the government is much too much involved and others, especially concerning the economy in recent years, where it is too little involved for our own good. Until one grasps the main principles of a sound *polis* and, conversely, the main errors of our own, all specific political action remains action in a pointless vacuum. It would be like running a school without any clear sense of where the education offered therein was headed.

The principles of a sound polity, from a classical and Catholic standpoint taken as a whole, are not that hard to master. I outlined them above, and they are the gist of Catholic Social Teaching of the nineteenth and twentieth centuries. Government, in all its actions, must remember that man is both natural and supernatural, both individual and social in character. The Enlightenment in its varied manifestations, including the one ruling the United States, denies this. If one participates actively in American politics without an awareness of this basic contrast of views, then he will be sucked up into the existing system and becoming little other than a tool of whatever willful forces dominate it; i.e., under current conditions, that legion of moral and economic libertines and supporters of the Israel Lobby that, in different admixtures, controls both the Republican and Democratic Parties.

My preference is for the creation on the part of those who understand the ideological lay of the land to form a Catholic Lobby that would act like a kind of "shadow government." There are many precedents for this in the past, my favorite one being the Italian *Opera dei Congressi* of the nineteenth century. Still, I can understand that many young people might want to try a "hands on" approach politically. The one thing I would beg them under such circumstances is that they not become a cheerleading squad for either political party. I think that the pro-life movement in the United States has badly compromised itself by becoming just that—a cheering squad for the Republican Party under George Bush, thereby making itself look as though it has little or no concern for born life as well as unborn life; that it could care less about unjust warfare and an unjust economic order.

Question: Since several of us here are involved in one way or another in the academic world, we sometimes have conversations about the best way to handle being radically at odds with the assumptions and general tone of one's academic environment. Obviously for the purposes of getting promoted, it is best to hide one's Catholic convictions (or abandon them, if that were possible) but we are more interested in the best way to be a good soldier for Christ within a (hostile) academic sphere. Is it better to resign oneself to being an enfant terrible, *on the argument that it's best to fly the colors proudly at any cost? Or is it good to play nicer with one's colleagues, in the hope that this will present opportunities to argue for Catholic positions with a chance of being taken seriously?*

This is a difficult one for me to tackle. I have to confess that I have never even once had a problem at St. John's University as a result of my being openly Catholic, either with the Administration or with my colleagues. This may be due to the fact that, gradually, as Dr. William Marra at Fordham used to say, anything has become acceptable at some universities...even the Truth. Still, it is the case that no one has ever stood in my way or even slightly bothered me for my views.

Obviously, I know other people who have suffered in this regard, both at liberal and conservative universities, depending upon the nature of the Catholic issues in question. I know people who have suffered from being pro-life and others who have suffered from not believing that the Catholic Church is superior to the American Constitution. From what I have seen and heard, I would simply have to say that the man on the spot has to judge the particular problems that he faces and act accordingly. I have known individuals at Columbia University who have spoken openly in the face of criticism of their views and been treated honorably. I have known others in openly orthodox institutions who have been pushed out for doing something similar. But, here, too, it may be a question of the personalities concerned, both those of the enemy of and our own. It is hard to know who is most to blame without awareness of the particulars of each case.

Perhaps the best policy is to be guarded and yet—dare I say—open-minded at one and the same time; guarded, because nasty enemies are indeed there, but open-minded also because much hostility is due to simple deeply-ingrained ignorance regarding what Catholics (and especially Traditional Catholics) really think and love. Unnecessarily hard bitterness has to be avoided at all costs, because if we succeed in a bitter spirit we become part of that broader mystery of iniquity that goes far beyond the Catholic-Modernist battle.

Question: What, if you had to put it in a nutshell, is modernism?

Modernism is, of course, not simply what is modern as opposed to what is ancient or medieval. Modernism is the logical consequence of Enlightenment naturalism. It is the willful, *a priori* refusal even to contemplate, much less seriously discuss the possibility of there being anything above nature "as it is," totally on its own terms; it is the willful, *a priori* refusal to allow for God to be what a God must be and Christ to be what we are told He is. The result is that Modernism always must bring all things heavenly down to the purely natural level, without first proving that this is necessary. Moreover, Modernism spirals ever downwards in its understanding of the dignity of that natural world it seems to honor, the more it loses a sense of the God who, in fact, created and redeemed it.

Question: In your articles in the Remnant, you've discussed the evils of the modernist, individualist understanding of "human rights." What would be the building blocks of a more correct, Catholic understanding of human rights? Or, in a rightly ordered Catholic society, would we not talk about human rights at all?

There would be no effective concept of human rights if it were not for Catholic Christianity. Our religion teaches the value of the human person, offering that supernatural completion and confirmation of similar arguments concerning human personality and dignity on the part of natural philosophers. More importantly still, it gave them the grace and the courage to *believe* in their own Reason.

A psychological problem rooted in the question of the hierarchy of values also should be noted here, and introduced with reference to current problems concerning the liturgy. The Mass is of supreme value to the individual, but not because it is primarily intended for this purpose. Its primary purpose is the due worship of God. It is because it is the supreme prayer that its supreme value for the individual is guaranteed. When reformers placed the human teaching value of the Mass before its primary function of worshipping God fittingly they wrecked both the worship and the efficacy of the teaching tool.

Human beings do possess the substance of what we popularly call "rights," but these can be understood properly only when they flow from a proper grasp of divine and natural law. It is the law of God and of the nature that God created according to His sacred plan that compels other individuals to treat us in a proper, rightful, dignified fashion; as children of God with an eternal destiny. The language of rights has been a historical disaster. It has placed the emphasis, psychologically, on what is "owed me." When one speaks, first and foremost of divine and natural law instead of personal rights, the emphasis is on what I owe to God and to my neighbor. I would rather place my hopes in a political and social discourse based on the latter foundation. The language of rights leads straight to a Triumph of the Will disguised as "the victory of freedom."

Question: Returning to the academic world . . . do you think it's better for society and the good of souls for traditional Catholics to infiltrate secular (and sometimes more prestigious) universities or to gather themselves in enclaves where their fellow professors are like-minded conservative, if not traditional, Catholics?

I would prefer a policy of doing both, again, depending upon one's situation, personality, and specific opportunities that offer themselves. I see nothing wrong with teaching (or attending) the "best" universities, so long as one is honest with himself about whether he is selling out to the *Zeitgeist* or not. One of the best ways that honesty can be maintained is simply by securing one's lifeline to other intelligent Catholics in or around the university in question. Based on what I know of New York, this is not a particularly difficult enterprise. But, at the risk of beating a dead horse, I would still admit that the person on the spot would know better than I do what the local dangers or hopes are.

There are certain warnings that I would also post with respect to the idea of creating Traditionalist "enclaves." This is especially true under present circumstances, when the official Church is not fully "with us" and we are still thrown back primarily on our own resources. It is all too easy to define oneself as something—counterrevolutionary, progressive, and, in this case, Traditionalist Catholic—and then free himself from the task of seeing whether he actually is (and perhaps even more importantly will remain in the future) what the "word" labels him as being.

Quite frankly, I have become more depressed over Traditionalist (or conservative) Catholics deciding to escape into their little enclaves than over practically every other development in our movement. Many have fallen prey to all manner of non-Catholic thinking and behavior in consequence, none of which is investigated because, once again, the power of the name—Traditionalist Catholic—seems to stand surety for their ideas and actions. I have met all too many well-meaning Traditionalist Catholics who have retired to their "little houses on the prairie" and who, in everything from their dress to their intellectual life, have become nothing other than atomist modernists in Amish clothing. I have met some Traditionalist Catholic homeschoolers whose loathing for serious thought and culture is more naturalist and revolutionary than that of Jean-Jacques Rousseau. I have met stern traditionalists who out-Jeremy Bentham Jeremy Bentham. And, as noted in one way or another throughout this interview, I have met all too many Traditionalist and conservative Catholics whose Church Fathers are really the Founding Fathers; good-willed people who, *in practice*, show that they really think the main event in Sacred History came not with the birth, death and Resurrection of Christ, but with 1776. One can see this even on the purely natural level. Many of the homeschooling history texts produced by "our side" begin with America rather than Mesopotamia. I have even read statements by orthodox homeschoolers which proclaim openly the need to reject as heresy any work that mentions a criticism of an American political tradition firmly rooted in one of the most dangerous of Enlightenment thinkers, John Locke. We accept too much long-standing Anglo-American "custom" as though it were the real Tradition of the Church and the duty of Traditionalist Catholics to protect. This is exactly the same problem St. Gregory VII complained of in trying to strike at the Caesaro-Papism of the eleventh century. Christ, as he noted, came to teach Truth, not custom. Many Catholics did not know the difference between the two.

In sum I am very much in favor of setting up fully Traditionalist schools. Still, I would put them at the heart of things, where everyone is confronted on a regular basis with the realities of contemporary life, and not in little houses on the prairie. If we establish our centers as enclaves in the middle of nowhere, we will: 1) emphasize that wrongheaded individualism of American society which already exercises too great an influence over all of us, whether consciously or unconsciously; 2) aggravate any tendency on our part to ignore a real study of the fullness of Church Tradition, with the justification that, having already declared ourselves to be the defenders of Tradition, nothing more need be done to make sure we are correct in our judgment; and, 3) give up our chance to meet and convert the ever increasing number of people who recognize that something is rotten in Denmark, but have no means of judging what that is, and are light sheep without a shepherd.

Question: Do you feel as though you've been able to connect with the students at St. John's? That is, have any acknowledged to you that you were successful in steering them in a more traditional direction? Or does that aim even factor into what you do in the classroom? What deeper goals or aims, if any, do you bring to the classroom as a (traditional) Catholic professor of history?

As far as I know, I have had an impact only on about six or seven students at St. John's over nearly three decades. These have indeed all become traditionalists and are close friends. Others may have been influenced but never told me so. I know that this is possible, because one of those students who was so influenced only got back in contact with me after an absence of many years.

All my lectures are connected with my Catholicism, either directly or indirectly; directly, either a presentation of a Catholic vision of history, and indirectly through a presentation of the truths of a natural order created and offered redemption by God. I am constantly attempting to drill into my students the three principles I have repeatedly enunciated above: that man is both natural and supernatural at one and the same time; that man is both and individual and a social being at one and the same time; that efforts to try to separate man's earthly life from his eternal destiny are a disaster; that attempts to try to separate the individual from society, as with a materialist Liberal Capitalism or a materialist Marxist Socialism, are a disaster.

One other thing in this regard. I try to instill in my students a sense of the Drama of Truth. Drama involves the serious and the comic sides of life. Anyone who accepts the reality of existence as a Drama of Truth has to have both a sense of the magnificent heights to which God has called us, as well as a recognition of our failures in seeking to scale those heights. It is important to know that we slip on banana peels as we aim for heaven and treat that fact with a little patience and humor. Therefore, I teach my students to enjoy life and patiently recognize its comical character, striving all the more to reach God in the process. I think that that enters into what the *Cornell Society for a Good Time* has done and continues to do. That's why I like to look at your website!

Question: What do you think about Bishop Williamson's remarks on the advisability of undergraduate education for women? Are they sound enough, but unfeasible today? (When one needs a Ph.D. just to work a cash register at MacDonald's.) Or of perennial applicability?

I am not certain that I know everything Bishop Williamson has said about education for women. Absurd qualifications have indeed entered into the demands of our time, and, combined with the fragility of marriage these days, I would not wish to throw any woman into the world without them. I have also very much benefited from and been dependent upon the aid of educated women. Moreover, I don't know how any woman can take on the kind of responsibility homeschooling involves without solid preparation for this extremely difficult labor.

If I have the money, and if they want to go on to college, both my sons and daughter will do so. Moreover, I would not give the preference to my sons over my daughter if it came to a battle among them; the better one would have to win. In any case, the question may be an academic one. At the moment, I cannot see how I am going to pay for anyone in my family, male or female, to go to college. I am the first one in my family to have attended a university, and this because of the peculiar circumstances of Americans, especially children of veterans, after the Second World War and the foundation of our unfortunate Empire. I may well be the last as well!

Question: What sort of ideas do you have about your own children's undergraduate education? Which universities might you encourage them to attend and why?

I want them to get a good solid traditional liberal arts education, with the question of the career they might have coming second in their minds. I want them to enjoy themselves as they get this education. I do not believe that they have to mark themselves off in some peculiar way in order to function even in the corrupt world that we live in today. Like Pius XII, I think that they can dress and act modestly in 2008 without looking like they are from 1950 or living in Pennsylvania Dutch country. Therefore, I have no problems sending them to university in a city like my own. I have seen with my own eyes how, by choosing properly—and this among non-Catholic as well as Catholic teachers—they can still get a decent liberal arts education at St. John's University, at Columbia University, and at Oxford University. I would, of course, be very happy to see them go to Oxford, which was the academic love of my life.

Question: Finally, what are some of the major advantages and disadvantages for traditional Catholics living in New York City?

The advantages are: 1) permanent contact with a very large number of like-minded New Yorkers and passing contact with a very large number of like-minded visitors from all over the globe. I would have been overwhelmed by acquaintance with the Catholics who have passed through our living room, from Dr. William Marra to Michael Davies to Bishop Williamson to Msgr. Wach and many, many others; and 2) the Classical-Catholic cultural influence available to them here, much of it for free.

The disadvantages are: 1) space. We have plenty of parks for the children to play in, but small, rent-controlled apartments are not necessarily the best one-room schoolhouses for children of different ages. Hence, our desire, always, to find a decent elementary school for the children to attend, so far without success; 2) pretty obviously, the need to maneuver our children around the streets with public displays of pornography. This evil generally comes to the children of suburbs and country through television or the internet (or other kids).

Having myself been raised in a suburban town which has now become a batch of strip malls with an aesthetic teaching deadly to the True, Good, and Beautiful, I would rather die than send my own offspring to a similar environment. I don't run around saying this to people living under those circumstances. Unfortunately, I find that practically everyone from outside the city presumes a right to lecture me on the nature of the life that we live here. My neighborhood in New York was the first place in the United States where I encountered the warm community life that I do not see when life is led in cars on highways. And when I compare the rate of corruption and loss of the Faith among the children of friends here with friends elsewhere, I do not see the city mouse coming off worse than the country mouse.

28
Monsignor Ignacio Barreiro†

REST IN PEACE— TU ES SACERDOS IN AETERNUM! (APRIL 2017)

IGNATIUS BARREIRO, Presb.
22 Oct. MCMXLVII–13 Apr. MMXVII
Requiescat in pace

A Priest Forever, According to the Order of Melchizedek

Dr. John C. Rao
for *The Remnant*

† First published on the Rorate Caeli blog, April 2017.

MONSIGNOR IGNACIO BARREIRO-CARÁMbula, the chaplain of the Roman Forum, long-time head of the Rome Bureau of Human Life International, and dear, dear friend ended his earthly pilgrimage to God at 2:00 A.M. today. His soul follows that of another dear friend, John Vennari, into Purgatory and—God willing—as swiftly as possible into Heaven. Our Lord and Savior Jesus Christ cannot but deal as mercifully as possible with both of these good, good men.

To give you just a bit of information about my beloved friend, Monsignor was born on October 22, 1947 in Montevideo, Uruguay. After obtaining a doctorate in Law in Montevideo, he joined the foreign service of his country. From 1978 to 1983 he was a member of the delegation of Uruguay to the U. N. In 1983 he entered the Dunwoodie Seminary in New York and was ordained a priest by Cardinal John O'Connor on November 14, 1987, in St. Patrick's Cathedral, New York City.

In New York at the same time that he worked in a parish, he was involved with the pro-life apostolate. In 1991 he entered the University of the Holy Cross in Rome, obtaining his license in 1993 and his doctorate in Theology in 1997 with a dissertation on The Experience of God and of the Faith in God according to St. Thomas Aquinas. He was fluent in Spanish, English, French, and Italian. In September 1998 Msgr. Barreiro was appointed Director of the HLI Rome Office, which was inaugurated in November of that same year, with the blessings of Pope John Paul II.

That is what there is to say about him "officially." But that does not tell you Don Ignacio's full story, which I am going to relate to you now, not necessarily in the most elegant form, because I want to say this quickly and I am, as you may well imagine, a bit upset.

It is appropriate that he died on Holy Thursday, the Birthday of the Priesthood, because he was a heart-and-soul, 24/7 priest. He always wanted to be a priest, but certain circumstances propelled him into a legal career, one which involved him in very serious anti-communist labors in his native country, and then into diplomatic service. I met him thanks to an even closer friend of Don Ignacio, Fr. Richard Munkelt, who is now the main chaplain of the Roman Forum, taking our departed comrade's place. This was when he was working for Uruguay at the United Nations.

Don Ignacio loved his country, but he loved his Savior more. I know that it is hard for non-New Yorkers to believe how much those of us attached to this strange city feel about her, but it was appropriate that Monsignor Barreiro's vocation got the better of him in this town to which he also gave his heart and soul.

Monsignor was one of the most intelligent men I know, and one with an aesthetic sense that did not brook foolish things lightly. It did not take long after he became a priest for him to know that he needed to be one "according to the order of Melchizedek" in the service of the Traditional Liturgy. Good theologian that he was, he never dreamed of denying the legitimacy of the *Novus Ordo*; he simply knew which form of worship was superior.

Everyone who knew and loved Don Ignacio knows that he was a soldier in every field that he entered. He was a Soldier of Christ. He was a Commando of Christ. He fought for the Old Mass. He fought for the fullness of the Catholic Teaching, every iota of every doctrine. He fought for the souls of all who came to him for help. He dropped everything—everything—for anyone who needed spiritual help. Knowing that my father-in-law was near death a good number of years ago, he begged my wife to tell him the moment that she knew. That moment turned out to be 3 in the morning Rome time, and Monsignor got out of bed, vested, and said Mass for him "on the double."

In addition to being one of the most intelligent and aesthetically aware men that I have ever known, Don Ignacio was also one of the most humorous, amusing, and individual. Why? As we believers know—and non-believers can never grasp—this was because he was a Catholic, and Catholicism breeds true personality.

Please pray for this good and faithful servant of God, whose endless work in endless ways, both in the United States and in Rome, has been totally unsung. He did more for the Cause than people outside his close circle of friends can imagine. He will do even more for all of us still trudging through this valley of tears when he makes it into the Company of the Saints.

29

Malcolm Muggeridge, John Vennari, and the Prince-Bishopric of Bamberg†

MALCOLM MUGGERIDGE (1903–1990), THE great English journalist and Catholic convert, noted that the essence of humor lies in the recognition of the gap between man's goals and his efforts to achieve them. What this means is that there can be no real humor without acceptance of two basic truths: on the one hand, that there are indeed precious goals towards which human beings should be striving, and, on the other, the fact that people regularly do fail to live up to their promise. Where there is insistence *only* upon commitment to some supposedly unquestionable dream or prediction *only* of the inevitable slip on the banana peel on yet another hopeless path to yet another deluded fantasy there is room for grim ideological dogmatism or nihilistic cynicism alone. But where there is faithful and rational appreciation of the supremely true, good, and beautiful goal of all of Creation, and a simultaneous realization that everyone repeatedly stumbles in their pilgrimage towards it there is the greatest sense of humor that one can imagine.

Our dear departed friend and colleague, John Vennari, was a man of enormous good humor; a seemingly unceasing cheerfulness that made its unfailing presence known in his tireless writing and speaking—not to speak of his conversation at after conference dinners and over a good cigar. This is no surprise, given what has just been noted above. John was the happy warrior of Christ, the King of the Universe, in whom he had a total faith, and whose goals for mankind—the goals of the Incarnation—gave to all men *the* truthful, good, and beautiful purpose that cannot be surpassed. And he was this happy warrior because he also always recognized that Christ, his Redeemer, knew his sheep, their weaknesses, their constant stumbling in faith, hope, and charity, on their path to eternal union with the Trinity through Him.

† First published in the *Catholic Family News*, May 2017.

In case you have not noticed, perhaps I should point out that our times are not exactly the most joyous in Church History. The consequence is that anyone casually encountering John by stumbling unwittingly into the ordinary Traditionalist conference or inadvertently picking up an issue of *Catholic Family News* would most likely have heard or read him rendering an account of appalling betrayal of Catholic teaching on faith and morals with behavior following suit, and no villain, cleric or lay, left untouched. What else could he, masterful observer of the times and journalist to boot, be expected to do? And how could he not deliver his Philippic without that talented combination of zealous outrage and wit that left the condemnatory conclusion he wished to be drawn doubtful only to someone truly invincibly ignorant?

But, once again, John could only accomplish his professional duty with inner pain. His need to attack was rooted in his much deeper sorrow over the damage done to Faith, Reason, Truth, Goodness, and Beauty by those either consciously or childishly ripping all of them to shreds. Catholic realism and journalistic responsibility demanded Blitzkrieg against the Modernist enemy. John's Catholic spirit desired the peace that passeth all understanding and is only satisfied when allowed to do what it really is supposed to do: exalt the Triune God, together with His saints. The *desire* and the *responsibility* were answered by going about his business in this valley of tears with the good humor defined by his English Catholic colleague.

The great Catholic historian, Ludwig von Pastor (1854–1928), also comes to mind in this regard. Anyone familiar with von Pastor's forty volume *History of the Papacy* knows that he is not the man conservatives or sedevacantists, both incapable of imagining a "true pope" doing something wrong, would wish to keep on their bookshelves. Too good a scholar to mince words, von Pastor presents the reader with an account of failures to live up to Catholic truth over which even traditionalists, all too familiar with fumbling from the Holy See, would blush. But this chronicler of case after case of ecclesiastical woe also was aware of the reality of Faith, Reason, Truth, Goodness, and Beauty, and the historical fact of many proofs of loyal commitment to them, from the top on down, popes as well as peasants. And that is why Professor Dietrich von Hildebrand, standing beside him at a canonization ceremony one day in Rome, saw tears streaming down von Pastor's cheeks as another Catholic saint was raised to the altar. The man who knew the sinner knew the saint. I could easily picture John reacting in exactly the same way, with his tears of joy falling upon an issue of *Catholic Family News* with a lead article by him attacking one or the other contemporary fall from grace.

Allow me to finish this brief piece with an at first glance seemingly strange digression; a detour to the city of Bamberg, in Upper Franconia, a part of present-day northern Bavaria. Barely touched by the ravages of the Second World War, this extraordinary place was once one of the great Prince-Bishoprics of the Holy Roman Empire, home to some of the Emperors themselves.

The visitor to Bamberg already thinks he is in a magical kingdom when strolling towards the center from the train station. But then he arrives at the lively Regnitz River, making its way to the greater River Main and filled with boaters paddling under a splendid bridge adorned with grand, Baroque religious statues. This bridge ushers the traveler through the splendid city gate into what can only be described as a Catholic Oz. His steps take him through one breathtakingly charming narrow street after another, up to the medieval cathedral that houses the tombs of the Emperor St. Henry II and his wife, St. Cunigunde of Luxemburg. Higher still, above the lovely palace gardens across from the cathedral and overlooking the city, the former Benedictine Abbey of the Michaelsberg irresistibly beckons the tourist. Its Michaelskirche offers incomparable Gothic, Baroque, and Rococo riches, with the grounds providing a glorious view of much of the Prince-Bishopric, and, along with it, perhaps even a glimpse of yet another nearby Baroque-Rococo gem: Balthasar Neuman's pilgrimage Basilica of the Vierzehnheiligen (the Fourteen Holy Helpers), a short distance away.

If readers of *Catholic Family News* want an "historical" photo analogous to the soul of our dear departed friend, John Vennari, they will find such a photo in the city of Bamberg and its surroundings. This Bavarian Catholic Oz, built upon a solid, orthodox truth, productive of incalculably diverse riches artistically, everywhere exudes a joyous Easter spirit that makes one want to lift a glass of Franconian wine in honor of all the great men and women who made the place possible—two of whom, Saints

Henry and Cunigunde, continue to pray for the conversion of those inhabitants who inevitably continue to "slip on banana peels" and soil its promise.

It was his own personal Bamberg that John was building in his soul, and, through his faithful soulful work, along with his music and delightful stories, in the world that he helped to construct for his wife, his children, and his friends. It is his own personal Bamberg, united with that of all the other servants of Christ and the cities of God that they have built and are building, that we pray his soul will reflect into eternity. It was the outrages done to this Catholic Oz and faithfulness to the message of the Incarnation that made its construction a possibility that alone made John—like Henry and Cunigunde in their own time and place—into the Soldier of Christ that duty demanded he become in his earthly existence. It is John Vennari as an ideal Prince-Bishop of Bamberg—fearless in his defense of Orthodoxy, eager for his subjects to benefit from Truth, Goodness, and Beauty, sorrowfully aware that they needed a serious verbal thrashing for their failure to do what alone could make them happy in this life, while saving them in the next, and maintaining his good humor throughout his chastisement—that will live on in my mind's eye, my prayers, and my memory of this fallen comrade.

ABOUT THE AUTHOR

John C. Rao obtained his doctorate in Modern European History from Oxford University in 1977. He worked in 1978–1979 as Eastern Director of the Intercollegiate Studies Institute in Bryn Mawr, PA, and was Associate Professor of European History at St. John's University in New York City from 1979 to 2021. Dr. Rao is also director of the Roman Forum, a Catholic cultural organization founded by the late Professor Dietrich von Hildebrand in 1968. He writes for numerous French, German, Spanish and Italian journals. Perhaps the most important of his works are *Americanism and the Collapse of the Church in the United States* (Roman Forum Press, 1995), *Black Legends and the Light of the World* (Remnant Press, 2012), *Removing the Blindfold* (Angelus Press, 2014), a discussion of Catholics rediscovering their own heritage in the post-French revolutionary era, and *A Centenary Meditation on a Quest for "Purification" Gone Mad* (Arouca Press, 2019). He has also written a companion volume to his collected works, *The Unrepentant Catholic's Cautionary Calendar* (Arouca Press, 2022).

www.ingramcontent.com/pod-product-compliance
Lightning Source LLC
Chambersburg PA
CBHW020452130626
46549CB00001B/386

9781998492343